CLASSICAL MUSIC:

EXPECT THE UNEXPECTED

CLASSICAL MUSIC

EXPECT THE UNEXPECTED

KENT NAGANO

WITH INGE KLOEPFER

TRANSLATED FROM GERMAN BY
HANS-CHRISTIAN OESER

McGill-Queen's University Press
Montreal & Kingston • London • Chicago

© McGill-Queen's University Press 2019

ISBN 978-0-7735-5634-8 (cloth)
ISBN 978-0-7735-5753-6 (ePDF)
ISBN 978-0-7735-5754-3 (ePUB)

Legal deposit first quarter 2019
Bibliothèque nationale du Québec

Printed in Canada on acid-free paper that is 100% ancient forest free
(100% post-consumer recycled), processed chlorine free

Funded by the   Financé par le
Government   gouvernement   Canada Council Conseil des arts
of Canada   du Canada   for the Arts   du Canada

We acknowledge the support of the Canada Council for the Arts, which last year
invested $153 million to bring the arts to Canadians throughout the country.

Nous remercions le Conseil des arts du Canada de son soutien. L'an dernier,
le Conseil a investi 153 millions de dollars pour mettre de l'art dans la vie des
Canadiennes et des Canadiens de tout le pays.

Library and Archives Canada Cataloguing in Publication

Nagano, Kent, 1951–
[Erwarten Sie Wunder! English]
Classical music : expect the unexpected / Kent Nagano with Inge Kloepfer ;
translated from German by Hans-Christian Oeser.

Includes bibliographical references.
Issued in print and electronic formats.
ISBN 978-0-7735-5634-8 (hardcover). – ISBN 978-0-7735-5753-6 (ePDF). –
ISBN 978-0-7735-5754-3 (ePUB)

1. Nagano, Kent, 1951–. 2. Conductors (Music)–Biography. 3. Music–History and
criticism. I. Kloepfer, Inge, 1964–, author II. Title: Erwarten Sie Wunder! English.

ML422.N33A3 2019   784.2092   C2018-906119-7
                                            C2018-906120-0

This book was typeset in Sabon.

"That's the pentecostal alphabet – the letters of fire – that God gave us: His *greatest gift*, the ability to talk and to communicate. And a big part of communication is music."

Leonard Bernstein (1918–90)

CONTENTS

PROLOGUE

What *is* classical music? It is an adventure we embark upon once we are willing to engage with it. Classical music transports us to another world. There it unfolds its tremendous power. And because of this power it can enrich us immensely, especially today in these troubled, accelerating times. That's what this book is about.

There is another way to answer the question. Classical music is a universe that expands as soon as you enter it. There you will come across everything that this art form has produced in the course of almost a thousand years: medieval music, renaissance and baroque music, music of the classical and romantic periods, finally new music; opera, symphonic works, church and chamber music. When I speak of classical music in this book over and over again, the universe to which I refer encompasses all aesthetic forms of expression that have been, and are being, created through the arrangement of tones. In classical music lies our entire Western tradition, the great concept of development up to the modern era, and the "canon" with its treasure trove of works from different periods. In it lies our never-ending human creativity, which constantly brings forth works in this art form. But it is also where community experience lies, as well as social encounters in opera houses and concert halls. And last but not least, a consensus on the significance and value of this art form. That's what I mean by classical music.

This book is not merely about music as such, but also about ourselves and why we should not allow classical music to lose its social relevance in our fast-moving, high-tech world that is mainly shaped by the visual. What else would remind us of our traditions – traditions that we so desperately need in our post-modern state of disorientation? What else could inspire us more comprehensively, enhance our ideas more forcefully or drive us on – far into the future – without letting us forget who we are?

Kent Nagano, September 2018

CLASSICAL MUSIC:

EXPECT THE UNEXPECTED

CHAPTER ONE

ON CATTLE BREEDERS
AND TRUMPETS

"The spoken language is always connected to statements, arguments,
politics or asking questions expecting answers and responses. The musical
language does not have arguments; it is free and always ready to be shared,
always ready to become a part of everyone."

Wachtang Botso Korisheli,
Memories of a Teaching Life in Music (2010)

A FISHING VILLAGE FILLED WITH SOUND

I have a dream. Perhaps it is misleading to start a book with a
sentence that will inevitably bring me in close proximity to the
"dreamer." However, I am not just a dreamer; I am a realist. And
that is precisely why I am writing this book. For my dream. This
dream takes me far back to my childhood, to the fifties and sixties. It takes me to the West Coast of the United States, somewhere
in the no-man's-land between Los Angeles and San Francisco, a
four-hundred-mile stretch that even today would take seven hours
to cover – and only if you chose the highway.

Flush against the wild shoreline, about halfway between the
two metropolises, lies the unremarkable village of Morro Bay, at
the time just a small fishing village with around two thousand
inhabitants from all over the world. When I think back to my
childhood in that village, my memories are invariably filled with

music – Bach's preludes and fugues, Beethoven's and Mozart's symphonies, chorales for big choirs, cantatas. It may not be unusual for a conductor to associate memories with music, given that sound determines his or her everyday life. Who does not know the suggestive power of melodies capable of conjuring up landscapes, edifices, situations, individuals and entire phases of the past in one's imagination?

But I don't mean that. I can hear music that was actually played by our orchestras and sung by our choirs at the time, because the constant presence of classical music defined daily life in our village as a matter of course. Music was part and parcel of our existence, simply always available – to practice, to pass the time, to gain social recognition, to enjoy community experiences. Without music, the lives of my siblings, friends and classmates, and my own life, were inconceivable. We made music for the sake of music. At the time, none of us ordinary children envisioned a career as a musician. In my childhood and youth, there was nothing to suggest that one day I would earn my living as a conductor.

Choir and orchestra rehearsals, piano lessons and, along with them, music theory – all of that determined the seven days of the week, even though my siblings and I were anything but special. Almost everyone in our rural community was involved in musical life one way or another: the children of the cattle breeders as well as those of the farmers and fishermen, the craftsmen and grocers, the teachers and the school principal. Morro Bay was a village filled with sound, something strange and unique between rocks, fields and the Pacific Ocean. As for the intensity with which the children devoted themselves to classical music and drew their parents into that world, our village was unusual, perhaps even a little weird. Music united us all, that society of immigrants from completely different ethnic and cultural backgrounds. Looking back it seems almost like a dream.

Perhaps I should reach back a little further: my grandparents on my father's and mother's side had emigrated from Japan to the United States at the end of the nineteenth century to try their

luck in the "land of opportunity" and had settled down as veg-
etable farmers on the West Coast. Our family has lived in the
United States for more than one hundred and twenty years – half
of the time span that has elapsed since the foundation of the
United States. So, regardless of my Japanese last name, I'm a true
American. My grandparents ran a farm that was later taken over
by my father and his brothers, after my grandfather fell seriously
ill. Neither my father nor my mother were trained as agricultur-
alists. According to their parents' wishes, both were supposed to
go far and learn professions that would allow them a livelihood
beyond agriculture. That is why they pursued completely different careers. My father studied architecture and mathematics at
the University of California, Berkeley, and my mother graduated
there as a microbiologist and pianist.

But in the end they did become farmers – out of necessity, because
my grandfather wasn't able to cultivate his land himself anymore. It
was not until much later, in 1976, that they were given the opportunity to engage in professions suiting their academic education.
At that time, our arable land was converted into building plots
as part of a regional development program, and purchased by a
food company. Today, some of our former fields have been built
upon. From then on my mother worked as a microbiologist for the
public health authority, and my father planned and designed not
only private homes but also large commercial centers. When that
happened, I no longer lived in Morro Bay.

I am, so to speak, a peasant child, the child of an artichoke
grower, one who saw little of his father, as he was mostly out in
the fields. Only in the evenings, when he returned home, did my
father concern himself with architecture and design concepts,
later more and more often with commissioned work. He had
begun early to establish a small architectural practice alongside
his agricultural activity, and would often retire to his "studio,"
where he prepared designs and pursued his dreams. My mother
made sure that we children never disturbed him while he was
working. She was not only a passionate scientist, but also an

excellent piano player. Furthermore, she was extremely well read and brought her fascination for science and her love of the fine arts of music and literature into our family.

The landscape surrounding us was rough and vast. The Californian metropolises of San Francisco in the north and Los Angeles in the south were each more than two hundred miles away from Morro Bay and thus almost inaccessible to us children in the fifties. When, on those rare occasions, we did travel there, it was always a very special excursion. We literally lived at the very edge of the United States, a sweep of country where the coastline plunges into the Pacific Ocean, where rocky scenery alternates with long beaches, where in stormy weather huge waves come rolling in. However, in our early years my three younger siblings and I spent fairly little time on the seashore, considering that it was right on our doorstep. Our life took place mainly in the two microcosms of our home and our school.

MOTHER'S DETERMINATION

When I was four years of age, my mother sat me down at the piano. She did this with the same peculiar determination with which she looked at books with us, read to us from them or took us to church on Sundays, leaving no doubt that we had to endure even the most tedious sermons. Each of us started our apprenticeship with her from that early age. We were not asked whether we wanted to or not. And so we didn't ask ourselves that question. We practiced whatever she required of us. We learned how to read music and how to listen – to ourselves and to others – and we internalized the difference between noise, jingles and serious music.

Music was a grave matter of great importance to my mother, more than just a gimmick and as essential as reading, writing and arithmetic. Practicing formed part of our everyday schedule as children. It was an irrefutable fact of life we never questioned, maybe because my mother did not seem overly eager to train us at the age of four to become child prodigies and later professional artists. In her view, the upbringing of her children had to include music; it was a natural part of any humanistic education and thus of our domestic life. It was never a means to an end. I would not go so far as to claim that as children we were excessively motivated to devote ourselves regularly to the piano. Did we really like practicing?

At any rate, I didn't. But I didn't resist it, either. It was a matter of obedience, which automatically sets in when someone commands you with unwavering determination to do something that they themselves practice day in, day out. Perhaps it is something that today would be termed "gentle force" – in certain matters one doesn't give children a choice, but decides for them. Music was not an option; it was an essential ingredient of life. When I think back, my siblings and I seem to have been surprisingly compliant, compared to other children at the time.

My parents were slightly unusual, as far as rural life is concerned. It wasn't just my mother's appreciation of art. My father, too, made his real vocation noticeable in family life. Sketches, architectural drawings and models were strewn all over our house. When we were a little older, he took us more and more frequently to his construction sites. Not only did he explain to us the way buildings were constructed, but he also left no doubt that he considered architecture to be a genuine form of art that aesthetically reflected and shaped its time and, at its best, transcended it.

One of my sisters, three years younger than me, and I mostly played the piano. My brother, on the other hand, developed a preference for brass instruments and learned to play the trombone; my youngest sister, the viola. None of us ever thought of giving up an instrument. Such an idea would simply not have occurred to us, all the less so because our daily life offered few diversions. We lived a secluded life, didn't engage in any organized sports, just went to the beach now and again and tried to learn from the bigger boys by watching them surf. In the mid-fifties, my parents bought a TV set. But there wasn't much to see. In Morro Bay, surrounded as it was by mountains to the east and by water to the west, reception remained poor for years. My father was chiefly interested in the weather report, on which he, as a farmer, was naturally dependent, since the daily forecast improved his ability to plan ahead. Most of the time, however, he relied on the radio.

Classical music certainly played a role in our family of six at a comparatively early stage. It was simply because my mother loved music. But apart from that, we hardly differed from our neighbors and other parish members in the fairly conventional United States of the fifties and sixties, where going to church, visiting relatives and meeting friends was just as much part of everyday life as school and sometimes, on weekends, going to the beach or the mountains.

There are some crazy stories about artists' childhoods. According to the ideas of modern education, more often than not they are sad stories, akin to those about outstanding athletes. There is the stern father, who for days on end demands relentless commitment from his son, hours of practice and training, without regard for the physical and psychological consequences of such unnatural torture. There are many examples like that to be found among classical music artists. Or it is the mother who, driven by boundless ambition, wants to turn one of her children into a soloist because from a very young age he or she showed great promise or at least keen interest. Children quickly arouse parental fantasies. And then it all starts: one performance after another, children are sent off to take part in competitions and introduced to musicians and well-known teachers. This is not a phenomenon characteristic of our time, but it was like that centuries ago.

As a child, Wolfgang Amadeus Mozart was taught by his father for many hours a day and presented to the world on numerous journeys, to the point of physical exhaustion. The young Ludwig van Beethoven endured a similar fate; his overambitious father is even alleged to have reduced Ludwig's age by a few years so that the child prodigy would shine all the brighter at the piano.

People don't like to talk about the suffering of child stars. Yet many autobiographies testify to it. Perfectionism quickly destroys the idyll of a carefree childhood. In any case, many a star, whether in classical music or in sports, whether in the past or in the present, did not enjoy an idyllic childhood or youth. The world of Morro Bay, however, was different, one that almost seems unreal to me in retrospect.

THE MIRACLE OF MORRO BAY

The musical miracle in our village began with the arrival of an exceptional pedagogical talent who changed everything. It was the Georgian-born Wachtang Korisheli, whom we, his students, still call Professor Korisheli with affectionate reverence. In my memory he came out of nowhere, pulling up in his small, rattling Volkswagen. All of a sudden he was there and began to transform our elementary school into a kind of musical laboratory. That was in 1957. I was no more than six years old.

Korisheli, at the age of thirty-six, had an eventful past. He hailed from Tbilisi, where he was born in 1921, the year when the Soviet Union forcibly annexed Georgia. His parents were actors; his father soon became a stage hero well known throughout the Soviet Union, who even attracted Stalin's attention and gave a performance in his honor in Moscow. But then the tide turned. As a Georgian he opposed Russian supremacy, and so he was declared an enemy of the state, arrested by the People's Commissariat for Internal Affairs (NKVD), interned and, in 1936, executed. His son Wachtang was only fifteen years of age at the time. He had met Stalin in person when his father was in high favor with the dictator. Once Stalin even put his arm around the little boy and spoke a few words to him. Before his father was executed, Wachtang and his mother had just twenty minutes to bid him farewell through the bars of his cell.

In the Soviet Union, the children of an enemy of the state were not given many chances. Wachtang could not train as a musician.

This became apparent in his final school year. Stalin subjected the sons and daughters of political adversaries to ever new restrictions. And even then Korisheli knew what that meant: he would not be permitted to complete any training and certainly not to study, and later on he would not be allowed to work in important institutions, let alone take on a challenging or responsible job. And, of course, these children would not be accepted into the Red Army, either.

His mother, who had worked as an actress at the Rustaveli Theater and gained regional popularity, lost her job and joined a traveling theater company. The pressure Stalin and the NKVD exerted on the families of declared enemies of the state was clearly felt by the whole family. There were no prospects for the talented pianist, who would have loved nothing better than to study music, and the outlook was gloomy, so gloomy in fact that he might have ended up in a labor camp at some point. After finishing school he was assigned to a work unit and soon transferred to the Polish border. In anticipation of an invasion by the German Wehrmacht, he and his comrades were to dig defensive trenches there.

The Wehrmacht wasn't far away, and a confrontation with German soldiers wasn't long in coming. He was taken to one of their prisoner of war camps. Thanks to his good knowledge of German and the fact that he was not Russian but Georgian and, more crucially, the son of an enemy of the state, he survived both the camp and the war. He translated for the Germans and he made music. In the confusion of the ending war, he traveled via Salzburg and Bad Reichenhall to Munich. At the conservatory in Munich, which after the war was trying to recruit young students, he was finally able to start studying the piano in his mid-twenties.

But he stayed there barely more than a year. As a refugee from the Soviet army, he had been granted the status of "displaced person," someone who had been catapulted out of his home country by the turmoil of war and for whom, because he could not be repatriated, resettlement programs had been negotiated at an international level. Korisheli was to travel on to Los Angeles, where the authorities had located relatives of his. With the encouragement of his professor he turned his back on Munich and boarded a ship. The resettlement program brought the piano student to the West Coast of the United States. He was never to return to Munich.

Perhaps his story and his origin, so strange and mysterious to us, were part of the magic attached to his personality. Georgia was unimaginably far away, and not only geographically. At that time it was still behind the Iron Curtain. And in the raging storms of the twentieth century, Wachtang Korisheli had indeed been blown further and further west from home, just like a leaf – a life without pity determined by chance or fate.

Professor Korisheli was an exceptionally gifted teacher who must have felt his calling quite early on. As early as during his training as a pianist at the University of California, Los Angeles, where he had enrolled after his arrival on the West Coast, he changed his plans and said goodbye to a career as a pianist. He switched universities, enrolled at the University of California, Santa Barbara, learned the viola, received instruction in pedagogy and graduated as a music teacher. Next he got into his VW Beetle and drove northward along the Californian coast, passing various places and conducting interviews at schools that had advertised positions for music teachers, and finally stopped in Morro Bay. A stroke of luck for us children, because in no time he managed to transform our village into a musical oasis.

There are many reasons for the success of this exceptional teacher. It was not only his extraordinary, almost exotic appearance; above all it was his authentic and utterly unconditional passion for the arts, with which he, almost like the Pied Piper of Hamelin, gathered very nearly all the children of the village around him, driven by the deep conviction that he had to bring music, and thus a little happiness, into their lives. He addressed himself to that task in a thoroughly strategic manner. Even during the interview in our elementary school, he asked if the school board would allow him additional time for aural training and music reading so as to benefit the younger pupils, not to mention various orchestras and ensembles that he intended either to continue or to establish.

He was convinced that music belongs in schools, that is to say, in a learning environment that the children themselves define as such. For him, as it was for my mother, music was no game, no entertainment, no gratuitous pastime, but a very grave matter indeed. Whoever wanted to study with him or make music with him had to take him utterly seriously. And that was best done in a place where children showed up day after day with a predetermined attitude toward learning. We all did take him very seriously. There was no other way. Professor Korisheli knew exactly: whoever wanted to discover the power inherent in music first had to make a proper effort and invest sufficient time in technical skills and some cognitive abilities. And those could only be developed by careful listening and by reading sheet music.

Those proficiencies were anything but self-evident at the time. Korisheli took over a kind of school band composed of about seventy students who were well able to play marches and so on. However, he soon found out that they could hardly read music, but were dependent on someone writing the fingering above the notes. It was impossible to hand these students a sheet of music and immediately start rehearsals. However, he did not let himself be deterred, rolled up his sleeves and began to demand more from the children than they were accustomed to. They were expected to learn how to read music, to sight-read and to listen to each other. Two thirds soon gave up. They left the ensemble and pushed the professor to the brink of despair – his first big failure, and that only a few months after he had joined our school. After all, the school board hadn't hired a teacher to decimate the school band in such a short time.

Korisheli was about to throw in the towel, hand in his notice, get back into his Volkswagen and drive off. However, younger students had already flocked to him in droves and made good progress in his aural training and theory classes. The remaining third of this strange ensemble did not get discouraged, but took him on. They learned to read music, gave a highly impressive presentation of their new skills after his first year at our school and seemed inspired by the fact that Korisheli had brought them out of their musical illiteracy. The parents and the school management were enthusiastic. And the professor stayed on. His great charisma soon captivated the entire village.

I think it was in his second or third year that I became his student. My mother entrusted us children one by one into the care of this magician. And that was a good thing. Everything we had learned at home was suddenly placed in a larger context. The real purpose of all those piano lessons, the hard work of reading music and practicing those pieces revealed itself in less than no time. Like most of the other children, we had but one goal: we wanted to participate in one of the ensembles that the new teacher had founded. At any cost. All of us did. Korisheli began to recruit more and more students for the orchestra. Over the years there were so many of them that they soon formed three orchestras. I myself learned the viola and the clarinet for good measure in order to be able to play in those orchestras. I was taught these instruments by the Georgian professor.

MUSIC – SCHOOL – MUSIC

Our everyday life was – not least because of the music – quite tightly organized. In the morning before eight o'clock, Korisheli started teaching those who had registered for his class. In order to support his musical ambitions for the school, the board had granted him his own building, which he converted into a conservatory for us elementary school pupils. After our regular school lessons, which were usually held from nine to half past two in the afternoon, we walked back to his building. Orchestra rehearsals and additional individual lessons followed. At six in the evening we finally went home.

Admission to his orchestra, for which one had to make quite an effort, meant an increase in social prestige as a member of a – supposedly – select community of children with whom he worked intensively. But we weren't a select community, for he managed to enlist literally everyone. Dan, the son of a cattle breeder, was made to play the trumpet. He never really got good at it during the time I spent in the orchestra. But he was so keen that he participated in all three orchestras. I can't even count how many hours he must have sat in rehearsals. On the other hand, my friend Noël, son of a very Catholic family of Italian-Swiss descent, had real talent playing his tuba. He produced a warm, soft tone. At some point he disappeared from my sight. Very quietly. It was rumored that he had moved to another school where he was to be trained as a priest.

I also remember the weekends. We would visit our teacher at his home, and again and again there would be other children rehearsing chamber music in the most diverse combinations of instruments. That was unbelievable fun. We worshipped the professor. At home we had never played much together, at least not in the form of trios or quartets, which one usually thinks of when talking about chamber music. That's what we did at Korisheli's. In his private music studio he had built a staircase with twelve steps leading up to a kind of mezzanine. Each of the wooden steps represented a half tone or half step of the chromatic scale. I don't know how many of the village children were taught the basics of harmony on those very stairs.

In his home he also occupied himself with sculpting. For that, too, he had a dedicated studio where he created sculptures from logs and blocks of stone. He painted and he talked a lot about philosophy. We often used to travel with him. On the excursions he undertook with his students, we learned much about painting and sculpture, about the importance of aesthetics and, of course, about the great thinkers of the West. He shared all his knowledge with us. He let us participate in everything.

School, music, visual arts and private life merged into one another in an almost organic way, for us children as well as for our teacher. We learned with him, and he learned with us. He even involved the parents. His doors were always open. Any mother or father who wanted to could attend – and, above all, take part in – his lessons.

He turned the parents into enthusiastic teaching assistants, so that the children were not abandoned to their own devices once they left his conservatory. Parents, he once told me, had to become part of the child's success. When a child whose parents had had no previous access to the world of music had been won over by him to learn a certain instrument and been recruited for the orchestra, it was virtually a dogma for him that the whole family should enjoy his musical education.

For almost all the children at our elementary school, music had become an organic part of their everyday lives. Korisheli had opened the door to the fine arts for us and shaped our approach to them. But he not only influenced *our* artistic sensibility, but rather that of an entire community, in which music seemed to occupy center stage. That had always been his intention. He metamorphosed Morro Bay into a village of sound where music helped overcome the numerous conflicts that would flare up again and again in a community of immigrants from very different ethnic backgrounds.

When, at the age of twelve, I completed sixth grade, the musical idyll was almost over. I went to secondary school, but Professor Korisheli remained my teacher for another two years. But in high school that also changed. And when I think back to that time today, I realize that I plunged into a crisis of sorts. During that time there were lots of changes in the United States, and a social transformation began that left none of us untouched. It was a time of uncertainty. Music faded into the background. Other things became more important to me, especially school itself with all its demands. Professor Korisheli taught me the piano only sporadically.

In the second half of the sixties, when I was fifteen or sixteen years old, there were more turbulent times in the United States. The country had not yet come to terms with the assassination of John F. Kennedy when, in 1965, the controversial civil rights activist Malcolm X fell victim to a murderous attack. And I vividly remember the news that put me in a state of shock in 1968

– first Martin Luther King Jr. was shot dead, and two months later Robert Kennedy was also killed. The United States was already deeply enmeshed in the Vietnam conflict, which by this time had escalated into a fully fledged war, a cruel course of action, which the public initially followed with mere incomprehension, then with growing horror and finally with strong street protests. The hippie and flower-power movement, whereby the country's youth expressed its opposition to the politics of the establishment, had gained my attention.

In general, the American populace was highly politicized, something that, in retrospect, exerted great influence on me as a youth. After rehearsals, we often had long and heated discussions with Professor Korisheli about current affairs. The focus of my musical involvement shifted to the church. It seemed to me that my environment had more urgent matters to address than for me to continue to care for my musical education as an individual. True, the seeds had been sown in the first years of my life, and the small plants that grew from them had been carefully nurtured for a few years. But after that, from one day to the next, they were abandoned to wind and weather. I myself had to make sure that these plants would eventually bear fruit.

That I would do so could not be taken for granted. And so, in my youth, there was little indication that one day I would become a musician. From a layman's point of view I was probably quite a good pianist, but by no means an excellent one. In 1969, having acquired my high school diploma, I enrolled at the University of California, in sociology – and in music. I didn't want to give it up completely.

The days in college were long. I not only attended social science lectures and seminars, but also many courses in music, including analysis, theory and composition. Regular piano lessons, too, were a feature of my musical studies. I practiced a lot – this time of my own accord. Music remained a pivotal part of my life. At that time I didn't conceive at all that it would soon play such a dominant role that within a very short period of time not a day would pass when

I wouldn't play music, reflect on music or speak about music. My music professors in particular made a major contribution to this development. The world was my oyster. It had, it seemed to me at the age of about nineteen, so much to offer.

ON TEACHERS AND STRUCTURE

Why am I telling you all this? It's not fits of nostalgia or sentimentality that make me do it. I'm writing this down because, looking back at my own story, I realize what it is that's required to prevent society from losing its connection to music and the fine arts over generations. And because there is hardly a better example of this than us children from Morro Bay.

The arts can be socially alive only if people, actively or passively, participate in them, preferably from childhood. The prerequisite for this is a good infrastructure, one that is not only used by the social elites who haven't lost interest in classical music and who have sufficient private means at their disposal to pass this art on to their children.

By infrastructure I do not mean the philharmonic temples that carry our music out into the world as if under a spotlight. San Francisco and Los Angeles, the two Californian cities on the West Coast that were musically important, were far too remote for us as children to attend concerts all the time. Neither am I speaking of the sometimes very extravagant outreach programs for young people, which almost every philharmonic orchestra has created in order to keep tomorrow's audiences favorably disposed toward it. We children from Morro Bay never experienced any of that.

Instead, I mean an infrastructure that ensures a lasting presence of art forms such as classical music in the everyday lives of children and young people. And that works best when everyone can be reached, regardless of their social background, their parents' educational attainment or the financial circumstances into which they were born.

Professor Korisheli's conservatory was part of our school. There was a permanent supply of music, all the time people went to see him, took lessons or rehearsed in one of his ensembles.

Sounds, voices and cheerful laughter issued from the building. It was almost impossible not to be lured in. And this applied to nearly all pupils, not only to those whose background in German would be called "bildungsbürgerlich," i.e., coming from the educated middle class, like me. My siblings and I probably attended Wachtang Korisheli's courses with a little more prior knowledge than some of the neighbors' children. But did it really matter? In Morro Bay, art did not depend on members of the educated middle class at all. It only depended on one single person who was capable of filling others with enthusiasm.

Infrastructure is one thing; the other is teaching. Interest in music that is more than just entertainment is passed from person to person, from old to young, from teacher to student. Through self-study alone, one can develop neither the art of listening nor an awareness that it is worth learning more about music in order to be able to gather new experiences from its very depths. The same is true of active music-making.

If you want to appreciate music or make music, you need teachers. In classical music, the oft-cited importance of the influence of teachers cannot be overestimated, the most prominent stars by no means being the best teachers. Wachtang Korisheli the artist preferred to take a back seat. He didn't make music for his own reputation; he taught out of a sense of vocation because he couldn't help but share the music that had given him so much in life. He well and truly yearned to make music a part of everyone's life so that everyone could lead a more fulfilled, inspired, contented existence based on heightened perceptive faculties.

"What have teachers got to do with music?" Leonard Bernstein, in November 1963, asked his young audience in the Philharmonic Hall at Lincoln Center during one of his legendary concerts for young people, which were regularly broadcast on TV, in a rather provocative manner. It was a rhetorical question as was usually the case with Bernstein. "The answer is everything!" he called out to the assembled children and their parents. "The trouble is that we don't always realize how important teachers are in music or in anything else," he continued. "Teaching is probably the noblest profession in the world – the most unselfish, difficult, and honorable profession, but it is also the most unappreciated, underrated, underpaid, and under-praised profession in the world."

We all know what he's talking about. And we also know what an extraordinary teacher Leonard Bernstein was. He had made it to the top of the international classical music business and yet spoke of music in words that everyone understood. Due to his frequent appearances on television programs, he enjoyed an enormous presence in the United States and was a welcome guest in many a music-loving family's living room.

But, of course, he on his own could not bring music into the daily lives of millions of children and young people, especially not those whose parents had no palate for tuning into classical music programs on TV. To achieve that end, another type of teacher is much more important, namely teachers who are willing to descend to the drudgery of everyday life and, in the way they themselves live, set children an example of how the arts are an indispensable part of our existence. Classical music is something that is negotiated between the generations: it must be handed down from teacher to student, from parent to child. Wachtang Korisheli was in no way inferior to Leonard Bernstein. He, too, was a gifted teacher in Bernstein's terms, probably more so than Bernstein himself.

At university I was strongly influenced by two other teachers: one of them, Grosvenor Cooper, instructed me mainly in composition and music theory. In the subject "piano," I took lessons with Goodwin Sammel, who showed me, among other things, how vital and worthwhile it can be to deal intensively with the sources of a piece of music. After completing one's conservatory training and graduating from college, learning certainly doesn't stop – least of all in music. Afterwards, in San Francisco, the famous cellist and conductor Laszlo Varga became my teacher. He was unrelentingly strict and unforgiving as far as mistakes were concerned. He never forgave carelessness. From him I learned that access to music implies lifelong hard work and effort, but that one will be amply rewarded.

THE GOLDEN AGE OF CLASSICAL MUSIC

In my case, it was not just the encounters with those teachers that proved a stroke of luck; it was also the times that I happened to be born into. The Second World War was over. The deep recession into which it had tipped the United States abated and was superseded by an economic boom. The so-called "economic miracle" was not confined to a vanquished and destroyed Germany (where the term "Wirtschaftswunder" had been coined). The United States, too, experienced this positive "pull." The economy grew – despite new political crises that plagued the United States in the wake of the Cold War. It is true that we children of the fifties and early sixties lived in an idyllic world of economic miracles and education expansion – albeit with a certain counterpoint. We were confronted with a peculiar threat that was clearly perceptible. The fear of an extension of communism to the West was all-pervasive. The aftermath of the McCarthy era with its vociferous anti-communism did not fail to make an impact on us children. The United States had a veritable enemy. One had to be afraid of Russia and of communism.

But the economy was booming. Production levels were high, and there was an incredible amount of building activity going on. People purchased homes, automobiles, TVs. Those years were characterized by a marked growth of the middle class. California was at the forefront of this development. The economic momentum there was stronger than in any other state. Prosperity allowed the education system to thrive. The public sector invested heavily. The universities, steadily expanding or newly founded, soon enjoyed an excellent reputation far beyond the borders of the United States.

With a rapidly expanding middle class, education assumed special importance. Californian schools followed suit and were soon considered exemplary in the United States. Music and art education played a significant role, likewise dance, literature and theater. In any case, money was plentiful, and California became a place of longing, not only for the many Americans who moved there during those years. Great European musicians fostered the development of classical music and helped it to flourish, including composers of the stature of Arnold Schoenberg, Igor Stravinsky or Ernst Krenek, and conductors like Bruno Walter and Otto Klemperer.

In the seventies the situation changed considerably. The oil crisis of 1973 and the "second oil shock" of 1979 did not fail to affect the United States' economy. Tax reforms that had been introduced to relieve the burden on the citizens had a noticeable impact on the education system. In schools, the fine arts gradually fell victim to the decline in state revenue. All of a sudden they were no longer that important. In the early eighties even our teacher had a hard time. In 1984, when the allocations for music were no longer sufficient to guarantee the position of this subject as a valuable part of the curriculum, Korisheli left the public school system, and with it our elementary school. He transferred to a private school in the larger neighboring town of San Luis Obispo. For those who could not afford private music tuition, let alone a private school, the arts and classical music largely disappeared from their lives.

In Morro Bay one could not only observe which conditions were necessary for everyone to find their way to the arts. It was also easy to study the impact classical music can have. It created public spirit in a small community that couldn't have been more heterogeneous. The parents and grandparents of the children playing music had come from all over the world to make their own way in the American West. Many families had emigrated from Europe to the

United States in the late-nineteenth and mid-twentieth centuries. They had built new lives for themselves, like my grandparents and parents, and yet maintained and cultivated the lifestyle habits and the culture of their countries of origin.

My hometown, which belongs to San Luis Obispo County, has officially existed only since 1870. The original settlement, of course, was older. The land was fertile, the sea teeming with fish. People came from England, France, Switzerland, Germany, Latin America and Asia. Many different languages were spoken, and many different festivals were celebrated. Of course, from time to time disputes arose among inhabitants of such different ethnic backgrounds, not only among parents, but also us children and adolescents. Yet when we learned about music in Professor Korisheli's classroom, when we sat in the orchestra or, on the weekend, played chamber music at his house in very different formations, those conflicts vanished and social differences lost their significance.

Music held us together, instilled a sense of community, was a place of encounter. And it set a common goal: the next concert, toward which all of us worked together in order to give the audience, consisting for the most part of our parents and relatives, a unique experience. There was an unbelievable number of concerts. These brought the parents together again, who had at least two things in common: the joy of music and pride in their offspring, whether they played well or perhaps not quite so well.

Once, a man I had never heard of came to see me in my theater box and claimed to remember me well from earlier days. It took a while before I was able to place him – after all, we hadn't met one another for almost half a century. It was Noël, the tuba player from my childhood, who happened to be in Munich and dearly wanted to see me again. At the time I was general music director of the Bavarian State Opera.

It was an amazing encounter – for me more than for him, as he had always been able to follow my career in public. What had become of the gifted tuba player? Noël was not a priest, but a high-ranking FBI agent who, in the service of the customs investigation authority, specialized in combating the illegal tobacco, alcohol and arms trades. When I met him, he was already retired, and had hung up his gun and immediately bought himself a new instrument. He played again, day and night, was involved in various bands and toured the world with his tuba, perhaps with even greater passion than in his childhood years and with all the fervor of a retired person who no longer had to worry about school, career, life planning and livelihood. Music, he said, had always remained a part of him, even though he hadn't had a sheet of music in front of him for ages. Those years in Korisheli's laboratory had shaped him for life. We agreed that any child who is drawn into the world of fine arts will never lose it again. They become an integral part of his or her life – in whatever way.

What have my childhood experiences in this musical wonderland at the end of the world in Morro Bay bestowed on me? On the surface, everything. My life as a musician, as an artist – all of that is rooted in my childhood: an international career as a conductor; at some point the courage to stake everything on one card, on music – presumably because the world of sounds had fascinated me to such an extent that I could not do otherwise; the meticulousness with which I delve deeply into the world of music, never to be fully satisfied with what I experience in it. All of this I internalized in my childhood.

But all of this is just part of a mixture that professional musicians probably cannot do without, just as they cannot do without lucky chance encounters, which leave their mark and propel them on, even in difficult moments. And it only touches the surface. In a deeper sense, it's about something much more important. The naturalness with which we children of Morro Bay, that mixed bunch of immigrant offspring, discovered the music surrounding us and applied ourselves to it, that naturalness opened the gate to another world: the fascinating, infinite world of aesthetics.

From what perspective do I write this? From that of a well-known conductor who, at the age of sixty-six and therefore rather late in life, is beginning to worry about his future audience? No, forget that. Nothing that moves me in my heart of hearts has anything to do with it. I write this as a man of convictions, who – like many others – is bothered by a few simple questions. Why does music touch us so profoundly? How does it unfold its power? Why do aesthetic experiences in particular enable us to endure more easily the vicissitudes of life and that ever-present question associated with them – the why and wherefore?

Why is serious music involved whenever we are faced with almost unbearable circumstances? Why did prisoners in Hitler's concentration camps draw, sing and, if they had the opportunity, play music in their inhumane barracks? Why, of all things, did art make them not lose heart? How could French composer Olivier Messiaen, in 1941 a German prisoner of war, create a masterpiece with his *Quatuor pour la fin du temps* (*Quartet for the End of Time*)? And how could Professor Korisheli have endured the imponderabilities of his fate – the execution of his father and, shortly afterwards, bidding farewell to his mother in that agonizing uncertainty whether he might ever see her again? When he boarded the train to the Polish border, when that train slowly set in motion, when his mother ran beside his car waving to him, he couldn't have known that this was his last glimpse of her. There was to be no reunion. As children we understood that it was music that had given him the strength to bear all this.

MY DREAM

So I dream of a world in which everyone has the chance to find access to classical music. Maybe not only to classical music, but to the arts in general. The arts, the most mysterious of which is certainly music, make everyday life more than just bearable. They inspire us, open our minds. They help us to take on the incomprehensible and unbearable, and to accept it as part of our lives, to draw strength from it and not to despair of it. Now, call me a dreamer, a utopian, if it is my wish that everyone be able to experience the meaningful power of classical music in his or her life, regardless of their background or level of education. And if I try, with this book, to make a plea for the unconditional presence of the arts in the life of each individual.

This longing has its source in my childhood, when the arts played such a momentous role in an almost joyous way. I have never found aesthetic experiences *not* to be part of everyday life. But access to the arts does not happen automatically. It requires a willingness to get involved and to concern oneself with them. Classical music entails more than just entertainment. Those who do not acquire that willingness will find it much harder to discover the depth of classical music. Perhaps they will never find their way to it and will not even miss it, because they have never experienced how much it has to give. But would it be fair if they didn't know anything about it? Not only artists like me must feel concerned.

I am very often asked about my favorite composer – a question typically asked by laypeople, one that we musicians rarely ask each other. Maybe because we perceive it to be superficial and banal. Maybe because, to tell the truth, a straightforward answer is impossible.

Music has become my life. Nothing I do has *not* to do with music. I have rehearsed and conducted works by famous and lesser known composers from very different periods. I have tried to come to grips with them. For countless hours, I have thought about how the orchestras I conduct could play those works in such a way that the audiences are made aware of the statements contained within them. I have endeavored to get to the heart of those compositions and to unveil their mysteries. I still do that today. Therefore, it is those composers whose works I'm most occupied with at any given moment that are most familiar and perhaps nearest to me at that very moment. But are they also the ones dearest to me?

I don't know. My voyage of discovery through the world of classical music, which began sixty years ago in a fishing village on the West Coast of California, is far from over. On the contrary:

every day, my artistic curiosity drives me further and further into this fascinating world, which grows ever larger the more I probe. The world of music resembles our ever-expanding universe. The more I delve into it, the less I believe I know about it. So how could I possibly answer that perhaps not quite so banal question about my favorite composer?

Perhaps by putting it differently: "In your spare time, during those hours that are not allocated to projects or activities and that are completely yours – what music would you play for yourself?" The answer to that question is much simpler. It has to be the music of Johann Sebastian Bach. I say that without the shadow of a doubt. From my earliest childhood, Bach has followed me and I have followed him. To this very day. His music won't let go of me. Its depth is infinite. It combines everything that constitutes classical music. And to this very day I have been searching for the why and the wherefore. Are we to allow more and more people to live without ever hearing of this unparalleled composer?

BACH

Through the Heart to the Head

The first chord hits me with full force, bouncing off the walls of the nave and filling the entire space within seconds. That chord, which so abruptly emanates from the organ, is potent, powerful, majestic. Nothing remains untouched by it; everyone can hear and feel it. My whole body feels it. The vast space seems to resonate. That first sound penetrates deep into the farthest corner of the church, instantly charging the building with its tremendous energy, straining it to the bursting point.

All of a sudden, a single voice separates itself, escapes the tension of that stunning chord, seems to run away from that group of notes, returns and beckons the next. That one, deeper, follows it. They chase each other, unite and part again. Suddenly, a third voice rings out. I gasp for air. What's this? I hear a play, a conversation. Sometimes like a chat, then again like serious talk. I now think back to that time, remembering that first chord, which shook me so deeply half a century ago. I see myself in our own church as a child, around five years of age and completely under the spell of that configuration of tones. It is the music of Johann Sebastian Bach.

Our Presbyterian community church, which in my memory strikes me as enormous, was in fact a small white stone building, whose narrow gallery could, of course, not accommodate a mighty organ. But the instrument was sufficiently powerful to flood the nave with its sound.

As a child, I had no knowledge of the principles Bach used to compose his music. Nonetheless, in one of those first encounters with the composer there might already have been a sense of something absolutely extraordinary, of an orderliness that gave a solid foundation to that music, and to myself a feeling of profound security. The flow of the various voices, all of which went their own way without ever accidentally clashing, had a soothing effect. I sensed that there would be no collision, no crash. No arbitrariness, but rather a structure of impressive clarity. This is how I recall those moments. I see myself as a child in our church, stirred by my first encounter with the composer and emotionally shaken – how else am I to describe my feelings during those childhood moments? Bach moved me deeply. This is how I explain to myself my completely unreflecting response to his music as a child – I now am in full cognizance of the complexity and perfection of Bach's cosmos, without which I am no longer able to listen to his music.

The child's naïvety has, of course, disappeared. However, it must have been the impression of order that thrilled and captivated me, as well as the enormous energy within the system that drove the tones forward. Further and further forward. I fancied that even in my breathing I could feel the tension that Bach built up in his part writing, as well as the drama that he put into his music. Behind those tones, endlessly strung together, I heard and felt a helmsman, a ruler who, as a matter of course, assumed responsibility for the overall sound as well as the individual voices, not leaving them to their own devices but guiding them with utmost prudence and care.

In addition to the orchestras, the vibrant music scene that developed during my childhood in Morro Bay also encompassed church music. All this blended into one. Soon the church of my first encounter with Bach became too small, and two new, larger buildings were erected, to which congregational life moved along with its music. There we sang Bach chorales and cantatas, children and adults together. During the rehearsals I often had the association of different drawers, into which the individual voices were neatly assorted, clearly and distinctly separate from each other and yet part of a great whole. I followed those very independent melodies, uniquely arranged to form a steady stream. Bach's choral compositions, the famous cantatas, the oratorios for Christmas and Easter, swept me off my feet as a child. It was impossible to imagine my life as a child and as an adolescent without them. In the choir I was not merely a listener, but, even as a young singer, quite naturally part of that steadily coursing river, its swirls and shoals, its surprising rapids and, at other times, its majestic flux.

Those early encounters with Bach and the deep attachment that sprang from them throughout my childhood may form a first, decisive part of the answer to the question as to why Bach, over the decades, has remained an unshakable constant in my personal, and indeed intimate, life as a musician, and has kept me in thrall to this day. To a certain extent, it is a result of "childhood imprinting," of the circumstances into which I happened to be born. Evidently, those early childhood experiences were highly formative.

But did it necessarily establish a lifelong fascination with the music of a single composer? Or with the fact that, when I travel and venture through the world of classical music and beyond, I always return to Bach and his music as though I were coming home? When I'm in California, having some time to myself and standing in front of my shelf with all the sheet music that has accumulated over a lifetime, I instinctively reach for Bach, perhaps pulling out one of his cantatas, an invention or *The Well-Tempered Clavier*. I sit down at my grand piano and play his music. Sometimes for fifteen or twenty minutes, sometimes losing myself in his world for hours on end.

In the course of my life I have thought more about Bach and his music than these pages could ever contain. And there has been more research done on him and more written about him than I could ever read or contemplate, in order to get to the bottom of the riddle that the centrifugal force of his music represents. But if I were to try and explain at least a little, I would begin with Bach's great educational skills.

Johann Sebastian Bach was not only a great composer and cantor but also an exceptionally gifted teacher. Today we no longer perceive him as such. In his day, however, instruction was nothing unusual. On the contrary, those who made music professionally, earning their living as cantors in a church or as Kapellmeister at a princely court, were teachers of music. Music-making and composition were learned as a craft. Until recent times, there were no courses at music colleges or conservatories on offer. Music was deemed to be a kind of artisan trade that required formal training. If you were very lucky, you were apprenticed to Bach.

The composer repeatedly admitted apprentices into his house. During his time as Thomaskantor in Leipzig he is said to have taught up to sixty university students as a sideline, not to mention a number of pupils from wealthy aristocratic circles. Leafing through the literature, one comes across many reports by his pupils about the way he – mostly through his own compositions – opened the world of music to them, his world. Learning under Bach meant not only studying pieces and playing them as consummately as possible on a keyboard instrument; it meant musical education in a far broader sense. His students, provided they were willing, talented and ambitious enough, also learned the art of improvisation or the art of composition.

Bach knew that, for this purpose, not only were the technical requirements of an outstanding pianist necessary, but above all a music-theoretical basis, which gave his pupils an understanding of characteristic features of the compositional art of his time. Genius that he was, he provided those compositions himself. For his sons and pupils he composed the thirty piano pieces known as two-part inventions and three-part sinfonias, which he collected in *Clavier-Büchlein vor Wilhelm Friedemann Bach*, the name of one of his sons. Three years later he revised them and compiled them in a new sequence in his primer *Aufrichtige Anleitung* (*Honest Method*). Here, the individual inventions and sinfonias are arranged systematically in such a way that major and minor keys strictly alternate, starting with the basic key C major and moving through all the other keys.

Bach himself clearly stated the intended purpose of this primer, arguably his first: amateurs of the clavichord, especially those "desirous of learning," were not only to learn how to play cleanly in two parts and even handle three obligato parts, but also to "acquire a strong foretaste of composition." Anyone can listen to music; anyone who has mastered an instrument can play music. But only those who have at some point internalized the theoretical foundations of music are able to compose, and thus to create something new. Bach wanted to achieve precisely that: in a recognizably systematic fashion, yet enwrapped in wonderful melodies.

At the age of twelve or thirteen, I studied these little compositions for the first time in earnest, and, frankly, in those days I saw in them no more than requisite piano études my teacher had set me as a task.

At the time, of course, I couldn't intellectually grasp, and could possibly only intuit, Bach's conceptual thinking as the foundation of his creative power in these miniatures. Today I know better. These miniatures are, so to speak, a distillation of his compositional art, since they contain everything that belongs to a basic understanding of our tonal system. It is actually possible, with the help of these miniatures, to learn virtually anything essential to music.

The passionate pedagog composed these little pieces, in spite of their being extremely structured, in a lively, extraordinarily colorful and contrasting manner, for learners, musicians and listeners alike. Yet all of these little works conform to the fundamental principle of motivic concentration. They grow out of a basic musical idea, but in so sophisticated and elaborate a style that I would confidently call them a completely new form of art.

Bach's pupils must have been enthusiastic anyway, and fascinated. Many of them went into raptures over them. The students learned predominantly from Bach's own works. At first they worked with his miniatures, the inventions and sinfonias, and after that they dealt with some of his suites. Finally, after they had studied those to their master's satisfaction, they gained access to his expanded musical cosmos: the sublime piano cycle *The Well-Tempered Clavier*.

In 1722, Bach created the first part of a total of forty-eight preludes and fugues; twenty years later, the second. Each part contains twenty-four sets of pairs of movements, namely a prelude and a fugue arranged within the key notation system, in both major and minor. The work begins in C major, the next pair of movements is written in the minor key of the same name, that is, C minor, and all of the others follow chromatically and thus half step by half step, ascending to the key of B minor. One pair per half step of the octave (which consists of twelve half steps), all of them in major and minor, so that it all adds up to precisely twenty-four preludes and fugues.

That Bach was able to write preludes and fugues so euphoniously on every half tone of the chromatic scale has a reason: he knew how to tune his instrument perfectly. "Well-tempered" translates to well-tuned. What we mean by that is a way of deliberately impure tuning, which is contrary to the natural law of physical sound vibration behind pure intervals, so that all keys sound pleasant to the ear. This was not feasable until well into the seventeenth century. In 1681, the musical theorist Andreas Werckmeister devised the idea that certain intervals had to be slightly altered, so that triads built on any root of the chromatic scale sounded agreeable rather than dissonant.

Bach was the first to make full use of this; he tuned his instrument with a healthy portion of pragmatism and henceforth composed in every key of the scale. Tempered tuning was like an act of liberation. The language of music had been released from its last fetters. Now, at last, Bach could pick from an embarrassment of riches and let his musical imagination run free in any key. And he was a consummate master. He had perfected the Western musical idiom of his time.

What is it about Bach that fascinates not only us musicians so much? Perhaps it is first and foremost the order that Bach created and that we humans need, and not only when we listen to music. Bach gives us a sense of bearing within this order – with its keys and roots and triads stacked on top of those roots, both in major and in minor.

The systematic way in which Bach composed these works for his pupils is impressively lucid. His piano cycle is a compendium not only of all the keys, but also of various compositional forms. This is unique in music history. It reveals, on the one hand, the composer's perfectly logical thinking, and demonstrates, on the other, his pedagogical aptitude, and his passion for making available to his pupils something that would help them to internalize the world of tones and melodies, of keys and their configurations once and for all. The students learn, so to speak, Bach's tonal system and thus his language, a language that is still spoken in classical music today. And all of this is done with the help of tunes and themes, whose diversity seems to know no bounds. In a fascinating way, this cycle combines both logic and creativity, a closed musical system and artistic inventiveness, Bach certainly giving free rein to his vast imagination. With this piano cycle, composed within the space of a few years, he reached an apogee in the art of composition.

How I would have liked to hear him play himself! How often have I imagined how *he* would have played his compositions, and envied his students, who could listen to this genius and enjoy their most impressive hours of instruction whenever Bach happened to have no desire at all to teach them. In those moments he sat down at his keyboard and made his musical cosmos vibrate. He played *The Well-Tempered Clavier* and turned the hours he needed to do so into minutes. No wonder – Bach's music cannot possibly become boring. On the contrary, it is full of surprises, which you sometimes don't even realize unless you have played a prelude or fugue many a time.

Why, at a certain point, does he use an ascending melody, even though our natural feeling would expect the exact opposite? Why does it not fall? Sometimes I am so perplexed that I have to laugh while playing. Especially when I believe that I know a piece particularly well. Then again, Bach suddenly changes from one key to another so that his composition is given new color, and a new atmosphere is established. And I marvel. Perhaps it is to that element of surprise his music owes its magic. Perhaps it is the fact that Bach's music gains in depth the more you devote yourself to it.

In any case, *The Well-Tempered Clavier* is not only a magnificent "transmission belt" for the musical language of the baroque, a language in which we communicate to this day as far as classical music is concerned, but also a coupling of two contrasting types of musical pieces: prelude and fugue, the first free and playful, the second stricter and more complex or sophisticated. While Bach's preludes show a wide range of forms of expression, the fugues follow a fixed pattern whereby the voices imitate each other. Together they turn the piano cycle into an encyclopedia of musical knowledge. When playing, I am acutely aware of this combination of the composer's intellectual capacity and the creative emotionality that he puts into his music, aware of how he manages to keep these two inner forces in perfect balance. If it didn't smack of pathos, I would argue that something divine inheres in Bach's musical creations.

Bach's music casts a spell over people throughout the world – completely independently of the cultural space they inhabit. Is it only due to the perfection of his musical idiom, his resourcefulness, his imagination? No, Bach's music contains stories, purely musical stories, which can awaken a plethora of concrete associations in the listener. If you are somewhat familiar with Bach's œuvre, think of his orchestral suites. Surely you know Suite no. 3 in D Major and its solemn second movement, entitled "Air" (a song-like melody), which immediately draws you into a kind of dramaturgy. Or the Brandenburg Concerto no. 4, involving a solo violin and two recorders, in which the three protagonists continuously relate to each other.

However, Johann Sebastian Bach was able to compose in a much more existential fashion than he did in the cheerful cycle of his six Brandenburg Concertos. He was a deeply devout Christian, an orthodox Lutheran, who placed all of his creative energy at the service of God. From this self-conception, and with his high measure of sensitivity and his mastery of musical language he took a closer look at the human condition. In his music, like an existentialist *avant la lettre*, he dealt with all those big life-defining questions that again and again occupy our minds. Bach refers to the opposing forces that determine our existence, and that is why his music is so true to life. He plays with major and minor keys, contrasts brightness and darkness, light and shadow, portrays the struggle of good against evil, of love against hate. No white without black, no good without bad – these cross-cultural opposites are found in his music and make it intelligible to everyone.

His music is about the continual recurrence of human experiences, about fun, joy, sadness and despair, about conflict and reconciliation. Bach addresses man's wrestling with the Creator and His will. His cantatas, written for Sunday worship, are full of drama. He composed more than two hundred of these cantatas, not one of them of inferior quality. In his cantata for solo bass voice and orchestra BWV 56 "Ich will den Kreuzstab gerne tragen" ("I will my cross-staff gladly carry"), he set the words of Jesus in such a touching way to music that, at the very moment of singing, the suffering of the whole world seems to lie on the shoulders of the Son of God. No less profound is his Mass in B Minor, in whose chorales and arias our human existence is wonderfully represented.

Everything he composed was created for the greater glory of God. He understood man to be made in the image of God, and music, in its most perfect form, to be an opportunity to make God's grace present on earth. And yet, much as he worshipped God, Bach never lost sight of man with all his needs, which also includes recreation, the "recuperation of the mind." Bach himself felt obliged to place his outstanding musicality and creativity at the service of the Almighty. It was the baroque worldview of his time that shaped him, and that did not yet know the sharp distinction between the sacred and the profane. Bach saw himself as a creation of God, his music as part, and mirror image, of divine conception, with man at the center, all his strengths and weaknesses included.

Everything is interconnected: entertainment and profundity, pedagogy and creativity, logic and feeling. That Bach picked up ever-recurring topoi of human existence and "processed" them musically is only a logical consequence. And, in the end, it's precisely that which raised this musician above the constraints of his era.

Thus, it is two things that led Bach far beyond the baroque period, making his music an inexhaustible source of inspiration for us, his interpreters: the life-defining themes that he takes up and that have occupied mankind from time immemorial, and the perfect musical language he created. In his catholicity, Bach may be more modern than any later composer whose point of reference he remains.

In this way, Bach himself becomes the creator of his own cosmos – perfect, logical, multilayered and much more powerful than in his earlier miniatures. But even there it is already palpable: Bach is the ruler and navigator of his own universe. He completes a musical development, leading it to perfection and hence far beyond its time. Was he aware of the significance of the language he created? I don't know. Without language there is nothing; without language there is no thinking, no consciousness, no human existence. One of the first acts of God, at the very beginning of the process of creation, was to *speak*: "And God said, Let there be light: and there was light." God speaks even before man exists. John the Evangelist placed the existential relevance of language at the start of his Gospel: "In the beginning was the Word, and the Word was with God, and the Word was God."

For so much music, whether serious or just entertaining, Bach's musical idiom is the very foundation. And that's what makes this composer so unique. We do not know how music would have developed in the centuries after him had it not been for him. We cannot even imagine it. I have often asked myself why, even today, Johann Sebastian Bach should be so much beyond criticism. He is rarely challenged, and his works are not often subjected to the kind of comparative evaluation received by other composers – including Mozart, whose numerous symphonies are said to be of different compositional quality. Bach is revered and loved. His music no longer derives its universal validity from its theological foundations and from the Christian worldview that left so strong a mark on him. Bach's music requires no Christian justification. Its aesthetics, its worth, its importance has long since outgrown the religious sphere.

Toward the end of his life, the genius withdraws, deals only with his own creations, plays with the language he has accomplished, and employs it to compose a final, equally stupendous work, yet another cycle: *The Art of the Fugue*, a collection of fourteen fugues and four two-part canons. Working on the last, the fourteenth fugue, the composer, at this stage completely blind, dies. The cycle remains unfinished. Nevertheless, it once again provides an illuminating insight into the artist's intellectuality and immeasurable power of imagination. The compositional artistry of this work is unrivaled. Bach composed some of the fugues as mirror fugues, that is to say, as pieces of music where the notes mirror each other along an imaginary horizontal line. Or to put it another way: you could turn the notes upside down. Of course, there would be a different melody, but one that is in no way inferior in quality to the original one. It is as if a poet wrote verses that could be read backward and that would have a different but no less profound meaning, and lose none of their poetic quality. Bach arranged these fugues in three- and four-part forms.

But that's not all by any means. Bach's piano compositions contain innumerable messages, teeming with symbols he incorporated into his pieces in various ways. Once you are open to that, you will strike it rich; you won't be able to stop yourself, as though you were decrypting a code that gains in complexity with every step of decoding. Bach plays with numbers, with the number fourteen, for instance. In the last, the fourteenth fugue of the cycle, which he left unfinished, he used his own name as a theme – as though he wished to put the creator's stamp on his life work one last time before dying.

If you look closely at the preceding pieces, you will discover that the sequence B–A–C–H (in English notation B♭–A–C–B♮) had been used before, albeit not as a theme, but concealed. In the last fugue, however, Bach introduces his own name as a sustained motif. There is some speculation that the number fourteen, too, is a coded reference to his name. If you number the letters of the alphabet and add up the digits that make up Bach's surname, the result is fourteen. That number fourteen appears in many of his works. A mere coincidence?

The sensation that someone is bringing order to my world takes hold of me even today. Unlike when I was a small boy, I now know about the closed tonal system, on the basis of which Bach created his melodies and produced an almost endless stream of works. Anyone who simply listens to the music of Johann Sebastian Bach will inevitably be absorbed by it. They will let themselves be carried away by the stunning power of the sound itself and maybe can only guess at the underlying musical principles. The music will infuse them. However, anyone who embraces Bach and studies the theoretical foundations of his musical creations will embark upon a journey that will last a lifetime. They will recognize that the universal validity of Bach's musical statements elevates that ingenious composer far beyond his time, the baroque.

In his 1908 monograph on the composer, the famous physician and philosopher Albert Schweitzer wrote that Bach was "a terminal point" ("Nothing comes from him; everything merely leads up to him"), the climax of the great tradition of Western music, which found its master and consummator in Johann Sebastian Bach, in whose works the musical development of an important era was perfected and thus exhausted. At the time, Schweitzer may have thought so, greatly influencing the prevailing view on Bach's significance. However, Bach was no terminal point. Bach was an experimenter, an innovator and, above all, a superb musician whose creations paved the way for a new beginning, the dawn of a new age.

Bach is classified as a baroque composer. He may indeed have perfected the baroque style of music. But the musical idiom he created marked the beginning of an epoch that was later called the classical period. In the first place, it facilitated those new developments, putting them on track. It was the point of reference for Haydn, Mozart and Beethoven, whose output cannot be fully conceived without Bach's groundwork. His œuvre is the beginning of musical developments that stretch through the classical and romantic periods to the present. His music contains those future developments, some of which he even anticipated, in embryonic form. His cosmos poses a permanent challenge: to either break out of it or tear it down completely, as Arnold Schoenberg did later. It all begins with Bach, and he won't relinquish his hold on the listener.

CHAPTER TWO

DECLARATION OF BANKRUPTCY
IN PHILADELPHIA

"The disappearance of the old culture implied the disappearance of the old concept of value. The only existing value is now what the market dictates."

Mario Vargas Llosa,
Notes on the Death of Culture (2015)

CONCERT IN A GHOST TOWN

The concert hall is brightly lit. It sparkles. Festively dressed people pour through the foyer into the big hall. The orchestra performs cheerful music from the heyday of classical music. A symphony and a piano concerto are on the program. The conductor, the musicians and the pianist give their best, the latter playing with particular intensity this evening. In the end, hushed tension erupts in thunderous applause – as has been the case for nearly a hundred years, whenever the wealthier part of society arrives on Woodward Avenue in midtown Detroit. There is no palpable sense of an orchestra hovering on the brink of financial ruin.

The performance having finished, a limousine takes the pianist to his hotel, only a few blocks away from the concert hall that was built in 1919. After his gig he is hungry and asks the driver for a little detour. He would like to get a sandwich from one of those 24/7 shops. The driver shakes his head. He refuses to oblige. He doesn't want to turn off the main street, certainly not enter one of those dark back lanes where street lighting has been switched off for months due to the ongoing municipal financial crisis. In Detroit, he says, it has been far too dangerous to do so lately.

This small incident took place a few years ago, at a time when the menacing decline of the city could be seen and felt on every street corner. But not inside the concert hall, to which listeners in their best evening attire have shown their loyalty for a hundred years. Vacant buildings, myriad robberies – every American remembers newspaper reports on the subject and knows that "Motor City," whose once thriving automobile manufacturing industry used to co-fund classical music, has slipped into a major crisis. In 2013, the city was just a shadow of its former self, in debt to the tune of eighteen billion dollars. Almost eighty thousand houses stood empty. In the concert hall of the Paradise Theater, as the building used to be called, it wasn't noticeable at the time, the pianist tells me. Not yet.

The picture he painted of the stark contrasts within this battered city suddenly assumed an almost surreal quality in my mind: a metropolis threatened by an economic downturn, whose population has shrunk to less than a third, but on whose "upper deck" the orchestra, applauded by an audience dressed up to the nines, bravely continues to play as it is sucked into the city's financial maelstrom.

As I listened to him, I instinctively thought of the bourgeois concert and opera culture that had its flowering period from 1870 to the 1920s. For a brief moment, that stolid music industry seemed akin to an unwieldy ship moving in icy waters. Could it be that we musicians who have dedicated ourselves to serious music are the band that's playing on while the ocean steamer's hull has sprung a leak? Fiddling on undauntedly, we refuse to believe that the ship is already full of water.

The news currently surrounding the traditional music business clearly shows that much is changing – threatened by cost-cutting measures. For years, there has been talk of a shortage of money in many places. Every house fights for itself. Classical music is at stake everywhere because it is allegedly too expensive or – as is often claimed – not quite suitable for the times we live in, an art form preserved in a museum with exhibits from the eighteenth and nineteenth centuries that have little to do with the life models and working conditions of the people of today. The big ship has run into trouble. And those who, together with their instruments, haven't already slipped off the deck simply continue to play.

It has been almost forty years since I devoted myself entirely and exclusively to classical, i.e., serious or art music. After studying sociology and music at the University of California, from which I graduated with a diploma in both subjects, I continued my studies in San Francisco. Then I actually made something like a career decision. So for four decades I have been experiencing how the world of classical music is changing. I see orchestras disappear. I observe how our audiences are aging and how young people no longer encounter classical music at all or, if they do, approach it with a certain degree of reserve. This applies even to my own family: my nieces and nephews can hardly relate to classical music at all. And it can be clearly felt that many institutions of the arts are coming under pressure.

Over the past four decades, I think, we have experienced an ongoing decline in the significance of classical music. Our guild – or call it an industry – seems to be past its golden age and is in urgent need of a kind of redefinition of its role in society. Am I glorifying the past? Are these the first signs of aging that I used to notice, and shrug off, in others because people beyond the age of sixty commonly lament their lost youth, sighing that everything was better in the old days? I don't really know. Let me describe what I am experiencing, then compare it with your own experiences and judge for yourself.

DEATH IN INSTALLMENTS

In the United States, an unprecedented number of orchestras has been in – sometimes terminal – decline. Many orchestras, whether large or small, find themselves in an almost hopeless financial position. Some have disappeared completely (the German language even has a term for this: "Orchestersterben"). In others, the struggle for survival is fierce. In each individual case a veritable cacophony ensues: managers, artistic directors and musicians put the blame on each other. Strikes take place, events are canceled, artists are locked out in response to a strike. Houses remain closed for months. The orchestras usually come under pressure from two sides: rising costs and an increase in expenditure on the one hand, lower revenue on the other, due to declining private sponsorship and a fall in demand for tickets. All of this takes place before the very eyes of the general public. Music enthusiasts may be appalled by the widespread demise of our orchestral landscape, but a large portion of the public seems to be rather disinterested.

It was hoped that the most renowned orchestras in our country, commonly designated as the "Big Five," beacons of classical music culture, would not perish. As long as they could maintain their budgets, continue to pay big artists and come up with ambitious concert programs, serious music as an art form would at least remain visible. In 2011, however, there was a tremendous crash. The Philadelphia Orchestra, which together with the New York Philharmonic, the Boston and the Chicago Symphony Orchestras and the Cleveland Orchestra ranks among the top five in the country, went bust, shattering the illusion that everything could stay the way it was. This proud and brilliant ensemble, steeped in tradition, whose history began in 1900, had to file for bankruptcy protection, as granted by the American legal system under Chapter 11. How to go on?

I grew up in a time when classical music seemed to be part of everyday life. Not for everyone, but for a significant part of the American population. Classical music happened everywhere: not just in schools like ours or in the concert halls of big and small cities. The whole country was littered with the most diverse music ensembles, in which music-loving laypeople banded together, rehearsed and gave concerts. There was a large number of semi-professional orchestras in which professional musicians and excellent amateurs came together. The doctors' orchestras of New York or San Francisco were known nationwide for their quality. Concerts were often broadcast on television, and other TV programs dealt with classical music in general.

Unforgettable is the cycle *Young People's Concerts*, a series of regular family concerts given by the New York Philharmonic Orchestra. It was devised in the twenties and reached the peak of its popularity with Leonard Bernstein. From 1958 to 1972, the concerts hosted by him at Carnegie Hall and later at Lincoln Center were broadcast on prime-time television. They are emblematic of what I call the golden age of serious music. Seldom has classical music fared better in the United States than in the thriving economy of the sixties and seventies. Classical music was taken for granted and a constant in the everyday life of our society. For me as a budding musician these were wonderful times. We artists were needed, even artists like myself who were not trained as solo instrumentalists, but as generalists, as composers, arrangers, musicologists or music producers. There were many ways to find a job in the world of music. I worked at many houses, first on the West Coast, then in Boston, accompanying soloists and ensembles as répétiteur or assistant conductor.

As early as the mid-eighties, this idyllic world of classical music, in which things seemed to be going upward only, rather unexpectedly received its first dent. In September 1986, the Oakland Symphony Orchestra went into receivership, buried under a mountain of nearly four million dollars of debt. It was an orchestra with a remarkable tradition, founded in 1933 and, over the years, a counterpart to the orchestra of nearby San Francisco in terms of audience numbers. I still remember this dynamic orchestra where I worked as assistant conductor for some time at a young age. Oakland was a lively city. The orchestra played in the city center at the Paramount Theater, formerly a run-down cinema, now a performance hall boasting almost three thousand seats. In the seventies this magnificent building, designed in the art deco style, was elaborately renovated as part of an urban renewal program, in the hope of adding another attraction to the city center.

City life flourished. People met at many places, in the illuminated old town, at the harbor, in the football stadium or indeed at the concert hall. At some point in the early eighties, however, money became scarcer. The fat years of upswing seemed to be over. Local politicians were forced to save money, they cut expenditure on the education system and on municipal administration, and they had to decide whether they would rather promote sports or save the largely independent orchestra from ruin with a generous financial injection.

At the time, the sports scene in Oakland was dominated by the Oakland Raiders, a successful football team and the pride of the city. The orchestra had already fallen into a spiral of deficits and ever more debts. The city's administration and the orchestra management moved further and further apart. The city stood back, and the Oakland Symphony Orchestra had no chance of survival. It was shut down, its large in-house library was sold, the musicians were dismissed and the concert hall remained locked and was no longer a meeting place. With music coming to an end, even the streetlights darkened. The old town emptied because the citizens stayed away. Social problems got out of control. Oakland's crime statistics were pretty high.

As soon as the representatives of the United States' classical music industry had somewhat recovered from the shock of that bankruptcy, unique at the time, they began to interpret this event as an isolated incident. A study under the memorable title *Autopsy of an Orchestra* was commissioned to analyze the reasons for the decline and to learn from the mistakes. It read as excitingly as a thriller. The thrust of it was unmistakable: the Oakland Symphony's bankruptcy was caused by management errors, by unreasonable musicians who were only concerned about their wages and, above all, by excessive expectations of growing attendance figures. Fourteen hundred orchestras in the United States, the media kept repeating, would not disappear overnight – regardless of the financially strained situation of many a city orchestra.

The Oregon Symphony director's statement, "We don't need to increase donations, we need to raise awareness," was a little more forward-looking. We need to raise awareness of music and of how much it hurts when an orchestra founders. Orchestras are not artistically credible because they make millions of dollars, he continued. "They make millions of dollars because they are artistically credible." Representatives of the American classical music world met at congresses, pondered fundraising, audiences, programs and so forth, yet allowed themselves to be lulled into a false sense of security: that the arts would not lose their traditional place in society.

Looking back, the death of the Oakland Symphony Orchestra seems to me, and not only to me, like a turning point in the history of classical music since the time it conquered the United States from Europe. In that imbroglio, an attitude manifested itself that has become commonplace in today's Western industrial and post-industrial societies: so many things are so much more important than serious music; serious music is a nice-to-have, but by no means essential. In Oakland, it was first and foremost the football team to which the city paid attention. A few years after the concert hall had been closed and the orchestra's inventory sold off, a new stadium costing 220 million dollars was built. From a musician's point of view, that kind of cynicism could hardly be beaten. Still, at that time, in the eighties, I couldn't have imagined that around the turn of the millennium a great "Orchestersterben" would commence in the United States, forcing performance halls to close their doors, and driving musicians into unemployment. Looking back, Oakland only marked a beginning.

GREETINGS FROM LEHMAN BROTHERS

There are reasons for this "Orchestersterben," chiefly the recent financial and economic crises but also, of course, a handful of home-grown difficulties. The financial crisis of 2008, which plunged the United States into a deep recession, left its mark.

The endowment funds at the disposal of the large orchestras and opera houses have shrunk dramatically. The return on capital, i.e., the cash inflow with which these institutions finance themselves, fell sharply. Equally affected were the assets of those private individuals who commonly support orchestras with donations. And the third source of income didn't yield as much revenue as in the past, either: ticket sales. During the economic crisis, many people preferred to forgo the pleasure of concertgoing, in the United States a rather expensive one in the first place.

All this has catapulted several of the once lavishly resourced classical music institutions into an existential crisis. Of course, not all orchestras are affected. Some are even expanding, others are reinventing themselves – thanks to the skilled hands of their managements. Unlike in Germany, American orchestras receive hardly any public subsidies. Either the business pays off, or it accumulates so much debt over the years that it eventually becomes illiquid, and thus bankrupt. This is just what happened in 2011 to the Philadelphia Orchestra, which officially declared insolvency on 16 April 2011 at 3:30 p.m., only hours before the evening's highly acclaimed performance of Mahler's Fourth Symphony. For us musicians this had been unimaginable until then – it was a real shock. Up to that point, several small orchestras had gone bankrupt, but none of the size and with the reputation of the Philadelphia Orchestra.

The financial crisis caught many of the independent institutions completely unprepared. Musicians were expected to forgo significant portions of their salaries, and strikes were the order of the day. American capitalism, which had created and financed such a wonderful orchestral landscape, was in a state of crisis. And that crisis voraciously devoured the music scene. In many cities and towns, citizens were suddenly forced to think about what these institutions as flagships of classical music were worth to them. The "Orchestersterben" actually demanded a reconsideration of how much music society was willing to afford. And above all, how much music it believed it needed.

Financial bottlenecks, concert halls pressed for money and orchestras facing ruin are, however, not exclusively an American phenomenon. It is only particularly evident here, because in the United States the public sector hardly contributes at all to the financing of cultural institutions. The magnificent cultural scene in Italy also found itself in dire straits – in Italy, of all countries, where opera had flourished, what with Giuseppe Verdi, Giacomo Puccini, Gioachino Rossini, Vincenzo Bellini and Gaetano Donizetti. There are houses in Italy that are barely or indeed no longer able to pay their guest artists. A large number of opera houses have run into the red and been forced to close down. In the fall of 2014, the venerable opera house in Rome gave notice to all its musicians and singers. It then embarked on a painful course of financial recovery to turn things around, with considerable success. But the tight network of opera houses in Italy is still in danger. Eventually it might dissolve, leaving in place only those well-known houses that are still, or once more, financially stable: the Scala di Milano, Venice's La Fenice, the Teatro Regio in Turin and the Opera House in Rome. Officially, the reason for the demise of opera houses in Italy is the over-indebtedness of the country as a whole and of its local authorities in particular. There is simply no money left to fund culture. Across the country, the budgets for culture have been drastically curtailed.

A WASTING DISEASE IN WONDERLAND

And what about Germany – the world's wonderland of music with more than one hundred and thirty professional symphony orchestras, a country where I have been general music director since 2002? There, too, we find hard-pressed houses. Orchestras are being merged or dissolved, prompting the question of whether medium-sized and smaller cities actually warrant concert halls and orchestras, when the financial worries plaguing the municipalities in charge are growing year after year. There, the pressure does not come from private donors or investors, but rather from the public sector, which is obliged to enforce a policy of cutbacks. Often, the decision is whether to invest in physical infrastructure or in the arts.

In Germany, unlike in the United States, classical music is more likely to be ousted from daily life *pianissimo*. Rather than causing full-scale scandals like in the United States, it tends to be a drawn-out dying process, a consumptive wasting away. In terms of the number of orchestras, the German musical landscape, once so rich, has been reduced by a quarter over the past twenty years. This process of "market adjustment," as some cultural practitioners like to call it, is far from over. In Germany's medium-sized cities, more and more orchestras are jeopardized by austerity measures, be it in terms of their independence or even their very existence, not only in the financially weak municipalities of industrial areas that were once flourishing, but also in the prosperous south. What are the repercussions for the social life of a city when, together with industry and employment, musicians quietly vanish, and people no longer meet in concert halls?

Of course, the opposite could also be argued: there are signs of hope. Some institutions are modernizing, trying to reach new audiences. In addition, chamber orchestras, string quartets and highly specialized ensembles are being founded, bringing new momentum to the rather traditional world of classical music – on both sides of the Atlantic. New concert halls are being built and utilized, such as the Elbphilharmonie in Hamburg or the Pierre Boulez Hall in Berlin. The radiating power of these new beacons in the long run and for the whole of Germany will become apparent only in a few years' time.

For the United States, one may also hope that when endowment funds grow strong again and yield more returns, the orchestras' plight will improve, provided they haven't been closed by then. One could argue even more boldly: if wealth and confidence return to my country, people would once more like to afford culture, and new orchestras or other music initiatives might emerge. Why not?

But that's not what it looks like at all. In the United States, the discussion on the marginalization and ultimate extinction of this art form continues unabated. "Is The Symphony Orchestra Dying?" *Time* magazine asked back in 2001. Much later, in 2012, one could read in the venerable *New York Times*, "Is Classical Music Dying?" In 2014, the *Washington Post* asked, "Classical Music: Dead or Alive?" Again and again, observers of the scene were worried about the future of our art form. "Requiem: Classical Music in America Is Dead," "Classical Music Isn't Dead"; I could cite quite a variety of examples. In 2016, the *Huffington Post* once again dedicated itself to the topic on the Internet, using the telltale headline "From Bach To Beyoncé: Is Classical Music Dead?'

It is good that the discussion about the future of classical music is in full swing. Despite hopeful signs in some places, this particular art form has, in an often disturbing fashion, become far removed from the majority of the population in industrial and post-industrial societies. It's no longer part of the reality of people's lives. Local classical music events are no longer reported in the newspapers. Classical music radio programs disappear or are banished to the digital sphere, where one has to search for them specifically. Musicians are no longer considered indispensable members of our society. Without the stage, they have no chance of being noticed by the public, of winning citizens over to the art of music in the first place, of convincing them of its importance and of fighting for it. And this is true not only of the United States, where classical music's continued existence in a largely privately financed opera and concert landscape depends much more on the wealthy citizen, but also of Germany, with its highly subsidized cultural industry.

The disappearance of an orchestra, the death of an individual institution, whether tumultuous or quiet, is the expression of a societal decision: What are the priorities of our society? What matters more, what matters less? When an orchestra has to close down or merge, it is a clear vote against culture. That's why the disappearance of individual orchestras is so alarming, especially when it is due to the withdrawal of donors and sponsors or to the diktat of public austerity policies, and not merely to abysmal management.

Looking back at the changes in the orchestral landscapes of our Western industrial societies and the steadily decreasing presence of classical music on radio and television, regardless of the peculiarities of each individual case, I can detect a pattern, a shift in the overall status of classical music in society. In any event, it has lost further points on the ratings scale. Of course, it was never at the top of that scale, even when it was ritually celebrated, in keeping with an elitist understanding of music, and when opera and concert served chiefly to enhance social prestige. We musicians may not have recognized this loss of social significance early enough, maybe because classical music is a constant in our own everyday lives, and life without it is inconceivable. But should we really be so careless as to leave this art form to its own devices, knowing full well that access to it is initially much more arduous than enjoying a spectacle in a football stadium?

GRAY, AND EVEN GRAYER

It is not only the shrinking number of orchestras that worries me, but it is also the elderly audiences whose members have turned gray over the years, along with myself. Where are the many young people, those in their twenties and thirties, who used to fill the concert halls of the United States even a few decades ago? The rising average age of opera- and concertgoers is a general phenomenon that can be observed on both sides of the Atlantic. In the United States of my youth, one could see people of every age group in the opera houses and concert halls. Even earlier, in the forties, the median age was almost exactly thirty. Twenty years later, the median age increased to thirty-eight. The median age divides the age distribution into two equal parts: one half of the audience being below the median, the other half above.

According to various studies, the real rise in age took place in the eighties – a period, incidentally, that corresponds quite closely to the withdrawal of the arts from American schools. Many students grew up without ever encountering classical music.

Ten years later, listeners born between 1936 and 1945 formed the largest cohort of concertgoers. The proportion of young people sank dramatically, and the average age rose continuously. The age structure of operagoers was even worse. In 1996, a large-scale study was published in the United States. Even then, just over twenty years ago, the authors of the study pointed out that the figures showed a change in the leisure behavior of younger people that might affect the art forms of classical music and opera in the future. Gone were the days when opera stars could lure parents *and* their offspring to concert halls and opera houses and recruit their fans among younger age groups, even teenagers. It will be a hard task to win them back.

In Germany, it looks equally bleak – stalls and galleries tend to be occupied by older concertgoers. The average age of visitors to classical concerts and operas is somewhere around sixty. Of course, this is only an average figure. Some orchestras achieve averages well below that and manage to get young people interested again. Nevertheless, the overall development is anything but satisfactory: in recent years the average age of concertgoers has increased significantly more than that of the population as a whole. These are not personal impressions of mine, but calculations carried out by different institutes, and have to be taken seriously. Do we have to assume that in thirty years' time, when many of our loyal concertgoers are no longer alive, a large part of the public will have simply fallen away?

As always, one can argue about such studies and predictions. Each artistic or music director will interpret those figures in their own way. I myself observe the development with mixed feelings. I am worried by statistics compiled by research institutes that tell us of the lack of significance that classical music has for the age cohorts of our children and grandchildren. This art form no longer plays a major role for them. Children and adolescents are being educated with a strong emphasis on the visual. Even when they attend pop and rock concerts, the visual element is usually on a par with the music itself. What are they supposed to enjoy during performances of classical music, where the complexity of the music takes much longer to stimulate the brain than catchy songs – accompanied by spectacular pyrotechnics – that one can hum along with after only two minutes? In classical music one has to listen very carefully and for a pretty good while before the emotional kick sets in; one has to surrender to it. At first, it can be quite strenuous for those who are not used to that.

To this day there is a dispute as to what the increasing average age means: the disappearance of the classical concert format and the opera, or not? The optimists among us believe that this is quite a normal development: in their youth, people go to pop concerts, put on their earphones at every opportunity, whether at home or in the metro, or while walking down the street. At some point, however, with increasing age – so the theory goes – this gets too boring for them, since in a pop song the chorus is repeated six times within three minutes, and so the older ones lose any sense of fun. The music gets too loud for them, as does the theatrical screeching of the young people who abandon themselves to the spectacle. Then at last they discover the "old" art of classical music, which is more profound, more complex, more attractive and perhaps more fulfilling. After all, it's more appropriate for middle-aged people to be seated in a concert hall chair in a well-behaved manner than to stand in a crowd of people, all gesticulating wildly and casting glances at you that quite unmistakably ask, What are *you* doing here? That's one way of looking at it. And I am sure many people would like to see it that way. So would I.

But I'm too much of a realist to believe it. I am convinced that many people who have never been to a concert before, who haven't practiced this challenging form of listening to music, let alone played music at a young age at home or at school, people who are used only to music that is merely entertaining and easily consumable, will never find their way into a concert hall or an opera house. On the contrary, they are still attracted to gigs of aging rock bands that were part of their youth. Many of them might have never even considered going to a classical concert or an opera instead.

Love of classical music and its great tradition, this possibility of identification with one's own cultural heritage, doesn't set in overnight. Nor is it necessarily a result of aging and maturing. How wonderful it would be if we could inspire even a fraction of those grandparents, parents and children who flock in their thousands to Bruno Mars concerts in the new multi-purpose arenas to also venture to philharmonic halls! So here is the question: Is classical music, are the great symphonies, are these fabulous operas composed two hundred years ago still "up to date"?

It doesn't look like it when you survey the big and small temples of classical music. And if you are not dealing with audiences that have learned to grasp and value classical music as a sublime art form beyond fads and fashions, you've got to come up with some idea as to how to convince untrained listeners that this "antiquated" music still has something to say to them today. In any case, classical music confronts its recipients with an enormous challenge: to apply themselves intellectually, to be fully engaged, to contemplate. Perhaps it is precisely that challenge that prevents classical music from being "up to date," considering that in an age of effortless consumption everything must be easily and instantaneously accessible. This once again raises a question: Have we professional musicians – unbeknownst to ourselves – somehow fallen out of time?

The conviction is slowly eroding that the presence of the fine arts in society is indispensable, not only in the population at large, but even among those in charge. The cultural consensus within society is beginning to dissolve. The construction of a new multi-story car park has become more important than the preservation of a municipal orchestra. Classical music is perceived to be a bad investment because people want to be able to park their cars before they think about buying a concert ticket. We live in the hope that we haven't reached that stage yet, because there are still concert and opera performances, and there are critics who report on them in the newspapers. And there are foundations that are still committed to responding to that declining consensus. But this is just a drop in the bucket. It amounts to no more than trite lip service.

CHANGING VALUES, CHANGING WORLD

All over the world, there is a visible trend of questioning the arts – today perhaps even more so than in the past. Rhetoric about the importance of art and music for society, so often reiterated, ring hollow when economic and political decisions point in exactly the opposite direction. A canon of values has established itself internationally that places the economic above the social, expediency above inner fulfillment, and in which precisely those things are at the top of the agenda whose added value can be quantified in dollars and cents.

May I provoke you by citing a single example in which this very change in values can be clearly seen? It concerns the children and young people who are so dear to our classical music artists' hearts, but to whom society now prescribes and, above all, exemplifies a completely different hierarchy of values.

Every three years, a representative sample of young people throughout most of the world are tested and compared regarding their cognitive performance. Each time, the result is a ranking list of participating countries, which allegedly provides information on the quality of their respective national education systems in competition with those of other countries. I am talking about the standardized assessments of educational attainment operated by the Organisation for Economic Co-operation and Development (OECD) under the name of PISA (Programme for International Student Assessment). Nowhere is the lack of appreciation for aesthetic education more evident than here. Aesthetic education is simply a taboo. All the same, a country's overall performance in these extremely limited test series is equated with the performance of the respective education system as a whole.

The test series and their results wouldn't worry me if they didn't testify to the decreasing status of the arts. What is astonishing is the broad international consensus that only the knowledge required in these test series is essential. Mathematical and scientific skills are tested, reading comprehension is tested and very specific cognitive or combinatorial skills are tested. Not even a knowledge of foreign languages is evaluated in these comparative studies, although foreign language skills could be very important for a country's economic prosperity in a globally interconnected world.

Music and art no longer play a role in this concept of education. One could argue that children, adolescents and their parents are led to believe that skills acquired in the aesthetic field have no relevance whatsoever. Instead, under the aegis of an international network of education experts, an idea has developed of what young people at the age of fifteen must necessarily master. Of course, it's not wrong for states to occasionally account for their students' performance in certain areas of knowledge. But what in the world made them sign over the definition of our concept of education, and testing its national quality, to an economic organization, of all bodies?

The PISA studies have by now subjected entire continents to this new concept of education. In the United States, the United Kingdom, Australia, Japan, Canada and Sweden, wherever you look, teachers of mathematics and science are under severe pressure to motivate their students to achieve better results, so that the country as a whole gets good marks in education. This is because the international rankings of the OECD countries are interpreted as showpieces in the fierce competition for business locations.

NARROW EDUCATION

PISA has established an internationally accepted, hardly ever questioned doctrine of "good education" and its standardized implementation, which has become immensely effective. It is devastating to see such a narrow educational concept, determined by an international elite of – in some cases rather blinkered – educational scientists, being adopted by national policy-makers. The experts' concepts of "performance" do not deserve the term "education" at all, because neither the humanities nor music or art play a role. The level of a nation's education cannot be determined by such tests. Knowledge may be an economically important production factor. But knowledge in two or three special areas alone cannot be equated with education, least of all with "Bildung," whose definition is occasionally meant to include character formation. But that is precisely what the general public seems to believe. And that puts me in a pessimistic mood because the arts, and thus classical music, are degraded to the lower rank of a mere pastime, and no one seems to question this kind of truncated education.

The effects of all this can be observed everywhere in our educational institutions: the time allotted to music and the other arts is dwindling. It is particularly worrying that in many cases music lessons are neglected in our elementary schools, of all places. Children at elementary school age are much easier to infect with enthusiasm for classical music than young people in high school, for whom pop music is particularly relevant. Furthermore, school is the only institution where music is accessible to children of all walks of life, as was the case in Morro Bay. School brought most of us to music, and music to most of us.

The conductor Kurt Masur, whom I greatly admire, described in very clear terms what he had been observing for years on both sides of the Atlantic: "The whole musical education system must be brought back to life," he said. "It's incredible that there are schools where you don't have music lessons because of the lack of teachers." His résumé is bitter: "Things have been lost that were and are valuable to us, like the commonality of making music." We are probably heading for an era of musical illiteracy, the alarming extent of which will only become apparent in future generations of parents. They will consist of today's children who will have grown up in a musical diaspora.

Perhaps we aren't able or indeed willing to prevent this development. But at least we ought to assess the consequences. I prefer to think positively: What if we could teach more children music? Children, given their natural curiosity, are fascinated by any kind of music, even classical music. Conservatories and music academies all over the world are teeming with music-loving students and producing musicians of unprecedented quality. Technically perfect, passionate, committed, comprehensively educated and extremely risk-oriented, they are prepared to stake everything on one card – music. Admittedly, this is a highly specialized bunch of people. But they give me hope, at least in one respect: classical music has lost none of its attraction for young people – on the contrary. If only more children were given access to it!

Perhaps I am writing this book specifically for those young people so as to encourage them to persevere in an environment that, at this moment in time, doesn't grant classical music any social priority. I never tire of reinforcing those students' passion and their zeal to continue to devote themselves with heart and soul to the arts, because they are still in need of classical music, today even more so than before. At the end of the day, only the enthusiasm of young people will enthuse other young people for the arts.

WISHFUL THINKING, WISHED-FOR PEOPLE

Admittedly, our lamentations as artists are banal. Just as banal are our complaints about growing utilitarianism, economism, materialism or unfettered capitalism, all of which make it so difficult for serious music, as a completely immaterial art, to survive. Therefore I will for once take the side of the utilitarians and the economy, and try to argue from their perspective. True, this is a perspective that I cannot be entirely confident about, because art is first and foremost created for its own sake. Music is not composed with an eye to its economic usefulness, but rather to make existential statements.

What kind of people does today's economy want? They should be sociable, communicative, approachable, thoughtful, self-reflexive, value-oriented, disciplined, empathic, attentive – and capable of making professional, personal and ethical judgments. Not reckless gamblers – like those who, by 2008, had unerringly hurled their financial institutions into the abyss and plunged the world into recession. And they are already on top of the world again, alarmingly close to the cliff, over which the supposedly calm stream tumbles into the deep. You don't have to be able to play the piano to become such a person, neither do you have to be a member of an orchestra, or a painter, or a dancer. However, at some point such a person must have dealt with existential questions and thought about themselves and their environment. But where exactly does this thinking take place? Almost exclusively in a permanent examination of the arts, of music, literature, philosophy, painting. This is where such questions are negotiated and where growth of knowledge is made possible. Are we to do without that? Won't social costs increase infinitely if people no longer receive training in disciplines in which they can acquire and practice those very skills?

In addition, there is openness, creativity, inspiration and humility. These qualities can be acquired only by those who encounter things that are bigger than they themselves. All this will undoubtedly fall by the wayside if children and young people are taught only that which produces "output," and if they are drilled to come up with a "profitable" answer to every question they are asked. But that's exactly what's happening. Classical music has long since been pushed to the margins of social perception. We shouldn't allow this to happen, if only for the sake of society's material prosperity.

There's no better way to put it than Harvard president Drew Faust did. She acknowledged the widespread calls for measurable results and for an education that responds to the specific needs of the labor market. "But many of the jobs our students will take at a later stage have not yet been invented, the necessary skills have not been defined." It wasn't a matter of enabling young people to answer questions concerning us today, at some point in the future. "Rather, we must enable them to ask those questions that will change the world of tomorrow." The short-sightedness with which political and economic elites allocate only standing room to the arts in the concert hall of life will cost a society dearly in the long run. They bring forth young people who will be in a worse rather than better position to ask those questions.

I don't want to be quite so pessimistic. That would be wrong. Large companies have long understood the added value that the arts can bring. These companies promote the musical commitment of children and found youth choirs and youth orchestras. In the United States, corporations are even setting up company orchestras – and not just out of pure altruism.

I will not hide the fact that the arts have always been a little worse off because their usefulness doesn't reveal itself in a straightforward input-output calculation. As the great German poet and philosopher Friedrich Schiller bemoaned at the end of the eighteenth century: "*Utility* is the great idol of the age, to which all powers must do service and all talents swear allegiance. In these clumsy scales the spiritual service of Art has no weight; deprived of all encouragement, she flees from the noisy mart of our century." Cultural pessimism, it seems, is not a modern phenomenon. It has probably been a permanent concomitant of culture ever since culture has existed. Anything that is not directly measurable or exploitable is placed in jeopardy in a world that has, in the course of evolution, programmed mankind to fight for physical survival first, and then for an increase in prosperity.

Only, we humans need the arts. This is proven by history. And the arts are responding to crises. The most progressive works were created in times of great distress. Beethoven wrote his Third Symphony when huge achievements such as the right to personal freedom were destroyed by Napoleon. Art forms disappear and new ones emerge. Perhaps, during this crisis of classical music, it is the young people who will find completely new ways of making music flourish again, possibly quite differently from what we envisage today. I trust them, I rely on them and I don't want to desert them.

In Philadelphia, the music hasn't gone silent yet. After years of trembling in the face of an uncertain future, the protagonists of the orchestra agreed, in exhausting negotiations, on a new contract. And in Detroit, too, the lights of the traditional concert hall are still shining. There seems to be new life in town. Classical music is still around. It is as if the crisis-stricken metropolis has remembered that music must not be allowed to fall silent along with everything else. Does our industry need such crises to remind the public of that tacit social consensus on the importance of classical music for social survival?

Later in this book I will show you that there are other ways, that an audience doesn't necessarily have to grow older and smaller, and that orchestras with numerous performances and an ambitious program do not automatically get into financial difficulties. My assertion might seem almost audacious: there doesn't have to be a crisis of classical music. But I will stick to it and take you to Montreal, to my "laboratory," as I always call the Maison Symphonique and the Orchestre symphonique de Montréal, where numerous young people have gathered to work tirelessly for the arts. And here, after years of innovation and experimentation, we are experiencing a small miracle. But before that I will have to give you some good reasons why classical music should not completely disappear from our everyday lives, but rather find its way back there, by whatever means.

SCHOENBERG

Collapse and New Beginning

Arnold Schoenberg was an American. More specifically, a Californian. Whenever I mentioned Schoenberg earlier, one thing was beyond question: he had to be one of us. There were many people with German-sounding names living on the West Coast of the United States, but as a child I hardly ever thought about their origins. In Palm Springs there was Ernst Krenek, a Viennese composer. Then there was Bruno Walter in Beverly Hills, chief conductor of the New York Philharmonic, and Otto Klemperer, who emigrated to the United States in 1933 and conducted the Los Angeles Philharmonic Orchestra. In general, foreign-sounding names were not uncommon – certainly not in California. Igor Stravinsky, that brilliant Russian composer, had also settled there and was admired and loved by us Americans.

Whenever my mother, from whom I learned so much about music, mentioned those musicians, she talked about them as though they were Americans. During the last years of his life Schoenberg was indeed an American – if probably only on paper. In 1941, he became an American citizen. After fleeing Nazi Germany in 1933 – he first left Berlin for Paris and later emigrated from there to the United States – he never again set foot on German soil. I cannot remember exactly which of his compositions it was when I heard Schoenberg for the first time. The music came out of the loudspeaker of a record player. Professor

Korisheli had put on an LP record at his home. I remember the strange sounds flowing toward me. What were those sounds? Dissonances strung together, seemingly without structure. Every now and again, a pattern emerged that somehow seemed familiar to me. But no sooner had I perceived it in that jumble of tones, the moment had already passed and what I considered to be utter disorder gained the upper hand. I listened with rapt fascination – maybe for one reason only: my revered teacher had said that I must get to know this music.

I probably share this experience of disorientation with many who encounter the music of Schoenberg or his pupils Alban Berg, Anton Webern and others for the first time in their lives. Today, it's quite different: to me, Schoenberg means music in its purest form, impressive, very special and extremely moving. After years of intensive engagement with his compositions, I have developed an almost organic relationship to his music. It touches me deeply because his works and the musical ideas they express – in a language that is very different from Johann Sebastian Bach's – bring four things into balance without which music cannot work for me: spirituality, emotion, intellect and the purely physical experience of the vibrations reaching my body. Schoenberg's music appeals to a human understanding of music in the broadest sense; it enlivens me because it strikes a chord in me, in my "heart and brain," as Schoenberg would have put it – like the works of all great artists are able to do.

This may surprise you, as one will often perceive the works of this extraordinary composer in a very different manner: as strenuously dissonant, disorderly, perhaps even unsettling. But when I look at Schoenberg and his œuvre, he always remains for me a composer of late romanticism and of the beginnings of expressionism. To speak in images: *The Scream* by Edvard Munch – that is Schoenberg for me. Why? On the one hand, his earlier works are actually still tonal, and thus composed in a musical language familiar to us. On the other hand, even the later works are written within structures derived from romanticism: the concertos, for example, which sound so unfamiliar, draw on traditional forms of three or four movements with the usual characteristics of an allegro followed by an andante. His solo concertos comply with the traditional format: a violin or piano accompanied by an orchestra. And in his opera *Moses and Aron* you will find all the features that are typical of traditional opera. In the case of Schoenberg, it is only his musical idiom that is different or novel, or better still: we are not accustomed to it.

However, anyone who hears Schoenberg for the first time may be deterred, appalled, disturbed, frustrated. The high degree of dissonance, rhythms that are often very unstructured, the alleged aimlessness of the melodies – we might initially perceive all this as an imposition. Since Bach, our ears are used to hearing certain chords over and over again, based on triads that relate to each other. Our brain has learned to accept that tones are hierarchically arranged, that there are more and less important tones in a melody, leading-notes and keynotes creating a certain dynamic. We automatically expect musical motifs to develop, music to culminate in a climax, or indeed in the end of a movement. We learned this musical syntax the way a child learns a language, at first without any reflection. It is familiar, comprehensible, understandable. This intuitive understanding generates impressions of euphony, which in turn create a sense of well-being. Occasionally, a melodic line or a harmony may surprise us, but by and large we are on familiar territory.

In the works that Schoenberg composed after 1908, everything seems alien. Familiar sounds are hard to come by. The ear following the course of the music is downright disoriented, there seems to be no purpose, no meaning, no inner connection. Some people are so annoyed by it that after their first experience with this "new music" (which by now is more than a hundred years old!) they won't even venture to a concert if Schoenberg is listed on the program. They might to do so if it's one of his late-romantic works, still written in the familiar "tonal" language, but not if it's music written in "free tonality," not to mention "twelve-tone" music.

A hundred years ago, when concert halls were still places of lively debate, people didn't stay away from the music, but actively engaged with it. They protested at the top of their voices, and highly emotionally so. Traditionalists regarded Schoenberg's compositions and those of his students as mere provocation. His followers, in turn, considered those people's lack of understanding to be intolerable ignorance. Schoenberg agitated people; he made them extremely angry. They laughed, whistled, booed and shouted. There were tumults and serious punches.

Unforgotten is an event in the spring of 1913, when Schoenberg conducted the orchestra of the Wiener Konzertverein, later the Vienna Symphony. The program featured pieces for orchestra by Anton Webern, orchestral songs by Alexander von Zemlinsky and Alban Berg, Schoenberg's Kammersymphonie op. 9, and Gustav Mahler's *Kindertotenlieder*. When Schoenberg was conducting his own work, people began to hiss and jeer, while the musicians were still playing. Only a small section of the audience understood that this work written in "free tonality" did not yet formally break with all tradition, but had sprung from the aesthetics and the spirit of romanticism. The atmosphere in the concert hall became so heated that a fierce brawl ensued between Schoenberg's opponents and supporters on the second gallery and the Polizei had to intervene. But it was when two of Alban Berg's *Fünf Orchesterlieder nach Ansichtskartentexten von Peter Altenberg (Five Orchestral Songs)* op. 4 were premiered that a veritable riot erupted. The police couldn't handle the turmoil. Schoenberg paused to let people cool down – without success. On the contrary, there followed a battle of words, finally even a slap in the face, a few seconds of frightened silence, then real uproar – the concert had to be ended, and Mahler's songs were not performed. Because of that slap there were legal repercussions. The concert went down in history as the "Watschenkonzert" ("ear-boxing concert").

Schoenberg's music, completely different, completely new, was given no chance, and not only on that evening. For many years the critics tore Schoenberg's compositions to pieces, in accordance with their firm conviction that they weren't music at all. And Schoenberg suffered. But what had he actually done?

He had plunged the prosperous community of classical music lovers into a genuine crisis of meaning. With his music he had gone beyond the boundaries of the harmonic system and thus of the musical language in which the greats of classical and romantic music, such as Mozart and Beethoven, Strauss and Mahler, had expressed themselves. Henceforth, Schoenberg was regarded as a destroyer, as a heretic, as someone who had dismantled everything that was, and still is, dear to us. All of this happened within a very short space of time – in the year 1908. Before that he had still employed traditional musical language, writing works like the *Gurrelieder* or the symphonic poem *Pelleas und Melisande*, for which he was celebrated. But even those compositions already pointed toward the imminent collapse of the supporting walls of the traditional tonal system in terms of harmony, orchestration and structure. Schoenberg had exhausted that traditional system. In his tonal compositions he had stretched it to bursting point. And he realized that the new sounds he needed in order to express his ideas could no longer emerge from within that traditional idiom and structure.

The revolution took place in the area of harmony. Schoenberg began to dissolve tonal bonds and to break with traditional forms. The old tonal world he himself admired so much had become too narrow for him. It is well documented how painful this musical revolution was for audiences at the time. Even today we can sympathize with them. We still have major difficulties with this "dissonant" music, which can irritate us unbearably and cause us great physical discomfort. And yet Schoenberg's new music only followed the logic of his thinking. It came into being when it had become necessary because he wanted to make musical statements that he couldn't formulate by means of the old musical language. Nowhere can this be traced more clearly than in his Second String Quartet, which he composed in 1908 in the midst of a profound life crisis. It is the embodiment of a breathtaking turning point in the history of music. Try to listen to this piece with the knowledge of the circumstances of its origin, remembering that Schoenberg composed this pioneering work as a romantic.

The first two movements are written on the basis of tonal harmony. The third movement, however, paves the way for something outrageously new. This movement, in which he adds a soprano voice to the instruments, marks the point of departure for a whole new world of tones. Schoenberg opens the door to a completely novel understanding of music and crosses a threshold. The soprano sings verses by the poet Stefan George. "Ich löse mich in tönen • kreisend • webend" ("I am dissolved in swirling sound, am weaving"), so the poem "Entrückung" ("Transport") goes, the human voice floating almost weightlessly in space, liberated from the gravity of conventional harmonic progression. One might almost think that Schoenberg was referring to himself. There had never been anything like it before.

Tonal relationships had largely disappeared from the composition, and the customary framework of a string quartet, in which only four strings are involved, was blown apart by song. To the ears of advocates of traditional scoring, the use of the soprano voice was a transgression, indeed sheer insolence. Moreover, Schoenberg molded his musical ideas in a completely different form. In doing that, he was to shape the next century of music history – in "never-before-heard harmonies," as his student Anton Webern put it.

Anyway, 1908 was a remarkable year for music history. Gustav Mahler created *Das Lied von der Erde* (*The Song of the Earth*), Richard Strauss composed his avant-garde opera *Elektra* in a manner in which he would never compose again, Max Reger wrote his *Symphonic Prologue to a Tragedy*, perhaps his most important work, which begins with a "psalm" and reveals an almost metaphysical approach. And the American Charles Ives composed *The Unanswered Question*. The most groundbreaking work, however, was written by a self-taught artist in Vienna, namely Arnold Schoenberg with his Second String Quartet. Once he had overcome harmonic limitation, the composer worked himself up into a veritable frenzy: one year later he created his *Five Pieces for Orchestra* op. 16 and his almost expressionist, nature-related one-act monodrama for soprano and orchestra, *Erwartung* (*Expectation*) op. 17.

In the subsequent period, the composer pushed the traditional forms of harmony further back. He discarded them as one discards clothes that have become too tight. He did this in a ruthlessly systematic fashion, and without regard for anything people were accustomed to and had grown fond of. However, his music was not yet based on a closed system that offered a consistent alternative to the traditional language of music. It wasn't until 1921 that that happened. Schoenberg found a "*Method of Composing with Twelve Tones Which are Related Only with One Another,*" also called "twelve-tone music."

It seems almost paradoxical that I should still call Schoenberg a conservative. What he heard within him was those new tones and sounds for which he could no longer use the old harmonies. Yet the form in which he presented them was anything but revolutionary; it remained true to the traditional succession of movements known to us from the worlds of Brahms and Mahler. This immediately brings to mind his Variations for Orchestra op. 31 in which we hear a theme – albeit in a completely new musical idiom – that we can follow through its variations. Not only is the composition of variations one of the most traditional forms in the history of music, but is in fact hundreds of years old. In these variations, Schoenberg also cast a glance back at the famous Passacaglia in Brahms' Fourth Symphony. He broadened the harmonies of the tonal world, but he did not completely leave them behind.

In his musical idiom there was no longer a hierarchical arrangement of tones or triad structures in which one tone always functions as the keynote. Rather, all twelve tones of the chromatic scale enjoy equal rights. To this end, Schoenberg created a series of tones whereby all chromatic notes are arranged in different sequences. These notes must be played in the selected order, but not necessarily by the same voice. A series of twelve tones can be used forward or backward, or mirrored along an imaginary horizontal line. This does not affect the principle of equality.

Schoenberg himself knew full well what he was asking of his listeners. He may not have suspected at the time, however, that serious or art music would not fully recover from the "tonal crisis" to this day. "Of course, I was primarily regarded as the Satan of modernistic music," he later wrote in *Style and Idea*. But even as early as January 1910, he had stated the reason for choosing his particular path in a program note for the Verein für Kunst und Kultur in Vienna: "I am being forced in this direction not because my invention or technique is inadequate, nor because I am uninformed about all the other things the prevailing aesthetics demand, but that I am obeying an inner compulsion, which is stronger than any upbringing: that I am obeying the formative process which, being the natural one to me, is stronger than my artistic education."

Many listeners still have that sense of impertinence, even today. I've experienced it many times. It shows that, even a hundred years later, we artists do not really succeed in conveying to our listeners this composer's romantic attitude toward life, which, despite those twelve tones, manifests itself in his music. If the listeners are deprived of the keynote, we artists must at least try to emphasize those formal elements known to listeners, so that they are not completely disoriented in the music – for example, the natural vibration of a work and the organic tension of intervals. Try to hear the recurring sighs in Schoenberg's music – you will find them many times over.

All his life, Schoenberg couldn't get over the partly vitriolic reactions, the rejection and the caustic criticism with which every new work of his was greeted. A few years before his death he wrote in a letter to the National Institute of Arts and Letters dated 22 May 1947: "[T]here was nobody to help me, nor were there many who would not have liked to see me succumb. I do not contend it was envy – of what was there to be envious? [...] It might have been the desire to get rid of this nightmare, of this unharmonious torture, of these unintelligible ideas, of this methodical madness." Sometimes he almost despaired at the controversy he triggered: "I never understood what I had done to them to make them as malicious, as furious, as cursing, as aggressive; – I am still certain that I had never taken away from them something they owned; I never interfered with their prerogatives; I never did trespass on their property."

Completely convinced of the correctness of his path, Schoenberg always hoped to attain, at least posthumously, the importance which he believed was due to him during his lifetime – the importance of a musical genius who does not discard the old, but must develop it further because he cannot do otherwise. For this reason he did not see himself as a destroyer who, for the sake of provocation, "abused" the musical language perfected by Bach. Rather, he regarded the collapse of the traditional tonal system as the inevitable continuation of classical music, the rules of which he had mastered expertly. In his essays and books, the great works of the past always remained reference points of his own œuvre.

Schoenberg didn't only compose. He also painted and wrote, incessantly driven by that inner compulsion to express himself. Abstract in music, more concrete in pictures, lucid and precise in words. In his essays, he turned to aspects of music that occupy my interest. Again and again he thought about what "new music" actually means: undoubtedly those contemporary works that were composed beyond the rules of traditional harmony. Schoenberg always objected to defining one music as "new" and another as "old," something that is very much in line with my own understanding of art. In all the great works of really important artists, he wrote, one will detect novelty that never fades: "Because: Art means New Art."

So how could one come up with the idea of perceiving Bach's works as old music? For me they are always new, forward-looking, almost progressive. According to Schoenberg, Bach's music cannot be old, and his own music cannot be not new. They are merely different statements in different idioms. He wrote: "Bach sometimes operated with the twelve tones in such a manner that one would be inclined to call him the first twelve-tone composer."

Criticism of Schoenberg continued for decades. And even today his music is still controversial. His departure into free tonality and, finally, twelve-tone music earned him attributions that called his very artistry into question. "Adversaries have called me a constructor, an engineer, an architect, even a mathematician," he complained. "They pretended that I offered the product of a brain, not of a heart." We all want music to reach our hearts, to move us, to touch an emotional chord. Schoenberg had a lot to say about that. He always argued in favor of the use of reason when working on a piece of music in order to complete a musical idea, even if surface beauty might be lost to some extent. He spoke out against any kind of superficiality, against music without intellectual brilliance, against pathos laid on thick, against musical fashions, fads or attitudes that merely corresponded to the taste of the audience or the "zeitgeist." Perhaps it is the uncompromising nature of Schoenberg's work that fascinates me.

But Schoenberg was by no means someone who only applied the intellect. Some of his pieces were written quickly, others were not. Many things were the result of spontaneous inspiration, others of intellectual consideration. Some things that he had begun by using reason drove his intuition further. For Schoenberg, reason and feeling, intellect and emotion, brain and heart belonged together. They were mutually dependent. "It is not the heart alone which creates all that is beautiful, emotional, pathetic, affectionate, and charming," he wrote. "First, everything of supreme value in art must show heart as well as brain. Second, the real creative genius has no difficulty in controlling his feelings mentally." And vice versa – because the mind sometimes runs the risk of dedicating itself to the logic of a piece and of producing only "the dry and unappealing."

Schoenberg had a deep distrust of "works which incessantly exhibit their heart," lulling the listener into vague or even spurious feelings. In his opinion, such music could not belong to the great works in history, neither could it contain musical ideas whose power would not pale at some point. Such music would never be able to stay fresh – and thus be timeless.

For me as a musician, this stance is impressive and easy to understand. Schoenberg categorically rejected mere pathos: "Today, be it France or Germany, we demand a music that lives through ideas and not through feeling." Pieces written by the really great composers of the past four hundred years live on thanks to their underlying musical idea. I believe that what Schoenberg expressed in his essays is the essence of something that all of us musicians feel. It is the longing for the ideal of a perfect balance between "brain and heart."

If we musicians try to interpret a work in a way that presents the underlying idea, the heart will not remain untouched. Then music can be fully experienced: emotionally, spiritually, intellectually and physically. I know that in the case of Schoenberg and his descendants, it is not always easy to achieve this kind of comprehensive experience with the audience. To this day, many people find it difficult to orient themselves in his works. Schoenberg may never have quite understood how difficult that can be. He could not comprehend that in music, too, the established concept of beauty has to do with memorability and recognition. A composer has two sides to his personality, which Schoenberg himself didn't always combine: his passion and his rationality. His music poses the great challenge of asserting both and uniting them.

Perhaps listeners will not always be able to understand the depth of a musical idea. But they can still fully experience music if they are willing to open up to it. They can be exhilarated by the great choruses in Schoenberg's unfinished opera *Moses and Aron*. There they can experience the two sides of Schoenberg's character in deep conflict with one another. They can recognize the deeply romantic side of this presumed intellectual, who makes use of traditional opera forms as well as of moving choral passages. And perhaps they can also sense the drama and the despair of an exiled Austrian who began to compose his opera in

Germany and completed it as an emigrant to the United States. In his early String Sextet *Verklärte Nacht* (*Transfigured Night*) op. 4, later arranged for string orchestra, the listeners experience an almost cheerful weightlessness that is able to inspire and stimulate. Inspiration will sharpen their perception, their senses. The audience will be carried away.

These are the moments that can cause a suspenseful, almost stunned silence in an audience – something I have even experienced during performances of Schoenberg's works in free tonality. It's so quiet you could hear a pin drop, no coughing, no program falling to the ground – only the music, whose power moves musicians and audience in equal measure. The gulf between the musicians on stage and the audience is bridged. Everything becomes one, and the music flows through me. And the audience seems to be frozen in a state of high alertness.

The musical idea itself, the interpretation by which it may be conveyed to the audience – in such moments it all makes sense. Brain and heart, reason and feeling are in harmony. This emotional state triggers deep joy, perhaps even happiness, which is not imposed from the outside but comes from within. Sometimes a performance succeeds in that way; sometimes it doesn't. If it is successful, the tension at the end abates only gradually. The audience needs a moment to find its way out of its stunned state. At some point, one individual begins to clap, timidly, others follow suit. And when the audience becomes aware what kind of moment we have just experienced together, enthusiastic applause erupts.

Schoenberg was undoubtedly a person who could be called a musical intellectual or, better still, a music philosopher because he ceaselessly drove himself to continue on the path he had chosen, and because he reflected on music, on the meaning of musical ideas, which do not lose their validity even if lifestyle habits, viewpoints and values change. But he was also an emotional person, someone who had to discipline himself again and again in his emotionality so as not to be simply carried away by pathos and self-pity due to constant hostility and disparagement.

The question remains whether one can understand Schoenberg's music even if one doesn't know his twelve-tone system. Can it enrich us? I am deeply convinced of that. We can understand things without getting to the bottom of them intellectually. To put it bluntly: I can enjoy a ride in my new car without knowing exactly how it is built. But there must be other people who understand precisely that and make the car work.

Anton Webern, Schoenberg's pupil, had a much better, touchingly true answer to this question: "But theory does not bring you any closer to his works. There is only one thing that is necessary: your heart must remain open. Schönberg's work should be listened to without inhibition or prejudice of any kind. Put theory and philosophy aside. In Schönberg's work there is purely music, music as in the case of Beethoven and Mahler. The experiences of his heart become tones." It's worth a try.

In a speech to the National Institute of Arts and Letters in Washington, D.C., now known as the American Academy of Arts and Letters, Schoenberg settled a score with his critics. In short sentences full of emotion, he described his inner state in times of denied recognition: "Personally I had the feeling as if I had fallen into an ocean of boiling water, and not knowing how to swim or to get out in another manner, I tried with my legs and arms as best as I could. I do not know what saved me; why I was not drowned or cooked alive ... I have perhaps only one merit: I never gave up."

He had cut his own path – unswervingly, uncompromisingly, like all great artists. He had plunged classical music into a veritable identity crisis. He couldn't help himself; he just had to do it.

CHAPTER THREE

CLASSICAL MUSIC FOR
A TIME OF CRISIS?

"Art is water, and just as humans are always close to water, for
reasons of necessity (to drink, to wash, to flush away, to grow) as well
as for reasons of pleasure (to play in, to swim in, to relax in front of, to sail
upon, to suck on frozen, coloured and sweetened), so humans must always
be close to art in all its incarnations, from the frivolous to the essential.
Otherwise we dry up."

Yann Martel,
What Is Stephen Harper Reading? (2009)

OUTRAGE IS THE BEGINNING OF ALL THINGS

It's still lying in front of me on my desk in Paris, this unassuming little booklet. A couple of years back it probably would have
caused next to no furor, had not the title been an incitement and
summed it all up: *Indignez-vous!* This polemic pamphlet (English
title: *Time for Outrage!*), published in October 2011, was written
by the French resistance fighter and later UN diplomat Stéphane
Hessel. At the age of ninety-three, this old man – essayist, activist
and, above all, incorrigible optimist – once more sat down at his
desk and wrote this short essay that would soon become the starting point of a worldwide wave of national protest movements.

In Paris, I experienced the excitement around this angry essay,
which consists of barely more than twenty pages, at very close
quarters. Within a short span of time, more than a million copies

were sold in France. I was one of the buyers. One could argue over the quality of the essay. Two aspects, however, are undeniable: here was a man of Methuselah's age, on the final leg of his journey – "I'm nearing the last stage. The end cannot be far off," he says – who, for one last time, shouts out his view of things, enriched by a wealth of experience garnered during an eventful lifetime of almost a century, to the wider public. I found that alone deeply moving. In addition, he addresses a development that all of us are acutely aware of and feel most uneasy about: "[T]he power of money [...] has never been as great and selfish and shameless as it is now," he says, outraged. Outrage, he posits, is a prerequisite for involvement. This is how the latter is triggered. And this is exactly what Hessel's call for action was aimed at. The French edition is still lying in front of me and I cannot stop thinking about it: *Indignez-vous!*

What does the outrage of this militant Frenchman of German-Jewish origin and his call for involvement have to do with classical music and, ultimately, with me? A lot. More than I initially thought. More than you might suspect, because I ask myself why we aren't more outraged.

I, too, am outraged by the direction in which postmodernism has taken Western industrial societies, with all their materialism, consumerism and utilitarianism. One would think that our society had fallen into a veritable crisis of meaning. Did we all tacitly acquiesce? Or did we not even wish to know about it?

I want to show that, because of its powerful impact, classical music could play a significant role right now. Our Western societies' crisis of meaning, which also manifests itself in a loss of importance of the arts, could be a great opportunity for serious music: more than just a recentering, it could be a form of revitalization. We just have to make it happen: classical music for a time of crisis.

IMMINENT DISAPPEARANCE

If, however, serious music is being played less and less, and is being taught less and less in schools; if one barely comes across it on radio and on TV; if concert halls remain closed; then fewer and fewer people will know about it. It will vanish from their ken. And what is not in our consciousness does not exist. The laws of economics will then come into play, just like at a bazaar or in a department store: decreasing supply causes decreasing demand. When there is no one left to promote an excellent wine, when the good bottles are pushed to the back of the shelf, no one will ever think of purchasing and drinking them. It's not the musical ideas themselves, though, that are disappearing. Those were devised long ago; they are permanently fixed in scores, have been printed, digitalized and recorded, safely stored away in archives. Physically, music is well prepared for eternity. But what of it? Music is not music proper if scores are not played and heard. Of course, there will always be a few mavericks, oddballs and nerds, passionate or crazy people who will attempt to compose serious music and come up with new musical statements. Highly specialized virtuoso musicians will continue to exist. A few islands of classical music will not disappear all that rapidly, because, for as long as high culture is associated with social status, music can also be used to adorn oneself, according to philosopher Theodor W. Adorno. He once breathed fire and brimstone on those privileged consumers of culture: "Another reason why official musical life survives so stubbornly may be that it permits some ostentation without exposing the audience – stamped as cultured, after all, by its very presence in Salzburg – to reproaches for high living and showing off."

Classical music must not be allowed to disappear. If I weren't convinced that classical music, especially today, can foster social cohesion and enhance our quality of life, my outrage wouldn't be as fierce as it is. Music does exist, and heaven is filled with sounds. We just have to ensure that it is listened to much more often and understood much better. After all, composers once had very different intentions. They wrote their music for the common people; not only for them, but for their entertainment, too. They composed for people who wanted not only to listen to music, but to play music themselves. A visit to an Italian opera was a social event. In the era of the baroque, no composer considered his works to be timeless. Until well into the classical age, composers predominantly produced commissioned works, often for specific occasions – utility music, so to speak. That they were creating music for posterity, indeed for eternity, did not correspond to their self-image.

Even to Mozart, that very concept was foreign, and the prevailing attitude changed only gradually with Beethoven, who, in his growing awareness of being a preeminent composer, neatly cataloged his works for posterity. Playing music was a pastime, a wonderful way to occupy oneself, be it on one's own or with one or more fellow musicians. Competing in playing fast runs until one of the competitors hit the wrong key, imitating one another in an ironic over-the-top way during duets – all of this was great fun, a discovery of one's fellow player, but for the majority of people today, it seems, it is something from bygone times. I am shocked, even outraged, how quickly habits that used to be common practice back in my day have vanished. It has taken less than a generation. Does anyone still make music at home?

Needless to say, composers address topics that are relevant to everyone. Their music represents all human beings, highlights their worries and their fears, their pain and their joy, the fight for what is good. In my opinion, nothing justifies an elitist understanding of high culture. After all, it isn't *high* culture because it was accepted and absorbed by a higher class in society. For me, high culture represents a form of art that comes closest to democratic ideals: the purest form of human expression that strives for the essence of things and describes those things in their verity. Everyone should have access to it.

NOT JUST FOR ELITES

Advocates of a somewhat elitist understanding of art may feel provoked by this. In his book *Notes on the Death of Culture* Nobel laureate Mario Vargas Llosa bitterly laments the consequences of a democratization of high culture that appears to have failed. He admits that a democratic and liberal society was under a moral obligation to make high culture accessible to all: through education, through promotion, through subsidization. But he adds: "This commendable philosophy has had the undesired effect of trivializing and cheapening cultural life." Due to its complexity and at times abstruse codes, high culture was reserved for a minority. If it weren't, it would inevitably deteriorate into a spectacle. It would lose its dignity and substance the moment an opera by Verdi, the philosophy of Kant, a Cirque du Soleil show and a rock concert were regarded as equally valuable. Or, I would add, as soon as entertainment companies such as Sony Music unceremoniously marketed movie soundtracks as "classical music."

Hasn't the music we today refer to as "serious" music always been only for certain higher classes in society? I am familiar with that argument, and I come to hear it more and more often, combined with the follow-up: Why then shouldn't we abandon it to the upper echelons of society where it originated a couple of hundred years ago – the clergy, the aristocracy, the educated bourgeoisie? The majority of the population weren't really in a position to enjoy Bach's or Mozart's music during their lifetimes, nor even Beethoven's, in an era that is generally referred to as the birth of a bourgeois concert culture. It was not, however, because they didn't want to, but because they weren't able to. The dissemination of music happened exclusively in concert halls. The ability to read music was considered a high art, and despite the fact that the world of music had begun to open up toward minorities, such as women composers like Clara Schumann, Fanny Mendelssohn and Alma Mahler, the broad masses barely had the opportunity to gain access to it.

The historical exclusivity of classical music was owed to the circumstances. Today, however, the situation is quite different. Technically, the dissemination of classical music could be easier than ever – through music classes in schools, countless recordings and the mass media, right up to social networks. Anyone can listen to almost any documentation of classical composition and performance on YouTube at any time, or download any of them via numerous streaming services.

Theoretically, this should make us rejoice, considering all those modern possibilities and, occasionally, astonishing successes thanks to the new media. There is truly no real reason anymore why classical music shouldn't be more widespread and more passionately received than it is – by all social classes. Nonetheless, there are enough critics whose articles suggest that they are hardly upset about the dwindling presence of classical music in everyday life. This development, according to their argument, illustrates exactly what this music was not composed for: the enjoyment of the general population. The democratization of this art had proven unsuccessful, maybe even for its own good, as widespread enjoyment would amount to its trivialization.

My own opinion is diametrically opposed to this view. Such an elitist understanding of art is a red rag to me. My outrage at today's approach to classical music is not caused by the worry that an entire industry must fear for its very existence, and I am least concerned about that small group of starlets and stars doing the international circuit. Spectacle and visual enjoyment have always been part of our art and its attraction. My outrage relates rather to the fact that we are increasingly depriving ordinary folk of this music. To borrow sports jargon, I am not talking about competitive sport, but about leisure sport. And this deprivation starts on a small scale and with the youngest: when music is no longer practiced in schools, when it is no longer practiced at home and when it is no longer performed by local ensembles.

When that is the case, people no longer have any opportunity to encounter classical music in familiar surroundings, and to experience it for what it is: something that immensely broadens one's horizon, a source of strength and inspiration that appeals to us emotionally, spiritually and intellectually in equal measure. I do not accept the constantly repeated statement that it was no different hundreds of years ago. Today's conditions actually allow for something different. When our colleagues of the famous

Minnesota Orchestra weren't able to give concerts for fifteen months, or 448 days, because their bleak financial situation had embroiled them in an industrial dispute over wages and fees, and they were literally locked out, then for that period the city's 5.3 million inhabitants had no opportunity to listen to classical music performed on the highest level by "their" orchestra. During that time, there were no outreach programs, no matinees and no children's concerts, no young musicians who could infect an audience with their youthful enthusiasm. The inhabitants of the city were left to witness the demise of an orchestra and to complain about it for a few weeks, until one day they probably accepted as perfectly normal that the music wasn't playing anymore.

"Indifference: The Worst Attitude," Stéphane Hessel entitled a chapter of his polemic pamphlet. "The worst possible outlook is indifference that says, 'I can't do anything about it, I'll just get by,'" he writes. And he continues: "Behaving like that deprives you of one of the essentials of being human: the capacity and the freedom to feel outraged. That freedom is indispensable, as is the political involvement that goes with it."

In that same sense, I feel outraged – in my own field. I cannot bear the thought that so many people are being deprived of classical music, of all things, because all my life music has given me so much – even outside the concert halls – and because especially now, during the social crisis that Stéphane Hessel addressed as early as several years ago and that flares up in ever new manifestations of civic discontent, it could teach us so much. Let's make the most of it – let's transform "the crisis of classical music" into "classical music for a time of crisis." Maybe this period of upheaval is its biggest opportunity. Why?

THE SEARCH FOR MEANING

The Western world is undergoing an almost epochal transformation. We all sense it. Life is getting faster, competition more relentless, social cohesion is diminishing, the risk of individual failure increasing. The contexts within which we have to make decisions have reached a level of complexity that often bewilder us. The offices of the therapists who are supposed to help people deal with such a changed reality are overcrowded. People in Western post-industrial, possibly post-democratic, societies seem to have lost their orientation. I do not hesitate for a moment to maintain, without exaggeration, that our societies have slid into a deep crisis of meaning, which at least the Western world is dramatically affected by.

The old democratic order, which, under the primacy of politics, rested upon rights, the rule of law and basic moral ideas of social cohesion until well into the eighties, is slowly unraveling. On both sides of the Atlantic, people are worried about the future of an erstwhile "good" society, which we knew to be democratic, centered on the middle class and defined by a social market economy, and which we perceived as comparatively fair and open. The harmonious duo of democracy and market economy had brought the people of Europe and North America prosperity, security and, above all, the highest possible degree of freedom. But the deep social divides can no longer be ignored – and not only here in the United States. What seems to be missing is the "cement" that holds our societies together, a minimum of consensus, a basic accord that allows individuals to flourish in all their diversity.

The core question as to how people will co-exist and encounter each other in future and how they will – on various levels – organize their communities has not been answered. Not only in the United States, but also in Europe, the desire for societies to renew themselves democratically, socially and, above all, morally has been expressed in various forms. Over the last few years, numerous people frequently took to the streets and protested passionately, not only on Wall Street in New York or in the capitals of European states that were severely affected by the banking crisis. Even the economic recovery following that crisis has not produced a new social consensus. Under President Donald Trump, the United States is looking to redefine itself in national isolation. These tendencies have always existed – they are of a cyclical nature. At present, the number of countries is increasing whose governments are trying to rally the majority of the people behind them by promises of a nationalistic nature. On both sides of the Atlantic, national conservative parties are in the ascendant. In Europe, by the way, this began before the onset of immigration from Africa and the Middle East.

Very few people realized that, at the beginning of the new millennium, society was threatening to fall apart at the seams. Yet there had, in fact, been a number of early indicators of far-reaching societal changes that ought to have been taken more seriously. In 2004, for example, *The Working Poor* by Pulitzer Prize winner David Shipler was published, a book about the conditions prevailing in the American labor market, which already shed some light on the early symptoms of that nascent transformation: a new type of economy, driven by financial markets and ruthlessly profit-oriented, that forced millions of people into the low-wage sector. The opposite of the so-called American dream is the end of social permeability: it is social stagnation. Why else were people electrified by Barack Obama's first presidential campaign, which had its core message cleverly wrapped up in one keyword: *change*. In our yearning for renewal, we Americans followed him in droves; and people all over Europe matched our enthusiasm. He promised a lot, but – it would appear to me – implemented only little of it. Under his presidency American society did not become a blueprint for a process of societal renewal, a model for the future. On the contrary, it is paralyzed by division, incomprehension and distrust, disillusionment and resignation.

A couple of years earlier, in 2000, billionaire and financial speculator Georges Soros, one of the largest profiteers of the system, of all people, attracted attention with a book in which he warned of the excesses of unfettered capitalism. He began to look at the dark side of the economy at a time when no one could imagine that the wheel would not continue to spin faster and faster. Today, scientists at Harvard, Stanford and Princeton are debating with their renowned colleagues from other countries whether the industrial nations have not maneuvered themselves into a secular crisis, a whirl of depressions and ever new financial bubbles. Such a disastrous development would drive millions of people into poverty, and perilously undermine many people's faith in democracy and humanism.

I myself cannot proclaim what postindustrial societies should look like, what would characterize them and hold them together, how they could define themselves and how a new public spirit could emerge. Like most people, I have no idea how liberties and civil rights would have to be redesigned in the era of globalization and ever new technological advancement to ensure that they are not taken away from us, their beneficiaries. To use a very big word, so far, a new *vision* for society is nowhere to be found. Its very absence describes the vacuum that many people are struggling with because they can very clearly sense two developments: the menacing signs of decay in our societies, and the limits to their possibilities of autonomy. This is barely any different in the United States than in Europe. The frequently described omnipotence of the state security agencies and of Internet companies such as Google, Amazon and Facebook frightens me. And I am not alone.

What exactly do I see? The world is still in the throes of a sovereign debt crisis that stems from the failure of the elites in politics and finance. No one dares to rule out the possibility that the situation might escalate again. The United States and the European states have run into debts in the most irresponsible and unscrupulous manner. And they are not putting an end to it. These are debts that have no corresponding assets, loans taken out to wage futile wars, which have caused nothing but devastation and huge waves of migration, in order to cover gigantic speculative losses incurred by the financial services industry, and to pay for questionable economic stimulus packages, which became necessary after investment banks and insurance companies had pushed the global economy to the brink. These are debts for a tax relief program, which one already knows will mainly benefit the super-rich, including the president himself.

The latest crisis, which began in the United States in 2008, bringing the global financial system close to a meltdown and plunging the world's economy into a recession, could have been predicted early on by pointing out several social harbingers: the drifting apart of rich and poor; the shrinking of the middle class, as postulated by Nobel laureate Paul Krugman in a long article in the *New York Times* at the beginning of the century; the astronomical increase in manager salaries; the euphoric reaction of the stock markets when an internationally operating company announced its intention to make twenty thousand employees redundant, as if that were a reason to rejoice; or the company's success in making billions in virtually tax-free profits while its workforce labored in degrading conditions for the lowest possible pay. A small section of society was infected with gold fever, whereas another, significantly larger, portion was left behind. To this day, that hasn't changed.

MAN'S FOE

What worries me is this system's built-in misanthropy and destructiveness. When, for some centuries, capitalism was on a fairly sound footing, even the arts flourished. But in its unfettered form, it stops at nothing; on the contrary: all areas of society are consumed by it. An economic model has mutated into an overriding ideology. Somehow the idea got hold of us humans that not only should the economic system as such be less social, but that we, every single one of us, should adopt the attitude of the capitalist.

The idea that man can and must forge his own destiny has historically always been more pronounced in the United States than in Europe, albeit always coupled with the expectation that those who have the means to do so should fulfill their social responsibilities. But even in this land of seemingly endless opportunities, which was populated by idealists and adventurers like my grandparents, a change of values can be perceived that is turning out to be a profound paradigm shift. To put it simply: egoism instead of social responsibility, individualism instead of public spirit. Many people are increasingly frightened by the social pressure they are subjected to.

As a result, the appreciation for things that were once simply part of a good life has weakened: assuming social responsibility and thereby gaining individual gratification, getting involved in the community and, of course, experiencing art that shapes our way of thinking. Almost unknowingly, we have fallen victim to the misconception that it is not charitable experiences that make life worth living, but only those that are immediately profitable. All those big and small capitalists have internalized that casino mentality of high risk-taking, a constant weighing-up of resource input and probability of success and of costs and benefits. Capitalism has the potential to destroy entire communities. It has – as we all know by now – a serious downside. A meaningful life entails experiences that require us to refrain from this ongoing gamble with gains and benefits. In our own impotence, we have all become speechless. How do we want to live in the future? And what is important to us?

I see our society's crisis of meaning as an opportunity for a return to the arts and to classical music. Aesthetic experiences that profoundly touch us as human beings are essential for our survival. We just have to become more aware of their power again. The great symphonies of Haydn, Mozart, Beethoven, all the way to Brahms and Mahler, are not museum pieces that we should listen to only if we want to familiarize ourselves with some music history. They are timeless compositions that can still move and inspire us, especially today. I am convinced that they can support us in our search for meaning. We artists, however, have to work to that end. Let me clarify two issues: Firstly, how does music unfold its power? And secondly, what does music really evoke?

ON THE POWER OF AESTHETIC EXPERIENCES

For more than two thousand years, great thinkers have agonized over the meaning and significance of aesthetic experiences. Plato and Aristotle thought about this question, as did Martin Luther,

Jean-Jacques Rousseau, Immanuel Kant, Friedrich Schiller, Arthur Schopenhauer, Friedrich Nietzsche and Theodor W. Adorno. They propounded different concepts and approached the fine arts – often music in particular – from different philosophical angles. But they never questioned the import of aesthetic experiences for human existence as such; rather, they agreed on one fundamental idea, which will always hold true for me: aesthetic experiences will always lead to a gain of knowledge, so long as one is open to contemplating them. Then they can even shape one's character.

However, there are debates as to precisely how aesthetics facilitate man's gain of knowledge. It can be triggered by *affect*, to which Plato granted the highest status in his philosophy. Musical education was so important because "rhythm, and harmony, [...] sink most deeply into the recesses of the soul, and take most powerful hold of it, bringing gracefulness in their train," the philosopher from ancient Greece wrote. But gain of knowledge can also be achieved through an *intellectual* reception of the aesthetic phenomenon, as German philosopher Friedrich Nietzsche postulated when he rejected any glorification of music as a direct language of emotion. It was simply not enough to be always moved to tears, choking with sentiment.

Whichever way one views it, the effect is surely different for every person, even though it might be more common to feel it in one's heart before processing it in one's mind. Music moves us, mobilizing our senses and our sensibilities in such a way that we are almost mysteriously thrown back onto ourselves. Perplexingly, it was mostly not the composers themselves who invoked the power and potency of music. Perhaps they were not exactly aware of it, given that they cared more about the musical statement itself. It was the great thinkers, the poets and philosophers, who tried to unlock the secret of the power of music over the soul from different directions.

Thus far, none of them has managed to get to the bottom of it. And yet, all their attempts at explanation hold a kernel of truth. In 1810, German romanticist E.T.A. Hoffmann wrote in his

"Review of Beethoven's Fifth Symphony": "Music reveals to man an unknown realm, a world quite separate from the outer sensual world surrounding him, a world in which he leaves behind all feelings circumscribed by intellect in order to embrace the inexpressible." Two hundred years ago, the poet argued that the power of music might lie in its preconceptual abstractness. What it represented was not specific, not a *particular* joy or sadness, no clearly identifiable pain, horror, serenity or calm, but the emotion *in and of itself*, or rather, its very essence.

Let us hear some other witnesses. In his series of letters, *On the Aesthetic Education of Man*, Friedrich Schiller considered the powerful impact of the arts. "Art is a daughter of Freedom," he wrote to Prince Friedrich Christian von Augustenburg in July 1793 in the second of those letters, moving on to a whole series of philosophical considerations. And it is through beauty we arrive at freedom. "Art, like Science," he argued, "is free from everything that is positive or established by human conventions, and both of them rejoice in an absolute immunity from human lawlessness. The political legislator can enclose their territory, but he cannot govern within it. He can proscribe the friend of truth, but Truth endures, he can humiliate the artist, but Art he cannot debase."

These letters bear witness to Schiller's examination of the French Revolution, the results of which sorely disappointed him. He concerned himself not only with the despotism of an aristocratic state, but also with the concept of popular sovereignty. The people were bound to fail, not meeting the high expectations of political reason as postulated by the Age of Enlightenment. The French Revolution did not implement universal freedom, and it did not bring more humanity to the people; quite the opposite. And so Schiller posits aesthetic education against the brutalization of people who are evidently able to trample all over humanistic achievements.

In literature, one can hardly find a plea for the arts that is more passionate and more convincing than that of this great German writer. The fine arts are a necessary condition for humaneness

– but unfortunately, as history has shown time and again, by no means a sufficient one. According to Schiller, beauty paves the way for people to proceed from feeling to thought, "since the way to the head must lie through the heart." Schiller places primary importance on the "training of the sensibility [...], not merely because it will be a means of making the improved understanding effective for living but for the very reason that it awakens this improvement."

The French writer Jean-Jacques Rousseau, too, was convinced that man is changed by his feelings. "Man is modified by his senses, no one doubts it; but because we fail to distinguish between modifications, we confuse their causes; we attribute both too much and too little power to sensations," the philosopher writes in his "Essay on the Origin of Languages," which also discusses melody and musical imitation, "we do not realize that often they affect us not only as sensations but as signs or images and that their moral effects also have moral causes." Yet it requires a long process of familiarization to be able to perceive and enjoy both the sensations and their moral effects, hence what Schiller called the "training of the sensibility," and what Professor Korisheli worked on so tirelessly with us kids. In the arts, nothing simply falls into one's lap, neither in the case of the artists nor in the case of the recipients, as even they have to work hard to achieve proper fulfillment.

A downright homage to the power of music was written by Reformation theologian Martin Luther, who couldn't even have known music as it evolved at the height of the baroque period: "For whether one wishes to comfort the sad, to terrify the happy, to encourage the despairing, to humble the proud, to calm the passionate, or to appease those full of hate [...]; what more effective means than music could one find?" And on another occasion he stated that music "is one of the fairest and most glorious gifts of God [...]. It is one of the best of arts [...]; it expelleth melancholy, as we can see on King Saul."

A MATTER OF SOCIAL SURVIVAL

The visual arts, literature, poetry and music – those are the fields in which aesthetic experiences can be made that might have a lasting impact on life because in their works painters and sculptors, poets and composers address matters that mankind has sought answers to from time immemorial. Children are not consciously aware of this, but I am convinced that they can sense it. It doesn't necessarily have to be classical music, just because that was, and still is, the case for me. Classical music is, however, part of the realm of the fine arts that provide more than mere entertainment, the adornment of the everyday or, indeed, a superficially glamorous career as a performer.

Classical music always throws one back onto oneself; it deals with questions of whence and whither, of what we humans are, or who I am as an individual. It changes our perception of ourselves and thereby our interaction with others. It won't leave us alone if we have settled for a comfortable life, with only rudimentary answers to questions that have not been fully solved yet. For it is not answers that the great composers of classical music, the painters and sculptors, the poets and thinkers provide us with in their works. It is questions they raise – questions we are inevitably confronted with in the course of our lives.

The fine arts are more than a mere add-on, an embellishment, a relaxation exercise for the accelerated pace of adult life. They are more than what a radio station for classical music once promised when it devised the slogan "Classical music – your oasis of well-being." And making music during childhood does not only fulfill the purpose of furthering the children's ability to concentrate, their social competence and thereby their fitness for life. Music can achieve all of that – of course. This is also what is always being advertised when it comes to the musical education of children. But I am utterly convinced that this is not what music is for. The sole purpose of music is to be *experienced*. It can stay with us, move us, change us and much more. Aesthetic experiences are an indispensable component of life. They are part of our identity, connecting us to our past and to our social traditions, and offering us guidance for the future.

Today I know that I owe this insight to my childhood. But the arts are having a hard time. Dedicating oneself to the consideration of aesthetic matters in greater depth has never seemed essential for survival. First of all, humans need water, and bread and a roof over their heads. They need an income to secure their livelihood. In addition, they depend on social contacts. But don't the arts rank closely behind those fundamental material needs? Are they not an essential requirement of our social survival?

Empty phrases, you may think, nothing but yet another attempt at persuasion. "Attempt" is the right word because although the impact of music is so powerful, its effect on the individual is uncertain, unpredictable and unquantifiable. We do not know when, where and how it will unfold its power, when it will strike, when it will touch a person – not even as far as we ourselves are concerned. We do not know whether the idea for the solution to a conflict with our employer was triggered by a recital the previous evening, when the pianist and the violinist took us on a musical journey.

Music is different from all the other arts. It is an abstract, temporal and transient art form. This is what makes it unique among the arts. It is semantically undefined; the language of music is not a language in the literal sense of the word. And because it is abstract, it does not, like other arts, create a direct copy or portrayal of things. Rather, it aims at their essence, on a meta level. This is where its beauty lies, and its appeal.

"Music expresses that which cannot be said, and on which it is impossible to be silent." There is a whole array of quotes about music, which I will largely forgo in this book. This one by Victor Hugo, however, is one of the most beautiful ones. Of course, the non-concrete is not confined to music, it has its place among the visual arts, as well. Paintings and sculptures do not have to be representational or figural. What is special about music, however, is its fleetingness. Unlike a painting, music cannot be perceived in its entirety in one single moment. It rushes past us, so to speak. Its "pull" develops over the course of time that has to pass until the piece of music has ended, while simultaneously playing with expectations. Every new tone, the very moment that it rings out, raises expectations for the next one. It is part of what makes music so irresistible.

Nevertheless, these attempts to explain the powerful impact of music remain unsatisfying. I do not really know why it can cast a spell over us. But in a reversed approach, I can state with some certainty what is lost when music is being denied to children, for instance. These children will have one opportunity less to express themselves; they will lose the possibility to be successful with music, to bring pleasure to others, to shine. They will miss out on a game, on joy and on many a chance to make important discoveries.

Aesthetic experiences allow people a whole new view on the world. I will discuss the functional mechanism that may be underlying here in the chapter after the next. But this much is certain: aesthetic experiences can transform people. They hold the possibility of making those who are ready and, above all, willing to let it happen, consider other ways of living, though not every single one of those sensual experiences has to be a positive one. A concert can also unsettle, a painting can disturb. Those experiences can, however, only be made by those who have found access to aesthetics in the first place. Without a certain form of education, such access is not possible. Without a "training of the sensibility," which in turn facilitates aesthetic experiences, a person remains incomplete and even partly unable to find his or her way around our complicated world. They will lack the power of judgment, and not only in aesthetic matters.

WHAT'S YOUR MIND MADE OF?

When we listen to classical music, the daily rush and racket melts away, as does the shallowness of constant digital communication. As soon as we hear the sound of music, we enter a different world and the aforementioned playing with our expectations begins. It is an inner dialogue – whether consciously or subliminally. We listen, we evaluate, we anticipate the next chord, maybe a melodic line, which, however, might take a completely different turn. We get upset, we ask for the meaning behind the music and for the reason why it touches us, why it excites us with its wild rhythms, why its atonality frustrates us or simply why it transports us from the familiar sphere of the necessary and the useful to a state of the highest acoustic awareness. We listen to a piece of music that a stranger has written on sheets of paper and that others are now performing for us. Music creates its very own self-contained space for emotional, intellectual and spiritual experiences that are not normally triggered by our immediate social environment. These are evoked by art, and within that space we encounter ourselves.

Let me ask once again: Why should we listen to classical music at all? Why even make the effort? Does music enable us to think more clearly, feel more profoundly and thus live a fuller life than we could without it? Does it alter our sociopolitical attitudes and the way we treat our fellow humans, or maybe even our perception of ourselves? These are rhetorical questions because my answer is, of course, positive. They guide me whenever I devise a concert program. It is my objective that music performed by us should animate an audience to give a positive answer, too. Music ought to become a permanent, indispensable dimension of their lives. But why does classical music, or let's call it serious music, because it was not only written during the heyday, and in the style, of eighteenth- and nineteenth-century classicism, why does it have this effect?

One could assemble a number of explications from a wide range of disciplines, put forward not only by philosophers, poets and the musicians themselves, who for centuries have concerned themselves with the effect that music – as the most mysterious art due to its abstractness – has on man. But we also find some by neurologists and psychologists who tirelessly strive to find an explanation for this very distinct and yet elusive characteristic of music. In any case, to this day its secret has not been unlocked. And maybe it will forever remain shrouded the more answers we gather.

But I want to discuss one more argument with you, as it is compellingly logical and might provide an answer to the question I posed in the title of this chapter, "Classical Music for a Time of Crisis?" The late Canadian literary scholar Northrop Frye developed a different approach to the significance of the arts. Naturally, as a literary critic he mainly had fiction and poetry in mind. Yet what he had to say about the impact of literature could also be applied to classical music and to the question of why one should engage with it. According to Frye, there is a difference between the world people live in and the world they would like to live in. The first is reality; the second belongs to the vast realm of the imagination.

The natural sciences explain to us the world we are surrounded by. They are, however, not directly involved with the world of our imagination. It is here that the arts come into play: literature, painting and music. Art, as Frye puts it, begins at the edge of the world that we imagine, that we construct in our minds, not of the one that we see around us. It is the arts that influence our idea of how we want to live. They have a more or less direct effect on it, literature maybe more so than music, whose abstract form sets a different process in motion. This is precisely why the arts are so essential, especially now, during this profound historical turning point, this societal crisis of meaning, where it is paramount to develop ideas of the world we want to inhabit in the future.

Frye published these ideas in 1964, in an essay he called "The Educated Imagination," and with which he tried to highlight the relevance of literature and the importance of the arts, which so profoundly influence human thought. The purpose of literature was to educate people and to train them in imagining the possible. Could he not also have written this wise essay about classical music? Music achieves a similar effect, it strengthens our imaginative powers. To Frye, vision, fantasy and imagination are, however, not just relevant for writers, but for everyone. "The fundamental job of imagination in ordinary life is to produce, out of the society we have to live in, a vision of the society we want to live in." This is exactly what we are searching for right now. This is what it's all about.

The arts exert immense mobilizing powers, whose secret has never been fully revealed. This may be the reason why, for more than two thousand years, humans have not only created and experienced art, but also relentlessly philosophized about its impact. The power of music was a virulent topic in Greek mythology – Orpheus uses a lyre to soften the heart of the ruler of the underworld. This is the archetype of the potency of music and the beginning of reflecting upon it. Or think of the sirens who – a sinister effect this time – lure people into the abyss with their almost magical songs.

Musical experience creates a unique emotionality that facilitates cognition. Tyrants' hearts can melt – if not always. The evil spirits that possessed King Saul took flight at the sound of David's harp. The music inspired Saul's imagination, evoking a vision of how different the world could be. Music and song made him see or sense that God was on David's side; they effected a turn for the better in him. Rembrandt impressively captured Saul's life-changing aesthetic experience in oil. The stricken tyrant is moved to tears. His gaze is inward. His features, worn by hatred, reflect his change of heart.

Does our music industry need an existential crisis to shake society up and remind it of the tacit consensus on the importance of classical music? That was the question at the end of the previous chapter. Since then, I have gone one step further. I now want to rephrase that question: Does it require a societal identity crisis of epochal dimensions to realize that the arts, particularly serious music, really have a lot to offer in these dark times?

THE PROMISES OF MUSIC

At this point in time, I see incredible opportunities for serious music, for classical music, for those old and yet so timeless works written hundreds of years ago. But this also holds true for new compositions that haven't yet proven their timelessness, but address all the trembling and quaking, all the uncertainties and insecurities of this epochal change, and maybe also what it will all lead to.

Classical music holds wonderful promise. As a child, I neither knew nor understood this, even though I sensed it, just like everyone else. It is the promise of energy, strength, insight, inspiration, solace and happiness, of freedom of spirit that rises above all social conventions. But one has to make an effort. That goes for children and adults alike. Finding access might be easiest for children of elementary school age. Professor Korisheli knew this. It was no coincidence that he decided to be an elementary school teacher in order to start with the youngest. He showed us that it was worth our while to engage with music, to learn ever more about it and to search for things that were greater and more powerful than we were, and to which he didn't have an answer, either. In his classes, we jumped up and down the steps of his staircase to learn about the chromatic scale and intervals. We banged on tables to learn about rhythm and time signature. We had fun, but not for the sake of having fun. Above all, we experienced many of those great and small moments of happiness that are rooted in a growth of knowledge and skills, and in the inkling of something greater that is inherent in music.

In addition, music promises us participation – a word that has gained importance over the last decade not without reason. Music becomes music only through the interaction of creator, performer and listener. What good is sheet music when it is not brought to life? Therefore, performers and listeners are part of the process even at the moment of creation. Whenever musicians play a score, they become part of the genesis of the work. True, it is not reinvented from scratch at every performance. And yet, each time it does come into existence afresh – and always differently. And the listeners do their bit to transform sound waves or acoustic stimuli into music. That music is created, or at least recreated, in their minds. In this way, even the audience becomes part of the creative process of a performance.

Another promise is that of equality: classical music is not exclusive. It belongs to all, but not to anyone specific, least of all to a social class that would consider itself the educated middle class, or elite. In those moments of musical experience, people meet on an equal footing, for instance in Mozart's *The Magic Flute*. This is an opera that brings everyone together, regardless of their age or their socialization. Not everyone can be a famous basketball player or golfer, a big entrepreneur, an investment banker, a billionaire in the digital economy, a president or a superstar at the piano. But we can all enjoy the same experience when we go to a concert or to the opera, or when we make music together. It is an aesthetic experience where neither fame nor prosperity matters. Class differences disappear.

In moments of sensual experiences, the gulfs within our society close, borders are opened, cultural trenches are leveled. During my travels to Canada's Far North with the Orchestre symphonique de Montréal, the Inuit were clearly moved by Mozart's *Eine kleine Nachtmusik* (*A Little Serenade*), even though they had never heard anything like it before. To share a musical experience means to meet as members of the human race, regardless of rank, origin or nationality. No one feels this more immediately than a conductor when the orchestra's music flows out to the audience and fills the hall to the farthest corner, musicians and listeners alike carried away by a flood of sounds.

The most beautiful promise in music, however, is that of infinity. Just as we will not succeed in uncovering the last secret of the power of music, we will not exhaust its depths, and we will not find an ultimate answer to the existential questions that are raised by the great works of classical music. It would be impossible for me to allege of a piece of music that I am forever done with it. It would be just as narrow-minded to claim to have come up with the ultimate interpretation of a work, or to have perfected the one and only valid performance practice. Whoever approaches music with that aspiration is already alienated from it. Great works are inexhaustible. They expose the mania for "doability," so characteristic of our time, as pure hubris. In masterpieces, I hear different nuances every time, new shades of meaning that can shake me to the core.

BEETHOVEN

Superstar

The rhythmic blows of the axes are echoing through the woods. Unremittingly. Oaks and beeches are falling to the ground. The forest workers are diligent – and in good spirits. There is an air of optimism about. Napoleon has been defeated. By now, the first harbingers of the industrial revolution have even reached Vienna, a relatively sleepy place in economic terms. The city is growing considerably and is suddenly in need of enormous amounts of firewood and timber. The Vienna Woods have plenty of it. Merriment and confidence abound.

The second movement of Beethoven's Eighth Symphony, the Allegretto scherzando, comes along in a wonderfully lightfooted, almost mellow manner, as if the atmosphere in Vienna couldn't be any better. The tireless forest workers are whistling this little tune as they work. And the citizens of the musical metropolis of Austria are full of hope for better times that will bring them machines and, with those, completely new opportunities.

In this Allegretto scherzando, it is the wind instruments that provide the rhythm with their constant staccato. For several bars the Viennese world would seem to be in perfect order if the listener did not gradually become aware of those insistent chords that are driving the merry tune relentlessly onward with their sharply detached notes. The men keep striking the tree trunks with their axes. They do not stop. The winds' staccato is so predominant that everyone feels it: what Beethoven is portraying here is not an entirely perfect world. A certain menace is hinted at. The wonderful Vienna Woods are under threat. Their beauty, which Beethoven so wistfully praised in his Sixth Symphony, the so-called *Pastoral*, how long will it last?

Ludwig van Beethoven's music evokes images, images like those, for example. His symphonies are ideas that become paintings that reflect the thrilling events of the late eighteenth and early nineteenth centuries. Beethoven embeds something haunting, alarming, almost ruthless within the Allegretto scherzando of his Eighth Symphony. With their rhythmic staccato, the wind instruments outplay the strings. One could also imagine the thudding of a machine imposing its unrelenting beat on the people. But for a long time, those people will not notice that they are literally being overrun by their own technological advances – the ongoing irony of industrial history that started in the early nineteenth century. It was not only the Viennese who enthusiastically commited themselves to continuous economic growth back then. The entire Western world fell into a manufacturing frenzy. And Beethoven may have asked himself, perhaps even at the very beginning of industrialization, whether it would be viable in the long term. The provocative staccato is constantly being interrupted. At the end, it falls apart. The spook is over.

When I read Beethoven's scores, play his music at the grand piano or conduct it, I often think in images. Throughout the years, these images have always changed, just as my perception of his music has changed. Beethoven is probably *the* classical composer whose music has been most influenced by contemporary events and the history of ideas. That doesn't come as a surprise, considering that he was born into very exciting times with pioneering achievements. Beethoven is *the* composer of a turning point in history, when the old social order broke down and made room for entirely new concepts. He witnessed the French Revolution, the accompanying abolition of feudal absolutism and the "State of Estates," and the establishment of civil liberties.

He himself was captured by the immense appeal of the ideas of the Enlightenment. He admired Napoleon, initially as a soldier of the revolution, then as the magnificent field commander that he was, only to despise him later as the despotic ruler of Europe who had betrayed the ideals of the revolution and thus the human and civil rights that were so hard won. Beethoven celebrated Wellington's victory over Napoleon; he observed the Congress of Vienna and the restructuring of Europe. And he witnessed the beginning of the industrial revolution that would, only a couple of decades later, induce a whole new class society. Again and again he grappled with the issues of his time in his music.

For me, Beethoven is a kind of life companion. His compositions are always present. For decades now, I have regularly included his symphonies in my concerts. And when I ask myself why, the answer probably lies in those numerous images and ideas Beethoven's music evokes – new ones every time, without the earlier images becoming less important. The new ones are simply added. In my youth, I discovered Beethoven's humanistic statements, and later on his views on the individual. And today? For some time now, this increasingly mysterious Eighth Symphony has affected me in a completely different way than before.

During my childhood, I began to experience Beethoven's music first of all as an impressive nexus of notes and tones. Of course, as a little viola player in one of our orchestras in Morro Bay, I did not immediately ask myself what the composer was trying to tell me with all those notes and tones. I remember us practicing the *Eroica*, his Third Symphony, in which he deals with the French Revolution's idea of liberty. I can still recall how I sat with my viola in the middle of that large orchestra, among all those children and teenagers of different ages. And when you are part of such an orchestra, as a violist literally in the very center of it, you simply cannot resist the music's pull. Even physically, it makes a deep impact on you. My arm moved the bow in parallel with the other string players, my body swayed rhythmically and vibrations reached me from every direction: the deep sounds of the cellos to my left, the wind instruments behind me, the high-pitched violins to my right.

Every orchestra player knows the feeling of becoming part of a bigger whole during a performance, of being taken over by the music's flow, when all of a sudden nothing else matters anymore. Making music together is fundamentally one of the most formative experiences – much more intensive than mere listening. This is how, through Beethoven's music, I first experienced my belonging to a community in which every single individual has committed themselves to the same goal. We were all inspired to turn this symphony into a wonderful experience for our audience. Beethoven's music was a permanent feature of my musical childhood and youth.

As a young listener, it moved me completely differently. One of the two large orchestras on the West Coast – it must have been either the San Francisco Symphony or the Los Angeles Philharmonic – gave a concert at the high school of Morro Bay. The basketball gym was filled to bursting point. I had managed to get hold of a seat next to the timpani and found myself between the musicians and the choir. The orchestra was going to perform Beethoven's Ninth Symphony, and there was hardly a student who wanted to miss out on it. This time, I wasn't going to play music, but only to listen to it – but again I was seated almost in the middle of the orchestra, a kind of cauldron whose temperature seemed to rise continually throughout the night, until the choir's cue in the last movement.

When, with great fervor, the singers sounded out this grand utopia – the peaceful living together as equal brethren – it took my breath away. The timpani virtually hammered Beethoven's message into my brain. At the same time, I sensed how far the world was removed from this utopia. At the time, on the eve of the Cuban Missile Crisis, the Cold War was moving into a new phase. The public followed the unfolding of the crisis with growing anxiety. Every household was urged to excavate a bunker on their property. At the same time, Martin Luther King Jr. was fighting for his dream – the equality of all Americans irrespective of descent and skin color.

For young people in pre-adolescence, an experience like the one I had can be quite formative: peace and equality as a utopia, which even King David had spoken of in his psalms, a thousand years before Christ. But man is not peaceable, and of course I noticed and sensed back then that the longing for universal brotherhood would not be fulfilled that easily. I also knew that the hope for peace must never be allowed to fade. Maybe that moment in the high school's basketball gym did not mark the immediate beginning of my interest in Beethoven's symphonies and in the question of what he was really trying to communicate. But it gave me the first inkling of the existence of profound ideas behind his music. Later, his music pulled me deep into the history of nineteenth-century Europe and made me examine the conception of humanity that had then emerged.

What is man? What does the dignity of man mean? And in what kind of society should man live? These are all questions that are addressed in Beethoven's works. It was ideas like that, of an enlightened attitude of mind that allows for individual autonomy and necessitates social freedom, that became overwhelmingly important to me. This may have also been caused by the turbulent times that the United States slipped into in the late sixties, and the heated sociopolitical debates that dominated the seventies. Beethoven's symphonies represent an exploration of those big humanistic ideals, especially the Third, the Fifth, the Seventh and, of course, the Ninth. The statements Beethoven makes through the language of music are timeless. In those days, I realized for the first time that human freedom and the right to autonomy are not a given, but had been hard won and always had to be defended against the permanent threat posed by those who want to curtail them.

In another phase of my pondering over Beethoven's symphonies, I was fascinated by his conception of man, and the individualism underlying it. As one of the first composers, Beethoven was convinced that man has the capacity to change for the better, and to grow throughout life: by means of education, experience and one's own effort, but also through renunciation and self-denial.

This is why there is so much hope in Beethoven's music, why we let ourselves get carried away by it and begin to believe in ourselves. This is why at the heart of his music there is *development*, and not some end result. His music was meant to drive people forward. Although Beethoven, in his symphonies, employs the language of music to great effect, he always includes an appeal to the listeners to make use of their own reason and to reflect upon themselves and their actions.

All of that, which I discovered during my younger years, had already electrified Beethoven's contemporaries. Their desire for freedom and autonomy was simply too strong to leave them untouched by his music. Change was in the air. And Beethoven's music expressed that atmosphere precisely. It was new, different, ingenious. This may explain part of the Beethoven phenomenon, a composer who was a superstar even during his lifetime and who fundamentally transformed the music scene in Europe. After him, hardly anything was as it had been before. With his symphonies, he founded an orchestra and concert tradition that has shaped urban musical life to this day.

With Beethoven, the composer established himself as a freelance artist. He was no longer a conductor-composer employed by the church or by aristocratic circles. If he chose to do so, he could earn a livelihood by means of commissions and contracts – albeit with all the risks an independent existence entails. Certainly, Beethoven cared about the music itself. But his music was also a "business." He was constantly trying to negotiate the best possible terms and conditions for himself – haggling with publishers, fighting for high admission fees, investing his money in shares, blackmailing wealthy patrons into providing him with a kind of life annuity by threatening to leave Vienna – and, despite some precarious periods in his life, died a relatively prosperous man. Beethoven was the first to lead the life of a modern artist.

But that was not all. Beethoven turned composing into an art form in its own right, independent of conducting or performing. As his hearing became more and more impaired, resulting in total deafness long before his death, Beethoven – who, after all, had been one of the greatest piano virtuosos of his time – was no longer able to perform or conduct his own works. He had to leave that to others.

To me, the most fascinating development, however, is the fact that he reached a broader audience. From then on, it was not just a small social elite that had the pleasure of coming into contact with classical music, but also the new social stratum of the large urban middle class that had developed during those years of change in European history. Beethoven's concerts in Vienna were real events. The academies he organized were attended by two thousand people. They resembled today's pop concerts. At times, the listeners were so thrilled that they started to applaud frantically after the first movement of a symphony.

At an advanced age, Beethoven couldn't hear any of that anymore. He had already gone deaf. So people started waving their arms, hats or handkerchiefs. His concerts were discussed in the newspapers, sometimes for days. Beethoven was celebrated, occasionally criticized, rarely trashed. Of the approximately four hundred thousand inhabitants of the city, around twenty thousand attended Beethoven's funeral procession. Many had tears running down their cheeks. Imagine how many people would have to take to the streets these days, in cities with millions of inhabitants, if a pop star were carried to the grave. Beethoven, through his music, had not only made himself immortal, he had also turned the world of music upside down. Above all, however, he had instantly captivated many people with his musical thoughts and ideas.

This, surely, is the reason why his nine symphonies and the heroic piece about Wellington's victory over Napoleon, only rarely played these days, brought about a new form of concert culture that put music events at the center of a broader public life. Beethoven's music moved people during those times of change, when a modern, open society, no longer based on the three Estates, came into being. It conveyed the values of the modern age: liberty, equality, fraternity, civil rights and social cohesion. With his musical idiom, Beethoven expressed a new societal consensus: that the individual, regardless of birth and rank, possesses human dignity, and enjoys the right to participation, personal development and advancement.

Beethoven was the composer of the middle class, a strong protagonist of new bourgeois self-confidence. That he managed to do this in an ingenious way, and that his music appealed to the people directly, is surely one of the reasons why a completely new form of orchestra tradition and concert life could develop. People from different social classes could meet, find common ground and, through the music, have a chance to daydream. Nobody recognized better than Beethoven how necessary that was – and what opportunities arose when music was made accessible to larger segments of society.

Can we hear this even today when we go to a concert with a Beethoven symphony on its program? I certainly think so. The individual listener's level of musical understanding is not relevant. Maybe they are familiar with the sonata form or with orchestration, or maybe they know something about the musical conventions of the time, which Beethoven threw out in order to arrive at completely new soundscapes. Maybe they have studied the compositional techniques that this singular composer employed in order to give different instruments their very own significance, or how he changed tempi and dynamics, or brought musical themes to an abrupt halt to make room for new ideas. Maybe they don't know any of that. Undoubtedly, most concertgoers have never looked at a score. Some may not even be able to read music. But none of this is necessary. Beethoven's ideas can still be heard, felt, sensed in his music, with all its drama or, in the case of the Eighth, its lightness, provocativeness and irony. And every visit to a concert will prompt new ideas.

In his Eighth Symphony, which is occupying my mind so much these days, effrontery and irony come through everywhere. This work, which even at its premiere in Vienna fell short of the Seventh in its impact on the audience and the critics, has long had the reputation of being the lightweight among the nine symphonies. All the others seem to be more substantial. The Eighth has always been the "little" symphony, a serene piece, to be enjoyed before the listener would again be seriously challenged with the Ninth. You can hum along with the tunes, especially that of the Allegretto scherzando. And to this day, the Eighth Symphony is given very little consideration in the extensive body of literature on Beethoven that fills the library shelves.

I used to consider Beethoven's Eighth Symphony to be a kind of retrospection or return to earlier symphonies and their manner of composition, maybe even an homage to Haydn, whom Beethoven esteemed so much, or at least to his compositional style. It seemed to me as though Beethoven was falling behind his own modernity and expressiveness. The Eighth Symphony is written for a much smaller orchestra and is, in design and structure, much more compact and "classicist." I used to perceive the Seventh and the Eighth Symphonies to be a contrasting pair: a great dramatic symphony at the time of Europe's liberation from Napoleonic rule, and a jaunty follow-up piece.

Today, I no longer see the Eighth Symphony as a return but rather, in musical terms, as an enormous step forward. I am discovering it anew and experiencing it in a completely different way. This is a new phase of my examination of Beethoven's œuvre. Today, I claim that the Eighth is one of the most confrontational of all symphonies, immensely provocative in its demand to concern oneself with time and its apperception. At the beginning of the age of the industrial revolution, Beethoven already seems to have suspected that the modern era would make people restless and condemn them to always have to work faster, react more quickly and take swifter decisions. If Beethoven ever captured that momentum of acceleration in his music, he did so in the Eighth. In this way, it is more relevant than ever. The history of the modern age is one of constant acceleration, whereby the time we save, thanks to breathtaking technological advancement, is not handed back to us but, paradoxically, drives us on incessantly. In the twenty-first century – at least in free and democratic societies – the question of heteronomy versus autonomy is, above all, one of time.

But what is the composer really doing here? What musical elements is he employing to bring the question of time and our individual perception of it into focus? Of all of his symphonies, in this one, which is supposed to be so "classicist" and, on the surface, all about serenity and the joy of life, Beethoven composes against all convention and all moderation. In the first movement, the Allegro vivace con brio, he already prescribes a dynamic build-up that was unprecedented in the musical history of his time: fifty bars are constantly marked f *(forte)*, but that's only the beginning. Beethoven demands even more volume, first ff *(fortissimo)* and then fff *(fortississimo)*. In the next, particularly fast movement, he employs the almost unnerving staccato previously mentioned, played by the wind instruments. The third movement is full of sfz *(sforzati)*, heavily accentuated single notes or chords, used in such a way that they counteract the regular flow of rhythm. He makes almost lavish use of those accents. More than twenty of them can be found in the introduction of the movement alone. Once you pay attention to them, you cannot get them out of your head. Is this really supposed to be just a burlesque, nothing more than merriment, humor and a bit of entertaining musical satire?

One doesn't have to think in such concrete images as the disappearance of the Vienna Woods when listening to the Eighth Symphony, as I did at the beginning of this chapter. One can also discover Beethoven's works on a different, more abstract level. Here, he is discussing the phenomenon of time, and the way it is perceived and experienced by people. Time is being described as fast or sluggish, as quiet or hectic, as steady or disrupted, as speeding up or slowing down, sometimes also as ruthless, for example when time "runs out." One can attempt a review of the historical events and severe upheavals of the late eighteenth and early nineteenth centuries, when social conditions were screaming for radical changes, which in turn were reflected by the music. One can, however, also relate Beethoven's music to the personal level of the individual human being that is always confronted with questions of continuity and discontinuity during times of upheaval. This subliminal restlessness can be detected in the Eighth Symphony. It permeates the entire work, unlike the Seventh Symphony, which specifically relates to the moment of Europe's liberation.

I am currently quite preoccupied with the idea of time and duration, and how it can be experienced so differently. Maybe this is the reason why the Eighth Symphony has come to the fore. Or the other way around: it suggested that topic to me. It's probably a combination of both. It cannot have been a random decision of mine to once more get absorbed in this work, whose score I have studied and analyzed countless times. My own sense of time is changing and so is my perception of the world. Mature age prompts us to reflect upon the meaning of time, a reflection that is of little relevance in our younger years, when it is rather ideas that touch mind, heart and soul. Today it is the phenomenon of time for me.

Maybe the enigma of the Eighth Symphony lies precisely within this confusing game with time and how it is experienced. Being preoccupied with it challenges me to confront my own personal sense of time. My sense of acceleration doesn't seem to match my self-perception as an artist. In this little symphony, which is so unassuming at first glance, Beethoven impressively contrasts the experienced moment with the relentless progression of physical time, and our inability to hold on to that moment. Almost nowhere else does it become so apparent that music – as opposed to, say, a painting – simply flows by. In this symphony, time itself becomes the theme. Music *is* time. It passes, just like life itself.

Beethoven's ideas, on the other hand, are timeless. Man is struggling with technology, and at some point he realizes his own naiveté: he has made himself a slave of his own inventions – yet he cannot help himself. The taunting scherzo of this Eighth Symphony mocks our reliance on gadgets, today, for instance, smartphones that speed up our high-speed lives even further.

The finale of the Eighth Symphony is the opposite of what precedes it. Suddenly, Beethoven allows himself an incredible amount of time to come to a conclusion. After an almost restless Vivace, it takes the music all of fifty bars to reach the final chord. This disparity amounts to impudence, even though it is – at least in parts – the result of harmonic development. What is Beethoven trying to tell us here in this new version of his game with time? Is he poking fun at traditionalists, just as he stokes up his supposedly "classicist" symphony with incredible speeds and a large dose of irony? Is he perhaps laughing at those who haven't yet realized that a new era has begun, not just in the art of music, but in Vienna, in all of Europe, in the whole history of civilization?

We do not know for sure. The Eighth is simply the most cryptic of his symphonies. From a purely musical point of view, it is revolutionary in its own way. At any rate, in this work Beethoven turns around one more time, casts one last glance at the ordered world of the past, mocks traditional ways and breaks the mold never to put it together again. At the very moment when the last chord has died away, one thing becomes abundantly clear: the old days are over for good. Stop, period, finish. The stage is set for the Ninth – new, different, sublime. It is a symphony that eclipses everything that had ever existed in symphonic composition. A cesura in the history of music. The almost outrageously charged Eighth has paved the way for new music. Now the epoch of great utopias can begin.

"Art demands of us that we shall not stand still," said Beethoven. He lived according to that maxim. He experimented, he changed and revolutionized musical forms and, especially in his later chamber music works, he composed in such a modern and dissonant way that his music was no longer comprehensible to some of his contemporaries. When you deal with Beethoven's music, it is as if you move along the edge of a volcano. The ground is too hot to linger. The fast tempi, the abrupt changes, the dynamic surprises, the explosive wealth of musical ideas – all this pushes the listener onward. "Art demands of us that we shall not stand still" – it is not art that demands that of us, but Beethoven. He simply doesn't permit stasis and stagnation. His music challenges us, over and over again.

Many feel that way, not just me. It is just that you never quite know when and how the full force of his creativity will hit you, and guide you in a new direction. That is Beethoven's secret. You cannot predict which of his works will suddenly unfold its exceptional powers and lead you to a new way of thinking: about music, about time, about the people surrounding you and, ultimately, about yourself.

CHAPTER FOUR

HEROES ON ICE –
AND NO COMPROMISES

"[O]ne cannot avoid in America the question of whether the concept of culture in which one has grown up has not itself become obsolete; whether what today as a global tendency befalls culture is not what its very own failure brought upon it, the guilt it incurred by isolating itself as a special sphere of spirit without realizing itself in the organization of society."

Theodor W. Adorno,
Scientific Experiences of a European Scholar in America (1969)

STRANGE SOUNDS FOR YOUNG FOLK

The seven cellists of the Orchestre symphonique de Montréal did not fail to make an impression. As soon as they entered the stage, the young audience celebrated them like pop stars. There was frenetic applause, even though not a single note of the complicated work I had selected for the program of our concert had been played yet: Pierre Boulez' *Messagesquiss*, a composition for solo cello and six accompanying cellos. Finding access to this music is not easy, at least not for untrained ears.

The opening is an extremely quiet and almost provocatively static chord, demanding a great deal of patience from the listener during the first few minutes. For our ears, which are accustomed to tonality, the piece then proceeds in a rather disharmonious fashion. Gradually, the music becomes livelier, quite weird in some of the passages and finally virtuoso. But the young listeners didn't have the slightest problem with it. They didn't shy away from it but rather embraced it from the very first moment. The reserve we had feared was not in the least perceptible. And as soon as the musicians had played the last note, they were celebrated enthusiastically: exuberantly, euphorically – as is the case at youth concerts of very different musical genres. For a moment, our cellists were quite startled and stood almost a little awkwardly on the stage. At any rate, they had become stars in Montreal overnight.

With Pierre Boulez' *Messagesquisse*, we kicked off a rather unusual concert in October 2010, part of a quite extravagant series of concerts. We called it "Éclaté," after the French verb *éclater*, meaning "to smash," "to burst," "to explode." We designed that concert series as a number of events for a somewhat different audience, especially for younger people and young adults, who wanted to experience something other than the customary sedate classical music concert, and at a different hour. The concerts of this series started at 9 p.m., significantly later than our regular performances. And we moved the opening night from our concert hall to the former building of the Molson Brewery. In addition to Boulez, I included Mahler's First Symphony in the program. For the end of the concert, in collaboration with the MUTEK Organization, we had hired the electronic musician Thomas Fehlmann, who is somewhat of an icon in Montreal's unique electronic music scene.

Back then, I thought that if we were to have any chance at all of getting young people interested in serious music, we had to start out by presenting this music in a frame and a context that might be more familiar to them than a concert hall, so they wouldn't have to go out of their way to find us. We would have to question all aspects of conventional concert presentation.

The tickets cost only twenty-five Canadian dollars. The idea was simple: young people should be given the opportunity to listen to pieces that they would hardly be able to discover on YouTube or stream on Spotify. If we wanted to convince them to take an interest in classical music in the first place, we would have to bring the music to them and not wait for them to accidentally stumble into our concert hall. Molson has an enormous brewery building in the old part of Montreal, right by the Saint Lawrence River harbor, with an early-twentieth-century brickwork charm. If I were to use youth language I would say that this location is pretty "cool" and "awesome." Still, none of us were sure if the concert would be well received and who would attend it. In the end, it was packed. Many young people came, an entirely new audience. Among them, however, were quite a few of our many loyal listeners. The concert was sold out.

Even I was surprised by the young people's enthusiasm during our first "Éclaté" concert at the Molson Brewery. But what amazed me most was the earnest concentration with which they engaged with Mahler's First Symphony. Again, this is not a simple work that makes it easy for listeners, especially when it is their first time at a classical concert, and the symphony lasts for over an hour. But there was no sign of a lack of interest, of overload or incomprehension on the part of the audience. The only thing one could call "easily accessible" was the location, which might have helped to remove one or other of the reservations that usually keep young people from going to concerts. The performance by a star of the electronic music scene, which plays such an important role in Montreal, surely added to the appeal. One could even argue that we, as a symphony orchestra, were trying to curry favor with a youth that is basically not interested in classical music. On the other hand, I had thought that we were expecting quite a bit from those young people with our program. After all, we were not playing Mozart or Beethoven symphonies that some of them might have heard before – even if it was only during one of those unspeakable commercials for pickup trucks, lager beer or cat food. It was the first concert of the series, and it was the most exciting one.

Back then, I had already been chief conductor of the Orchestre symphonique de Montréal for a number of years. I had taken over this erstwhile internationally renowned orchestra in 2006, in turbulent and quite challenging times. Seen from the outside, the conditions I came upon might not have indicated that my appointment there would soon turn out to be a sure-fire success. I knew that we had a lot of hard work ahead of us. However, this was part of the appeal for me, and a great chance to show what can be done to reestablish an orchestra with so many excellent musicians and their concert hall as the cultural center of the city, and to bring it back to the top of the international scene.

Working with the Orchestre symphonique de Montréal was a wonderful challenge. We would have to try many approaches, turn the whole house into a "lab" or workshop, and see what we could offer and achieve with quite limited financial means. The optimization task was clear: within the same budget, I wanted to increase our seat occupancy rate and, above all, lower the average age of the audience. In their demographics, our visitors were to represent the overall population of Montreal. I wanted the sound of the orchestra, its appearance on stage and its repertoire to reflect the singularity of the city, the ideas and values of its inhabitants; the orchestra had to resonate with the perception that Montrealers had of themselves. The orchestra had to become competitive again within the city's particularly rich cultural scene, and make it to the top of the priority list for as many people as possible. Therefore, our relaunch in 2006 had something experimental about it, that magic of all beginnings and a considerable amount of excitement. Would we be able to convey to people that classical music is still up to date?

AN ORCHESTRA WITHOUT A CONDUCTOR

The Orchestre symphonique de Montréal (OSM), founded in 1934, has been conducted by many famous personalities, among them Wilfrid Pelletier, Igor Markevitch, Zubin Mehta and Rafael Fruehbeck de Burgos. But for many decades, despite its high quality, it seemed to fall a little short of the international reputation of the North American "Big Five." With Quebec's rapid economic development and the province's strong identification with the arts, a truly great period began. Under Swiss conductor Charles Dutoit, the orchestra actually made it onto the world stage. Dutoit began his position as chief conductor in 1977. During his nearly twenty-five-year period as conductor, he managed to forge a unique sound and put the orchestra back on the map. Dutoit was young, just about forty, when he took on the conductorship. With him, the orchestra went on tour, played in the most famous halls in the world and in 1980 signed a long-term contract with Decca London, with whom it released nearly eighty records that sold extremely well. *Daphnis and Chloé*, by Ravel, which inaugurated this collaboration, immediately distinguished itself. The orchestra then made it into the platinum category of record sales with their recording of Ravel's *Boléro*: that record sold more than a hundred thousand copies in Canada only.

Covered with awards and honors, Charles Dutoit and the orchestra stood in the eighties at the forefront of the international classical scene. They had attained, in the eyes of younger musicians and the population at large, the status of stars. On the occasion of the 50th anniversary of the orchestra, the Canadian government even issued a postage stamp in honor of the OSM. At an invitation from the orchestra, I met Dutoit and became friends with this man whose work I admired.

But these glory days gave way to a darker period in the 1990s. The exclusivity contract with Decca ended in 1997; the British label, which was in a restructuring phase, only kept a few recording contracts with the orchestra through 2002. In this precarious situation, tensions between the conductor, the orchestra and the management rose noticeably. It was going downhill: the seat occupancy rate dropped, the orchestra lost many subscribers, the audience became older and growing debts limited the house's scope of action more and more. The public was not blind to the increasing alienation between orchestra, conductor and management – which in itself is fatal for an institution that has to prove itself within Montreal's cultural landscape, whose diversity and quality is unparalleled in the world. There is ballet, the opera, several splendid museums, another orchestra, an electronic music scene and well-known festivals. In addition, there is sport, Canadians' great fascination with ice hockey, which has, of course, priority over going to a concert if the household budget is tight.

After many turbulent years, the situation finally escalated in April 2002, during Dutoit's twenty-fifth anniversary year, of all times. All of a sudden, after a nerve-wracking public dispute, the maestro and the orchestra went their separate ways. And nobody knew how things would continue from there. The management was successful at keeping the situation stable, and somehow holding the orchestra together without a chief conductor. But as you can imagine, the atmosphere between management and orchestra remained grim and tense.

It was under these circumstances that I was expected to start my position as chief conductor in 2006. Some colleagues advised me against it. The orchestra was unmanageable, they warned me. But they didn't know it firsthand; they based their opinions on what they had read in the papers. I, on the contrary, had already conducted the orchestra several times and knew that the musicians were capable of reaching top form. And that made the orchestra incredibly appealing to me.

In addition, I was also intrigued by the special characteristics of Montreal, Canada's second-largest city and, after Paris, the largest primarily French-speaking city in the world. With its more than 1.6 million inhabitants, Montreal is a metropolis that, to this day, clearly orients itself toward Europe. I perceive it as extremely cosmopolitan and international. Whenever icy winds blow the sea air over the Saint Lawrence River and into the streets, I think to myself: Montreal is a place where I can really breathe.

The city is, however, not wealthy. The question of sovereignty made many businesses and investors feel uneasy. As early as the seventies, Montreal lost its leading position to Toronto, when the economic focus shifted from transatlantic to intercontinental trade.

Capital flowed there, too. In any case, the money did not stay in Montreal, leading to two implications: public funds for the orchestra could not be as generous as in other metropolises where culture is subsidized in a similar fashion. And our audience's budgets were not unlimited, either. Ticket prices had to remain moderate.

So, in the summer of 2006, I took up my post, while at the same time attending to my commitment at the Bavarian State Opera in Munich. Montreal was, however, a great deal more challenging. There was a lot to cope with. First of all, we had to put an end to the decline in the number of listeners. The orchestra longed for stability, new ideas and leadership, for the musicians were ambitious, too, and ready to break fresh ground. An awful lot can be achieved in such a situation.

A disunited house with a strained budget, an open but not exactly wealthy city, an aging audience – given these circumstances, how can one turn things around? My answer to this question is much simpler than you might assume. The orchestra has to get closer to the people so that the music can reach them – in a spiritual, but also socio-spatial way. Therefore, one needs an overarching idea for one's own appointment, and individual concert programs that connect with real life. And one has to come down from one's Olympus, to literally play where the people are. Breaking with a number of conventions requires a good amount of creativity and a willingness to take risks. I was fully aware that I might well fail.

ANYTHING FOR THE TURNAROUND

My team and I decided to be brave and position the orchestra in a new and different way, for an orchestra has to be singular to its audience, unique so to say. To achieve this, its music has to be played in a context that reflects the country's history, the people of the city and the orchestra itself. To put it simply: in the francophone city of Montreal, Beethoven has to be placed in a context that is different from what it would be in Berlin, Munich, New

York or even Vancouver. If this is accomplished, Beethoven will sound different, too. Why does that matter to me?

Let me give you four reasons: Firstly, I am trying to use the uniqueness created through the regional context to establish a permanent link between the music and the people who live in the city where the orchestra is located. It connects the orchestra more closely to the people so that it becomes part of society. This is extremely important. We are, after all, recruiting our listeners from it. That way, in a best-case scenario, I am giving the citizens the opportunity to identify with their orchestra. The more the specific characteristics of a society are reflected in the orchestra, its sound and its repertoire, the more distinctive the orchestra becomes, and the greater the identification with it. Gradually, it will attract not only typical concertgoers but also new and, above all, younger listeners. At every performance, our audiences have to feel our esteem for them and their relevance to us. Without their interest, we wouldn't be selling tickets, we couldn't justify the public funding that makes up forty percent of our overall budget, we would soon stop being on stage and would no longer play. This deep connection with the local audience is the basis for the establishment first of a regional, then a national and, finally, an international reputation. Without being anchored locally, nothing can work.

Secondly, it is the only way I can show people that a two- or three-hundred-year-old work, for example a symphony or an oratorio, is not an exhibition piece from the glossy catalog of a venerable museum, but has retained its relevancy throughout time. If I cannot create a connection between a composition and the present-day reality of the people who buy the concert tickets and who are even funding us through the subsidies made possible by their taxes, as well, then the music cannot unfold any special sound. And I would forfeit my right to exist as a conductor.

Thirdly, it is only through context that the particular sound of an orchestra is developed. That sound is shaped by the overall idea behind an engagement, by the compilation of programs, the connection with the region and thus through the whole framework of experiences we are offering the audience. That way, throughout the years, the orchestra becomes unique. To use economic jargon, which has long become commonplace for us, as well, it becomes a brand.

And fourthly, through all of this, I gain the audience's trust to open up to new works. This is important so that new compositions, or a repertoire that hasn't been played much before, are reflected in our overall program.

If you were to ask me what the Orchestre symphonique de Montréal sounds like today, I might say *Québécois:* brilliant, very warm, lean, elegant, not very American, but not purely European, either. Or rather, this is how it comes across. For it requires a great deal of concert experience to be able to ascribe a pure sound discriminatingly. And it is no shortcoming at all if one is not able to do so. When it comes to international top orchestras that all draw on the same repertoire and use the same pool of internationally trained musicians, the differences in sound are only nuances, anyway. The positioning of the orchestra and the idea behind the programs are much more important because it is not the sound alone that creates uniqueness, but also the context in which the orchestra presents the works.

STRAUSS, OR THE PATH TO A PROGRAM IDEA

But how does such a program idea develop? Or to put it differently: How does one establish a connection between the music and the reality of people's lives, and thus the closeness that is so important to me? At the beginning of my appointment we included Richard Strauss' *Ein Heldenleben* (*A Hero's Life*) in the program. Although the orchestra had played this unique tone poem before, it had never studied it in detail. It had focused on the great French composers. The musicians had presented Berlioz, Bizet, Saint-Saëns, Franck, Ravel, Debussy, Fauré, Poulenc and many others in a very memorably impressive way. Russian composers could be found in their repertoire as well: Stravinsky, Mussorgsky, Tchaikovsky, Shostakovich and also symphonies by the Czech composer Antonín Dvořák. But Beethoven, Schubert, Mendelssohn, Schumann, Brahms, Wagner, Bruckner, Strauss – works by these composers had not been regularly performed for several decades.

Under my leadership, and following my vision, the orchestra's musical experience, and thus their repertoire, had to be expanded – to become more balanced. The only problem was this: How would the listeners, who were used to something completely different, react? The project was not without its risks. Still, I was determined to show these excellent musicians, and soon also the audience, how much the musical statements of great composers from other cultural spheres, and especially from the German-speaking world, could mean to them, and how new, progressive and visionary they were.

Even at its premiere, Strauss' *Ein Heldenleben* had polarized public and critics alike. While some described it as the pinnacle of the art of symphonic composition, others saw it as an excessive form of self-portrayal. They interpreted the symphonic poem as a hybrid act of self-definition, as an epic in which the artist challenges his adversaries. This was not entirely groundless. After all, a symphonic poem does not have any lyrics, and therefore allows for speculation. And by way of numerous allusions, the composer had given plenty of reason for that assumption.

But in the end it was Strauss himself who rescued his poem from the depths of such a profane autobiographical interpretation. For him, his music was not about the heroic life of a "single poetical or historical figure," but about something else altogether. He was trying to address the topic of heroism in an abstract way, outlining "a more general and free ideal of great and manly heroism," of a "heroism which depicts the inner struggles of life and which, through efforts and renunciation, strives for the uplift of the soul." Strauss put a message into sounds that still holds true today: heroism isn't that simple. Hardship, inner turmoil and even failure can all be part of a heroic story.

At all costs, I wanted the audience to take a different, contemporary look at this composition, which couldn't have been more appropriate to our times, in which we are all constantly searching for heroes we can to look up to. So, what makes a true hero?

As so often, I began the discussion of this program idea with a few questions to my Canadian team. "Who are your heroes?" I asked during a team meeting. "Whom do you admire?" Who might be important for Canada, for Quebec or for Montreal? Who might be a vital source of inspiration and leadership? Both management and employees looked at me altogether uncomprehendingly. I kept going. But what I got back was next to nothing. "Here in Canada, we don't really have heroes," they said. I didn't let up: "Come on, I don't believe you. You must have heroes, like us Americans who admire George Washington, Abraham Lincoln or John Glenn, the astronaut." Again, I was looking at blank faces. It went back and forth a little. I insisted, but the replies remained strangely vague. "What about military leaders, generals?" They shook their heads: "We are a peace-loving nation." I was quite astonished to learn that Canadians apparently do not have any heroes, or are not used to thinking in such categories. "We don't worship people that way," they added.

A few days later, I broached the topic again. This time, I asked about sports – football, basketball, there had to be some icons or pop stars. All of a sudden, it poured out of them: in ice hockey, there were big names who were admired by many. And unexpectedly, I became the listener to an excited conversation about a sport that apparently plays a very special role in French-Canadian identity. My team was deeply immersed in the topic. Again I learned something: ice hockey is more than just a sport, it is part of Canada's history and cultural heritage, it is a way of life, a philosophy.

They decided that they would take me to the arena to watch a match, so that I would be able to experience Canadian ice hockey live before talking about heroes any more. And in that arena, I instantly understood the logic behind the sport and the passion the people of this city have for it, a city that is locked in the depths of winter until the end of March. After all, Canada's territory reaches far beyond the polar circle. Afterwards, there were plenty of names that came up in our discussions, current heroes and legendary players from the past, who had shaped whole generations. In Canada, active ice hockey players are pop stars, icons. It was then that I realized: to convey Strauss' *Ein Heldenleben* in Montreal, it would have to be connected to ice hockey.

I commissioned a composition that was to be devoted to the phenomenon of this sport. As part of the new piece, ice hockey players were to recite texts that would discuss the sport and its heroes. We were able to bring on board Canadian composer François Dompierre and writer Georges-Hébert Germain. Together they created the piece *Les Glorieux*, which we performed in February 2008 alongside Strauss' *Ein Heldenleben* and a few short compositions by Erik Satie. Satie was a perfect fit, seeing as he had entitled his cycle of miniatures *Sports et divertissements*.

First, the Canadians heard *Ein Heldenleben*, and then the voices of their heroes: Yvan Cournoyer, for instance, the fastest player a team had ever seen, inducted into the Hockey Hall of Fame in 1982; Henri Richard, more than seventy years of age; or Guy Lafleur, the long-haired right winger nicknamed "*le démon blond*" thanks to his mane. For the audience, he was a hero whom everyone was talking about back then because he and his family were going through a deep crisis. A hero with flaws. "It ain't gonna be easy," it said in the text; not on the ice, and not in regular life, either, least of all as a hero.

It was a moving concert evening during which the audience listened to Strauss' music in a different context. Visibly touched, they left the sold-out Salle Wilfrid-Pelletier that we then still played in, before we moved into our new, acoustically unique concert hall in 2011. I was often told that that concert, for a brief moment, had changed the way people perceived and judged heroes. Evidently, it was the symphonic poem that had given rise to this change of attitude.

OUTSIDE THE DOOR

A year later, we brought music into the ice hockey arena, the so-called Centre Bell. The concert was, with pathos aplenty, designed to be *the* encounter of the century. The ice hockey team, the Montréal Canadiens, had been in existence for a hundred years, and the orchestra was celebrating its seventy-fifth anniversary. I will never forget how electrifying the atmosphere in the stadium was. In front of me, the current stars of the team were gliding onto the stage. Fifteen thousand people were screaming with excitement. Then my name was called, and the crowd continued to scream. To be honest, it certainly wasn't for me; they were just in full spate. We played a colorful mix of Beethoven, Rossini, Respighi and once again *Les Glorieux*, the composition from the previous year. The audience applauded and cheered. They gave us a standing ovation. I was very moved. At that moment, the orchestra belonged to the reality of their lives just as much as the sport did. I was aware of how many listeners we had reached, right there and then, who had never been to a classical concert before. It was a great opportunity to take classical music to the people.

A program idea is one thing, but it alone does not necessarily attract people. I always found it important to first bring the music to the people of Montreal. I wanted to get physically closer to them as well. Before a classical music artist can expect the people to come to him for his "product," he has to go to them. It is an offering – no more. The orchestra already has a certain tradition in this regard. For decades, it has been giving an annual series of open-air concerts free of charge in several parks in Montreal. The series is called "*osm dans les parcs*" and is a big event every summer. The citizens usually come to hear their orchestra. If it rains, they simply put up their umbrellas.

For many of the musicians, playing in a crowded stadium or park is one of the easier tasks. It brings glamor and happiness. These performances are positive challenges – neither the musicians nor I myself are confronted with the darker side of human existence:

with illness and death, violence, discrimination or lack of opportunity. But it is also part of my mission to visit places with the musicians where we are truly needed and where the music might be able to brighten up people's everyday lives for just a moment: cancer wards in hospitals, kindergartens and schools with teenagers from socially disadvantaged areas. We do this regularly, and I make plenty of time for it.

A few years ago, I was moved by a performance of ours in front of the Borough Hall in Montréal-Nord, a mixed *arrondissement* with a number of deprived areas. I was particularly touched a few years ago by an appearance by our orchestra in front of the Montreal-North town hall: a heterogeneous borough, some its districts could be described as sensitive. Many immigrants live there, youth unemployment is high, the crime rate is comparatively high, the phenomenon of gangs and clans, drug trafficking and violence are part of the daily reality for its inhabitants. Some sections of Montreal-North are said to be among the most dangerous in the city. I myself knew very little of this part of the city. Just weeks before our free concert, there had been serious unrest there. For reasons not fully clarified at the time, the police had shot an eighteen-year-old Latin American immigrant boy named Fredy Alberto Villanueva, who seems to have been only accidentally present when his elder brother and four young men were playing a dice game, which is illegal in Montreal. It happened as it so often does: the police spotted them and demanded to see their identification. One of them refused. Shots were fired that took the life of the one boy who was just an innocent bystander.

Civic protests followed soon after, and whereas they started peacefully as a silent march, things soon escalated and resulted in violent riots that shook Montreal for days. Cars were burnt, shops looted. The citizens watched aghast as one of their most ethnically mixed districts seemed to literally blow up. "Let me know if there is anything I can do," I told Mayor Gerald Tremblay. "Could you give a concert there?" he asked me. "Preferably right in the center of this quarter?'

We did, although I had left it up to every single member of the orchestra to participate or not. Everyone was to decide for themselves if, after those excesses, they wanted to play there on an open stage. The musicians' willingness to take part was overwhelming. Both young and old were up for it. We played in front of over a thousand people, of whom probably only a fraction had ever listened to classical music before. It remained peaceful, quiet, focused.

What was our intention with this concert? I cannot say. Maybe it was a token of empathy; after all, a mother had tragically lost her son and a family had lost a relative. It was possibly a sign of respect for a district whose youth appeared to have almost no chance in life, or maybe it was just an attempt to focus attention on this part of Montreal once more, four weeks after the unrest, so that it would not be forgotten as soon as things had calmed down. I knew that in the end it had to be a kind of self-obligation to bring our music to all the people of Montreal, and therefore also to areas where the primary purpose couldn't be to recruit future regular listeners. For a long time after the concert, I couldn't stop thinking about Montréal-Nord. I knew that one day I would want to do more for the people there than merely giving a concert.

We still try to be present outside our concert hall, as well – in very different locations. We don't do that only in disadvantaged areas, but also where the chances of getting people excited about our music are a bit better. To me, the most wonderful thing is the enthusiasm with which especially the older members of the orchestra are embracing many of our unconventional avenues and are thinking about how and where we can offer our music to the people, so that we might "tempt" particularly young people even more.

NOTHING LASTS FOREVER

We cannot afford to rest. The process of renewal is far from over yet. It can never be over, for if it is my aspiration to place old music within a context that at least partially reflects people's everyday reality, then we cannot stop changing. Society is changing, too. And if I, admittedly a bit sentimentally, describe the orchestra as a met-aphor for society, as its mirror, then it has to change just as much so as to lead our cultural heritage into the future. In Montreal we enjoy many liberties, and we have a team and an orchestra that like to experiment and to discuss ideas so that we have the opportunity to try out many new things. Our programs, besides the more tradi-tional concerts, come in very different formats, ranging from after-work concerts to symphonic matinees and "Musical Sundays," recitals, a series of special events, all the way to a ball for children and several performances exclusively for them called "Children's Corner." The "Éclaté" series is among these, as well.

This diversity works; especially younger people are noticing us more and more. By now, one thousand of our subscribers are under the age of thirty-four. Eight years ago there were none; back then young people never took out a subscription. Today every one of these young subscribers books tickets for several concerts a year in advance; eight years ago that was not the case. Their share has steadily increased over the years. And we are doing everything we can to increase it even further. The orchestra's financial situation has significantly improved as well, and debts have dropped. With a budget of twenty-seven million Canadian dollars per year, we are not making huge profits, but we are getting by quite well. The management has a strict policy in this regard. Everything has to be funded, even big tours. We are simply forbidden from incurring any further debt.

So, in our "brainstorming lab" we continue to experiment, and new ideas are being cooked up all the time. With an almost youthful enthusiasm, our team is working on new ideas, our appearance, our media presence and – in today's terms – the quality of our brand as a friendly, approachable and non-elitist world-class orchestra.

Two projects emerged that we are very proud of. The first is close to my heart: in November 2016, after years of meticulous planning and with the help of generous donations, our musical kindergarten, which we built in Montréal-Nord, finally opened its doors to the first cohort of sixteen children from areas where poverty, lack of education and a mix of ethnic backgrounds produce a population with little chance of participating in mainstream society. These kids are welcome eight hours a day and five days a week. My own childhood, with its intensive musical education, played an important role in the idea for this project, which started out with a budget of one and a half million Canadian dollars. It is my dream to give these children access to a world that was once revealed to me and my friends by Professor Korisheli in Morro Bay.

Two years later we followed this up by opening a Saturday school which allows the kids to continue their musical education a few times a week. We even loan them keyboards for at-home practice.

And by 2020 we plan to open a summer orchestra academy for emerging artists. They will be able to gain experience and attend master classes, but they will also prepare themselves for the eventuality that their studies lead to a professional life outside the world of music.

Our work is laborious, fragmented and exhausting. It consists of courting the audience continuously, of making a constant effort to get their attention, because they could always choose to be entertained in an easier, more superficial and more convenient way. Increasingly diverse activities with young musicians add to the workload. In Montreal we are not geniuses – though we might be excellent craftsmen – but are currently working quite successfully. We want to expand our commitment to society, we want to grow and we want to develop new projects, programs and formats. We have to do that because history has taught us that success and reputation are volatile in our increasingly fast-paced world. No formula for success lasts far into the future. Those who do not adapt are bound to become outdated in no time.

FRANK ZAPPA, OR THE
SERIOUS SIDE OF THE ARTIST

A few years after our concert at the Molson Brewery by the harbor, we designed another truly unusual evening. We combined

Beethoven's Fifth Symphony with one of the many symphonic compositions by Frank Zappa. The piece I had selected was called *Bogus Pomp*. I already knew it quite well, as Zappa and I had studied it together with the London Symphony Orchestra in 1981. *Bogus Pomp* was a clever parody on the rigid rituals of the traditional symphony concert. Every protagonist in a performance – the musicians, the concertmaster, the first cellist and also the conductor – were targets of cutting irony. It was Zappa's way of dealing with the concert performances of the eighties, in which, he thought, far too self-referential artists were not doing the great classical works justice. *Bogus Pomp* – the title said it all.

Beethoven and Zappa – it was a rather wild combination of two artists who, regardless of their individual roles and positions in music history, had one thing in common: a creative disregard for compositional rules and the audience's taste – and their own intransigence. In this respect, Frank Zappa taught me a true lesson in the eighties.

Beethoven's Fifth Symphony was well ahead of its time. It broke with the conventions of the past, was far too modern and perhaps reached a bit too far into the following period of romanticism for the audience to be able to grasp at the premiere in December 1808. Zappa, on the other hand, was a crossover artist between the two worlds in which he operated: rock 'n' roll and serious music. He did not let himself be defined by one or the other and did not care about other people's opinions, but followed his own path unswervingly. He pushed the barriers of the classical genre, made parts of his composition become a satire about that genre's rules and weaved references to rock music into his work as if he wanted to stick his tongue out at the establishment.

While the audience knew what to expect with Beethoven, Zappa was more of a surprise. This American superstar of the seventies and eighties was commonly known as a rock musician, a rock 'n' roll icon, brilliant on the electric guitar; and as someone who had mastered many musical styles in the realm of light music. It remained relatively unknown until well into the eighties that he operated in the worlds of both light and serious music and did not only land international hits on the electric guitar with "Bobby Brown" and "The Sheik Yerbouti Tango" on the album *Sheik Yerbouti*, but also composed entire orchestral pieces. And even today, the name of this unique and universal artist is primarily associated with the rock legend who was inducted into the Rock and Roll Hall of Fame long ago, and who defined the musical taste of an entire generation, and not with a composer of classical music who deserves to be taken seriously.

I still remember that my parents forbade Zappa's music in our house after watching one of his concerts on TV. In their opinion, Zappa was absolutely not for children. I discovered Zappa in the late seventies on a first short trip to Paris. Pierre Boulez wanted to perform several of Zappa's works with the Ensemble intercontemporain. It aroused my interest. I marveled.

At home in California, I decided to contact his manager so I could take a look at some of his scores. But for a very long time, I did not get any response to the message I had left. Then, all of a sudden, out of nowhere, Zappa himself called me. He first wanted to know what my interest in his compositions was based on. Then he invited me to one of his concerts, which was to take place in Berkeley. He wanted to meet me there and show me some of his scores.

Even as an adult, I had never in my life been to a rock concert. As a classical music artist I had grown up quite sheltered. Rock concerts were out of the question. The concert in Berkeley was a completely new experience for me, a mass event, teeming with thousands of people. One lightshow after the other, endless smoking – it was all entirely unfamiliar to me. During the break one of his gigantic bodyguards, named Big John, came up to me, ordered me to follow him and brought me to the superstar's dressing room.

There he sat, Frank Zappa, admired, controversial and as a symphonic composer by and large unknown. He was eating caviar with sour cream. After a short exchange, he handed me quite a number of his scores. I took a look and found some unbelievably complex orchestral music that I was barely able to evaluate at first glance. He let me take the scores home. I wanted to look at them more closely there. Given their complexity, it turned into a quite a challenge, to be honest. I was completely surprised to find incredible passages of serious music on many of those sheets of music, exciting, excellently written, tremendously colorful. I had his music in my head for days. However, I didn't hear from Zappa for weeks. I had neither his phone number nor his address, and thus no way of contacting him.

Then, suddenly, and again completely out of nowhere, he called me. "And," he asked, "what do you make of it all?" He wanted me to visit him at his home, so we fixed a date and time and he collected me from the airport, but then we didn't drive to his place after all; instead, we went straight to the university campus. There he had hired an orchestra, with whom I was meant to rehearse several of his works – as a trial run, so to speak. I caught my breath, yet I had no choice but to comply. After a lengthy rehearsal we drove to his home. There he told me about his big dream. One day, he wanted to have his symphonic works performed. This was why he had started looking for an orchestra and a conductor who could make his dream come true. I left deeply impressed with the seriousness of his request.

A few days later again, I received another call from him. Quite abruptly, he asked me this time if I wanted to accompany him to London to record his music with the London Symphony Orchestra. At that time, I was not yet particularly well known as a conductor – and I hesitated. A little too nonchalant, I told him I would think about it. Frank's response was both a shock and an impressive lesson about the intransigence of great artists: "I give you exactly fifteen seconds to say either yes or no," he replied calmly. "You have to decide now. If you say nothing at all, I'll hang up and find myself a different conductor." After less than fifteen seconds I said yes – accompanied by a feeling of deep shame for having hesitated, and not giving a straight answer to an artist who cared so deeply about his art. Those who really mean it seriously do not make a fuss and do not play games. That was a lesson I learned from Zappa. He is a fascinating musician, who in his day received relatively little recognition for his compositions outside the rock genre in the United States, but in Europe he had already electrified classical music audiences with his symphonic works.

For many years, I had scruples about including Zappa in my programs, not only because his music is very difficult to play, and therefore requires many rehearsals. I also wanted to avoid at all costs creating the impression that I myself was trying to dabble at "crossover," that ingratiating mix of two different music genres, only one of which I am a specialist in, and only one of which I represent: serious music. But Zappa's symphonic works *are* serious music that every musician ought to take seriously. His compositions are on an incredibly high level. He never saw himself as only a rock star, but as a universal artist. And that he was an artist gifted with an impressive creative power that had to express itself constantly in a relatively short lifespan.

The performance in Montreal ended. The audience's reaction was overwhelming, the concert turned into a cult event and people were thrilled. They wanted to have a real experience in their concert hall, and with Beethoven and Zappa they got it. And afterwards, in the foyer, there was music by DJ Misstress Barbara, who is a household name in Montreal's electronic music scene. She was the final act. The listeners stayed for a long time. It was a colorful mix of older and younger ones. Parents, who might have remembered Zappa but were essentially interested in Beethoven, came together with their teenage children, who were probably more excited about Misstress Barbara and were willing to accept Beethoven in order to see her perform. The generations mingled and both of them seemed to get something out of the evening. The house was on fire.

Of course, it's not exactly original to turn a temple of high culture into a dance floor after a concert. It had been done every now and again in the past. It works, of course, because after an aesthetic experience that, according to our conventions, requires a focused and almost unnaturally still way of listening, the accumulated tension is released into a barely controllable urge to move.

Dancing after a concert? After his concerts, Leonard Bernstein regularly went to New York's legendary Studio 54, in the seventies arguably the most famous discotheque in the world, to wear himself out for a second time after conducting, this time on the dance floor.

Can one risk such a thing? A concert with serious music at an unusually late hour, with an admittedly crazy program that even announces an after-concert party at which a well-known DJ is to play her music? Does this not debase "serious" music, because none of us artists can be sure that people won't just come to the concert hall in order to mindlessly abandon themselves to booming bass after their "work" inside the auditorium is done? Not necessarily. It depends on *how* it is accomplished. Misstress Barbara is not just any DJ. She is a well-respected member of Montreal's flourishing art scene. Even the older musicians in my orchestra, who have been members for decades, were excited. They find the unexpected contexts in which we present classical music wonderful. The concert hall is alive. People have accepted it as their own, they come and they stay. Anything goes.

There are only two things I remain firm on: with me, there will never be any of that popular crossover, no mix of pop and the classical genre, because I am not a pop artist but a classical music artist. And I will never lower my sights or accept compromises when it comes to quality, not only regarding our musical performances, but also the compositional standard of the works we perform. They have to be exceptionally well written. This I owe to our audience. It is my pledge, and my name stands for it. In this regard, I am intransigent myself. Were you aware how receptive and open especially young people are about the idea of absolute intransigence?

MESSIAEN

A Glimpse into the Beyond

It's always a little cold in Sainte-Trinité. And damp. In the winter time, our breath floats upward. Our fingers are clammy. On the other hand, in the summertime, when the sun turns Paris into a groaning monster of a city, it is wonderfully refreshing. Then the large church nave becomes a refuge from the heat, rush and noise, without which Paris is not conceivable. L'Église de la Sainte-Trinité in the 9th arrondissement, right next to the Place d'Estiennes d'Orves, was the church of French composer Olivier Messiaen. He was its titular organist. For decades, his playing accompanied Sunday mass, provided that his many trips abroad allowed it. And he was often there during the week as well, not only for the daily services. He, a master of improvisation, placed great value on practice and perfection.

Messiaen, his wife, Yvonne Loriod, and I are the only people on the organ loft. Deep beneath us, a few parish members have gathered for mass. They are significantly fewer than the enormous nave has seats. Messiaen is sitting at the organ, highly focused. He is improvising – as he always does during mass, when the priest prepares the Eucharist, or later, when the parish members are absorbed in deep prayer after receiving communion. Yvonne Loriod and I listen. On this Sunday, his improvisation is once again completely fresh and perfect. It is always as though one were listening to a story. Out of nowhere, a bird is suddenly soaring through the church. High above, light, agile. It is small and dainty. It flaps its wings, once, twice, and gathers speed so as not to glide all the way down before perching on one of the galleries in the bright light of the stained-glass windows. There it lingers for a moment, looks around and takes off again, up and away.

The highest pitches that can be elicited from an organ ring out. The tiniest pipes belong to the little birds. Messiaen has just conjured up that dainty bird with its gentle movements, a creature of his musical imagination that, for a brief moment as treble voice, joins the catchy lower melody, with which he began his improvisation. I remember that moment to this day. Suddenly, there was only nature around us: the bird, maybe a meadow, a few trees, a river bank.

The moment Messiaen's improvisation was over, the landscape vanished. I was back in the heart of Paris in a majestic Catholic church whose construction had commenced in 1861, commissioned by Baron Haussmann. Up in the loft is the famous Cavaillé-Coll grand organ, which was inaugurated in 1869 by Camille Saint-Saëns and César Franck, and which has since been regularly played by well-known organists. I was in the presence of one of the greatest composers of the twentieth century, who, in 1982, had invited me to come and stay with him in Paris for a while. For an American from the West Coast of the United States, that amounted to a culture shock. My senses were almost overwhelmed. I was already thirty-one years old. Never before had I been to Europe for a longer period of time.

When I studied Olivier Messiaen's music for the first time, in the seventies, I couldn't have known that one day I would be in Europe, standing right next to him, listening to him, working with him and learning so much from him. At that time, he was already one of the best-established composers of the twentieth century. He was greatly admired, not only in Europe, but also in the United States and in Asia. His works were performed relatively frequently as far as contemporary compositions go. Until well into the early sixties, the musical world had been fiercely divided over him – at times, performances of his works were accompanied by riots. He once told me that, on one occasion, members of the audience, enraged by his music, had waylaid him at the artist's entrance of the Théâtre des Champs-Élysées in order to beat him up with their shoes. He had to duck down to make it reasonably safely to his car. But that was well in the past. Among contemporary composers, Messiaen was a star from whom the most famous directors commissioned works, and whom the country's political elite regularly paid courtesy visits.

Messiaen was seventy-seven years old back then and had been through very different periods of artistic creation. Various influences had left their mark on his pieces, among them the musical impressionism of Debussy and Stravinsky. But Messiaen also concerned himself with Gregorian chant, as well as ancient Greek, Indian and Nepalese music. His works are reminiscent of Balinese gamelan music and the chant of Japanese Noh theater but, above all, of the sounds and colors of nature, and the endless diversity of birdsong. Out of all this, and over the course of decades, Messiaen developed a unique style that had long since reached its peak when I began to study his music. At the time, he was working on his only opera, *Saint François d'Assise*, which we would premiere years later. As a deeply religious Catholic, he addressed the great religious topics in his music – eternity and the beyond, as well as man's relationship with God and His creation.

Messiaen's classes at the Conservatoire de Paris, which ended when he retired in 1978, had been famed and in great demand. In Europe he was considered, alongside Schoenberg, to be one of the greatest composition teachers, whose classes in analysis, aesthetics and, later, composition produced composers of very different schools of thought, among them Pierre Boulez, Karlheinz Stockhausen, Iannis Xenakis and George Benjamin. As early as the forties, he had written a book about the technique of his musical language. Later, he worked on a treatise on rhythm, color and ornithology, which was completed and posthumously published in eight volumes by his wife Yvonne Loriod, and which documents his specific method of composition in great detail. One could even compose by following Messiaen's instructions, for example using the scales he compiled, the "modes of limited transposition." And if one takes a simple melody and uses his ametrical technique of "added value," whereby a bar is extended by an additional note, silence or dot, a bit of Messiaen and his unmistakable musical style comes to life. Unlike Schoenberg, however, Messiaen never founded his own school.

What I couldn't have known during my time at university was that, of all composers, it would be this one who would open the doors to Europe far and wide for me, and who would have a lasting impact on my understanding of music. I had first encountered Messiaen's compositions in an analysis class. Then, in 1975, I had the chance to listen to a live performance of one of his symphonies for the first time. It was the *Turangalîla-Symphonie*. I still remember that the work made an impression on me, but I cannot claim to have understood it. Later, during my time as assistant conductor at the Opera Company of Boston, I regularly spent time in the library. During one of my aimless rambles through music magazines, I one day came across Messiaen's name on the spine of one of the score covers. Instinctively, I pulled the score off the shelf. It was the *Catalogue d'oiseaux* (*Catalog of Birds*), a collection of compositions of birdsongs, which I had already heard about.

Without further ado, I took the score home to study it more closely. Soon I began to work my way through these compositionally difficult pieces – page by page. Although they were technically demanding and certainly could not be performed easily, I was quickly engrossed. Suddenly, I desperately wanted to understand Messiaen. I wanted to penetrate his new musical language, different rhythmics and perfect polyphony. Without my being truly aware of it, Messiaen had already cast a spell over me.

In 1978, I became music director of the Berkeley Symphony Orchestra and decided to perform the best-known pieces of this idiosyncratic artist in a "Messiaen cycle." The orchestra had only a small budget, but the musicians were ambitious and open-minded. I was convinced that I could dare to tackle something like this with them. In preparation, I had read everything available by and about Messiaen, I had learned his language and I had studied and understood the principles of his compositional style. Still, I was not entirely sure what his music was actually supposed to sound like, especially the way Messiaen himself would have liked to hear it. I was tormented by question after question. Nobody could help me. In my desperation, I took a leap of faith and sent Messiaen a radio recording of the first performance of the cycle. It was the song cycle *Poèmes pour Mi*. As I did not know his home address, I simply wrote his name and "Conservatoire de Paris, Paris, France" on the envelope. Had our music turned out the way he had wanted it to be? Had I even understood his music?

My letter actually reached him. Completely unexpectedly, I received a reply a month later in which Messiaen discussed my interpretation, bar by bar, on many crowded pages. Following his request, I also sent him recordings of the following concerts, including the *Turangalîla-Symphonie*, which apparently came so close to his own vision that – as he wrote to me – he would like to meet me in person and work with me. *La Transfiguration de Notre Seigneur Jésus-Christ (The Transfiguration of Our Lord Jesus Christ)* was scheduled for the last evening of the cycle, an oratorio written in the second half of the sixties. For this performance, Messiaen himself came to Berkeley – it had been his idea. His wife played the piano part. The performance succeeded wonderfully, and an intense and exciting collaboration began, stretching over many years.

Almost five years later, in 1983, Messiaen's first and only opera *Saint François d'Assise* was to be premiered. He had finally completed it – after ten long years and many lapsed deadlines. It is certainly his grandest and possibly most significant work. Rolf Liebermann, director of the Théâtre National de l'Opéra de Paris at the time, had commissioned it. Seiji Ozawa was to conduct it. Messiaen had suggested that I would oversee the extensive rehearsals and had invited me to stay with him in his apartment in the 18th *arrondissement* during the months of the rehearsal period. So, there I stood, on the balcony of Sainte-Trinité, an anything but worldly American with Japanese roots. To this day, the story of my encounter with Messiaen has something almost surreal about it.

I always say that Messiaen changed my life. He was like a father to me: he had brought me to Europe and introduced me there – not just geographically with his invitation to Paris, where I was able to live in his apartment and learn from him, but in a much broader sense. My French was terrible, and I had to quickly learn to speak it fluently in order to be able to communicate with him and his wife. In addition, many things in Paris were foreign to me. The different way of life, the mentality, the city's smells, the noise of the traffic and the completely different aesthetics, not only in music and in art. So much was so new and strange that I couldn't even form an opinion on it all. But in my early thirties, I wanted finally to arrive in the culture of Europe that had shaped my life through music and music history for such a long time. Without any doubt, it was Messiaen and his wife who gave me access to this world, to a European way of life and to a European appreciation of art. There was so much to learn about European history. Messiaen awakened in me a sense of the diversity of European traditions and the many languages. He and his wife showed me around Paris and put me in touch with other composers and artists. Yvonne Loriod gave me numerous private piano lessons so that I could understand Messiaen's works better. For someone from the other end of the world, these were extremely formative experiences. Rarely did I learn so much in my life.

Today I know how difficult, indeed almost impossible it is to gain access to Europe from a purely American perspective. Attitudes toward life, perceptions and people's self-image are completely different. Thanks to Messiaen and his wife, thanks to our many conversations, excursions and travels, I began to gradually understand Europe better. This experience was like a liberation, as though I had been given the key to a door that until then had been locked, and behind which I had longingly suspected another, much bigger world. My time in Paris transformed me. I am sure that in many ways, mentally and emotionally, I never fully returned to the West of the United States.

What is everyday life with a great artist like? Messiaen was modest, reserved and very private. In the evenings, we usually dined together and discussed the necessary details regarding the rehearsals for his opera, whereas during the day we went our own separate ways: I oversaw the rehearsals, and he retreated to his studio one floor higher, which was equipped with an organ and in which he composed. I never set foot in that room. I never saw him compose, and I never enquired about it, either. He did not show his pieces to anyone before they were finished – not even to his wife, with very few exceptions. Apart from his studio, the entire apartment was at my disposal. Sometimes, when we went on excursions into nature, I was able to observe the way he would write down birdcalls – in his by now famous *cahiers*, his note-books, that he always carried around with him.

What kind of music is it that Messiaen composed? What did he want to tell us? As with any great composer, it is almost impossible to answer those questions in just a few sentences. I am going to try anyway. I believe he wanted to lend an acoustic shape to timeless truths. To him, timelessness meant divinity. Messiaen was deeply religious, in fact, so far from any doubt that he always described himself as a "born believer." His way of approaching infinity, where space and time lose their meaning, was to dispense with a tonal basis and a regular meter in quite a few of his compositions.

The basis of Messiaen's music is a highly complex cosmos of music theory, developed over years, including his very own rhythmic system. In addition, there is color symbolism. Messiaen was a synesthete, that is to say, someone who can, indeed is compelled to, associate sounds with certain colors. But the most important feature of his music is birdsong. Throughout his life, Messiaen archived hundreds of birdcalls, referring to himself as an ornithologist. He registered the songs of the birds by way of words and notes, sometimes not just solo voices, but polyphonic harmonies, as well. Occasionally, Messiaen recorded them with his cassette recorder. He characterized the wren's song, for example, as "silvery, very rapid, pearly," compared the golden oriole to a "very large flute, almost a horn," and described the crow as "raucous, powerful, sneering, sarcastic." He noted the birds' awakening and their evening songs, both in his immediate surroundings and far away, when visiting other countries and continents. Birds inspired his melodies.

In his works, of course, he didn't just reproduce those birdsongs in a true-to-life fashion, but presented them in a modified artistic form. Birds had a special meaning for Messiaen. They were the origin of all music, a gift from God in their natural diversity and interaction. "Among the artistic hierarchy, the birds are probably the greatest musicians to inhabit the planet," he confided to Claude Samuel in one of their conversations. The birds were part of his experience with nature. When he set off for the woods in the early morning to listen to the first calls of the birds waking at dawn, when the light of the rising sun returned the colors to the landscape, those would always be spiritual moments to him. During those moments, philosophy of nature would encounter religiousness, just like the different ways of expressing those thoughts – in color and sound. Birds were his angels – lightsome, weightless, God-given.

In his *Saint François d'Assise*, Messiaen employed every composition technique and musical idea that he had developed over decades. This work, which we premiered following his instructions, is composed as a kind of credo, combining the wealth of all of his inventiveness. It is his overall musical résumé, an extraordinary work, not only due to its length of over four hours, but also because he wrote his own libretto. Toward the end of the twentieth century, it was quite unique that a contemporary composer would chose a religious theme for his only opera, but to Messiaen it was only a logical consequence of his Catholic identity. That he chose Francis of Assisi, of all people, might superficially be owed to his love of birds. But far more important were Saint Francis' humble attitude, the way he turned his life around and his reversion to the Creator and His creation. During our conversations, he often told me that he identified most with this figure.

In three acts and eight scenes, Messiaen traces the life path of Saint Francis, his transition from a life as son of a rich merchant family to one in poverty, devoted to God. The fascination of his operatic music, in which colors and sounds flow into one another, and its unparalleled spirituality, are best experienced in the final scene. It describes the last days of the protagonist. Francis of Assisi dies, and the opera ends with a long-drawn, radiating C major chord. C is the primal keynote of music, the beginning and the end. No key radiates brighter and purer than C major. Francis of Assisi dies bathed in white light – illumed by Jesus' truth.

During the months of preparation for the premiere, Messiaen was not feeling well. He was exhausted and sick, and he once told me that he had lived only to write this opera, after which he would most likely not be able to compose anything else anymore. At his advanced age, he wrote the end of the opera in the way he imagined the end of his own life: "I imagined myself in front of a curtain, in darkness, apprehensive about what lay beyond: Resurrection, Eternity, the other Life. [...] I try simply to imagine what will come to pass, which I can sometimes perceive in 'éclairs.' I speak of course of Christ, who will be the light of the resurrected: they will shine with the light of Christ."

The opera *Saint François d'Assise* was, however, not to be Messiaen's ultimate work. After that, he wrote his truly last completed composition, the orchestral work *Éclairs sur l'Au-Delà ...* (*Lightning over the Beyond ...*), his vision of paradise, even more devout, more spiritual. Messiaen is at the end of his life; his perception of the beyond has changed. Nothing here is euphoric and jubilant, as it was in earlier works. The music is supernatural, marveling, spherical, anticipating – beyond space and time. In death, man's sovereignty is taken from him. He doesn't have to make decisions anymore. He becomes weightless. He floats.

Messiaen's inspiration was based on his deep faith in God. Almost all of his works have a biblical content, or they address theological thoughts: the meaning of the Holy Trinity, the birth and transfiguration of Jesus Christ, His immortality. Messiaen never tried to conceal the source of his inspiration. His faith gave him the energy and strength to compose a sheer inexhaustible variety of works. When he composed or improvised, he did not reflect only on the creation. Composing and playing music had a much deeper meaning for him. It was his way of communing with God. Through music, one can experience God. Music possesses an incomparable spiritual power, perhaps the greatest among the arts. It builds the bridge to transcendence.

I rarely talked to Messiaen about his faith. I never asked him about it, and I never felt the need for it. Not that it would have been bad manners, but it was simply not necessary. He never asked me, either. We had a certain basic understanding in that respect, which did not require any discussion. I was able to relate to his thoughts and feelings. I, too, had grown up with the church; it was part of my upbringing and my musical education. It has shaped my worldview to this day. In the sixties and seventies, many people turned away from religion and left their church. They searched for spirituality elsewhere, and they experienced or lived it differently. This never happened to me. Spirituality and religiousness are one and the same to me.

Spirituality is an important part of my musical experience. It inevitably emerges whenever I am conducting or playing the piano, and when I master or know the piece so well that I do not have to think about my fingers on the keys, or about the technical challenges of conducting. When everything flows unimpeded, moments occur of a mental connection with the beyond or with infinity. This happens every single time. Maybe it is the reason why, throughout my experience of dealing with it, Messiaen's music has had such a captivating effect on me.

And this is why Messiaen was no different from me in that regard. He identified with Francis of Assisi and he loved the almost mystical religiousness of Thomas Aquinas. Outside of music, however, he was quite reserved about his faith and not at all excluding. For as long as I knew him, he never proselytized. He did not talk about his faith. He did not write his music to convert others. He wrote it as a dialogue with God.

Does one have to share this deeply religious attitude to understand Messiaen's music? Or to put it differently: Does one have to be deeply religious to experience the spirituality of his music? To be honest I cannot say, because to this day such a question has never arisen for me. Messiaen, on the other hand, was asked this question quite often. He always answered in the negative. He argued that he drew immense inspiration from his strong faith, that it was the foundation of his creativity and that it enabled him to write music in the first place. But once a work was completed and he had to let go of it and hand it to the public, to the musicians and the listeners, the music was no longer his. Then it belonged to whoever interpreted, conducted or listened to it; everyone had their own personal experience with it. At this point, Messiaen would always refer to Johann Sebastian Bach, whose œevre sprang from a deeply religious worldview and self-image. Does one have to be deeply religious to understand the messages of Bach's music? Messiaen used to add: "Would you have ever asked Johann Sebastian Bach this question?"

"There are moments in music, fractions of seconds during a performance, when I believe I can see what lies beyond the stars." This is how the great conductor Günter Wand once described to me that overwhelming moment of experiencing eternity. One cannot find more wonderful words to describe those moments when music carries us beyond our world and lets us divine that there is more than earthly life. Those moments are barely more than a short glint, illuminations of the beyond. They cannot be retained. Once you become aware of them, they are already a thing of the past. Musical experience has many facets. It is different for every single person, and even for me it is always new because music is not tangible or material. Messiaen once called it the "most immaterial of the arts." Music is entirely abstract – physically, it consists only of sound waves and vibrations. But those release unexpected powers.

I do not have a prerogative of interpretation of Messiaen just because we worked closely together for years and he invited me to Paris to spend almost a year with him under one roof. No one does. But there is one thing I know for certain, when I look from today's twenty-first-century perspective back to the twentieth century: his works have gained a secure place in the repertoire of us musicians. These days, his *Turangalîla-Symphonie*, which was such a challenge for me in Berkeley, and his *Éclairs sur l'Au-Delà* frequently feature on concert programs. They have been recorded numerous times. Many young composers have told me how much they were inspired by Messiaen. His opera alone motivated many to muster all their courage and devote themselves to opera as an art form that is still relevant today. The classical world is still discovering Messiaen's music. But even now, a review of the twentieth century with its many exciting composers shows that Messiaen's music will withstand the test of time. It has become part of, and is vital for, the musical canon. This is not going to change. Quite the opposite is true: more of his works will be added.

Once more we are climbing the steps onto the organ loft of Sainte-Trinité. First Messiaen, then Madame Loriod, and finally me. Once more, the old man is dragging himself up the narrow staircase, weighed down by countless sheets of music, of which he does not let us carry even a single booklet. There are only about fifty or sixty believers in the whole vast nave. This time the choir is present as well. Its task is to sing in alternation with the priest. The choir consists of motivated laypeople who sing passionately, but none of whom has a trained voice. The priest provides an intonation and chants his words instead of speaking them, as is often customary in the Catholic church. Then it's the choir's turn.

All of a sudden, the singers are struggling, not hitting the right note, and virtually stumbling into their passages. For several bars, the choir's response to the priest's intonation is off pitch. Luckily, they find their way back at a later point.

Moments later, it is time for one of Messiaen's improvisations. He takes up the priest's melody and imitates the choir's unskilled response – including their stumblings. Madame Loriod and I look at each other and can hardly believe what Messiaen is doing. The way he almost undetectably weaves this little passage into his improvisation is highly amusing and entertaining. He was a great composer and a serious, profound artist, blessed with a wonderful sense of humor. I am certain that none of the parishioners in the pews below noticed the little joke, so subtle was that improvised phrase. The moment we become aware of Messiaen's motivic variation, he has already moved on with his music and has turned the faux-pas, the choir's amateurish blunder, into a wonderful melody.

This side of Messiaen has stayed in my memory, his spirituality and his profound sense of humor, with which he knew how to make fun of human frailties and transform them into something hugely lovable. Though, when I think back to that brief moment today, I have my doubts whether Yvonne Loriod and I truly understood Messiaen back then. Maybe his cheerful imitation of the lay choir's dilettantism was not rooted in humor, but was rather a statement by this deeply religious man. By turning the singers' obvious clumsiness into a wonderful melody, he reminded us, full of gratitude, of one of the most central and maybe most beautiful messages of the New Testament: namely, that God does not love us because of our perfection and our strengths, but loves us particularly in our moments of weakness.

When I am in Paris, I return to Sainte-Trinité every now and again. To me, Messiaen is still present. I see him before me then, at the organ: this composer, unique in modern music history, who opened Europe's doors to me. Messiaen played this organ for sixty years. I see his gray, combed-back hair, his patterned shirt underneath the jacket, his almost motionless face as he plays, his gaze fully focused on the manuals, entirely immersed in his music, almost enraptured. To Messiaen, improvisation was more than just a meditation – it was a prayer, every single time.

CHAPTER FIVE

NOTHING BUT MUSIC
IN ONE'S HEAD

"Heard melodies are sweet, but those unheard
Are sweeter; therefore, ye soft pipes, play on;
Not to the sensual ear, but, more endear'd,
Pipe to the spirit ditties of no tone."

John Keats,
"Ode on a Grecian Urn" (1820)

DIABOLUS IN MUSICA

Did you know that intervals can scream, spray poison, sow discord? The tritone is exactly that kind of interval: a nasty, venomous combination of two notes whose distance consists of three whole tone steps of the scale. It is a very unstable interval that presses ahead and makes the listener want to beg for salvation: "Give me back harmony!" Someone who is at home in the language of music would call the tritone an augmented fourth, a leap from C to F#, for example, or from F to B. The tritone is powerful, demanding, menacing – an interval in which, as soon as it rings out, a catastrophe seems to announce itself. It is often employed in the musical accompaniment of horror movies or thrillers. It is the interval that Bach uses in his *St Matthew Passion* when Jesus meets a leper, and that Bruckner uses as a symbol for the Last

Judgment in the Credo of his Mass no. 1 in D Minor. And that Mussorgsky, in "The Hut on Hen's Legs," the ninth movement of his piano suite *Pictures at an Exhibition*, uses to set the siren calls of the witch Baba Yaga to music. In his *West Side Story*, Leonard Bernstein lets desperate Tony call for his lover Maria with this ominous interval. Jimi Hendrix based the beginning of his famous song "Purple Haze" on the tritone. It is used in the opening music of the cartoon series *The Simpsons*. British singer Adele begins her song "My Same," in memory of a broken friendship, with an unaccompanied repetition of the interval. She literally yells it at the audience.

And if today a composer were to summarize the eve of 15 September 2008, those hours when a few super-rich, powerful bankers desperately tried to save Lehman Brothers from collapse, and the world from a deep recession, he would surely resort to the portentous tritone repeatedly – redemption lies either in a happy ending or in an explosion: the aforesaid catastrophe. In the Middle Ages, this interval made people feel as though Lucifer was speaking to them in person. The color of the sound irritated the Catholic church to such an extent that it gave this "devilish" combination of notes the sobriquet "Diabolus in musica" ("Devil in music") and simply prohibited its usage. After all, the interval could throw people into turmoil and instill fear and terror. Until well into the baroque, people adhered to that ban for fear of conjuring up Satan. And yet, the tritone is nothing special. It's nothing more than an acoustic stimulus. But the exciting thing is what our brain does with it, making us become greatly perturbed.

How potent music can be, and how much it can press on our souls, invigorate our fantasies, awaken our imagination, make us think or open our eyes is shown by this little pair of tones alone. However, this is only one example – almost arbitrarily chosen from the infinite variety the world of music has to offer. Music can do much more than create moods. It evokes memories and helps to overcome mental blockages. It can relieve physical pain and psychological injuries. Doctors ascribe healing powers to it;

philosophers, a knowledge-enhancing effect; as moving sounds, through the emotion, stimulate the brain to think.

My relationship to music is so organic due to my lifelong occupation with it, and my great passion for it, that I would never question the power of music at all. For years it didn't even occur to me to think about why music is so potent – it was self-evident. When I was younger, I dealt with this question from a music-philosophical point of view and read a lot about it. Over the centuries, on a philosophical level, the phenomenon has been explained imaginatively, plausibly and often with a fresh approach, even though it has ultimately never been fully decoded.

Perhaps I wouldn't have looked again at the question of the power of music if it hadn't been for a number of really sensational publications in recent years that have tackled the phenomenon of music on a neuroscientific basis and asked what actually happens in our brain when we listen to music or make music ourselves, since the acoustic stimuli reaching our ears and penetrating into our heads have to be processed. Music, one could say, is created in the mind – of composers, musicians and listeners. Even if this idea seems a little reductionist, the tritone alone clearly shows how only the brain produces music. True, a mere interval doesn't add up to a melody; it's just two tones that can be played either simultaneously or one after the other. But even those two tones trigger sensations, longings and ideas in our brain, which, as soon as it processes the sound, begins to evoke sinister sensations. What in the world is going on in my head?

I make an arrangement to meet Daniel Levitin. Daniel is a neuroscientist, musician and author. He teaches at McGill University in Montreal and heads the Faculty of Arts and Humanities at the Minerva Schools at Keck Graduate Institute in San Fransisco. He also taught at Stanford. During the fourteen weeks I spend every year in the Canadian metropolis, we are almost neighbors, unless he is in San Francisco or traveling the world giving lectures. His institute at McGill University is just a kilometer from the Maison Symphonique de Montréal, the new concert hall and my office, as the crow flies. If two of his books hadn't caught my attention, I might never have thought of meeting him. A few years ago, he published a *New York Times* bestseller with *This Is Your Brain on Music: The Science of a Human Obsession*. Later, his book *The World in Six Songs: How the Musical Brain Created Human Nature* came out. So, not long ago, I went to his laboratory spaces to ask him that one question: Why does music hold this power over us, sometimes even with one single interval?

The neurosciences, as they are conducted today, are a comparatively new field of research. Since it has been possible to map the brain and determine the function of various semiochemicals, general interest in neuroscience has rapidly increased. Today we talk about dopamine, serotonin and endorphins as a matter of course, about the cerebral cortex, the cerebrum and the cerebellum, the motor, sensory or auditory cortex, and the hippocampus. The latter, by the way, is a region in the middle of the head where, as Daniel explained to me, the memory for music, musical experiences and contexts is located. So music has a lot to do with the brain, in fact so much that there is a philosophical consideration that music as such wouldn't exist if our brain didn't "construct" the music out of mere sound waves. Since I now know how far this fascinating science has developed, I naturally expected a clear answer to my question from Daniel. Who should know better than he, who played and produced music himself, and had been thinking about its cerebral effects on a daily basis for decades? What would he say?

MUSIC CAN ENGENDER MORE THAN WORDS

His answer astounded me: "Kent, I am not eloquent enough to even begin to do justice to this question." I must have looked at him in surprise, for he added: "How am I supposed to describe the power of music? It would be too one-dimensional. When you're moved by music, there's no words for it." A short, tense silence ensued. "But," he then said in a conciliatory way, "even if words are not nearly able to express the effect of music, music can help us to describe our emotional state of mind, because people don't just use music as some kind of emotional regulator to get themselves into a different mood when they're angry, or when they slump on their sofa at home, full of adrenaline after a stressful work day. Apparently, they also use music to *define* their mood." Daniel told me that he often felt exactly like the mood of Debussy's solo piano music, but couldn't find words for his state of mind.

I don't give up and try another way. What happens in the brain when music moves us, literally takes possession of us? Here, too, he is reticent: "I don't think we have precise knowledge of that," he replies. He says he didn't even know how close he and his colleagues were to deciphering the secret of the power of music. "We just always find modules that help us explain things." He says he knew where in the brain the pitch was processed, which regions recorded rhythm and timbre and where chemical reactions were triggered by harmonies. He could also locate the processing of tone length and volume. "We are such a young science that we are still trying to localize the regions in the brain where something is happening. But we're just beginning to understand how it works." There is only one thing we now know very well: that music is a stimulus that quickly reaches the entire brain.

Using various techniques to track brain activity, be it with electrodes or different methods of scanning, one immediately discovers in medical imaging that almost all regions of the brain are addressed by music: the right as well as the left cerebral hemisphere, front and rear regions, the cortex as well as the interior limbic system. Music is one of the very few stimuli that activate our whole brain. All regions are involved, and so is every neuronal subsystem. There is no music center as such in the brain. The various aspects of music, i.e., rhythm, tempo, volume or pitch, are processed in different regions and reconnected somewhere as information. According to Daniel, these areas work simultaneously, not one after the other. The matter becomes more complicated due to the brain's ability to reorganize itself.

Certain functions can be performed by other parts of the brain. Nothing is static. Scientists speak of neuroplasticity. "But where are all the processed pieces of information put together?" Daniel asks himself. The question as to why music touches us emotionally marks a limit to scientific knowledge.

Daniel shows me a series of colorful images depicting brain activity when listening to music. They are the result of a complex process of visualization, since a scan actually only produces heaps of figures, which in turn have to be made visible in a sophisticated way. But the pictures are beautiful: the whole brain glows in the primary colors red, yellow and blue. Our mind is in top form, so to speak, thanks to music. Looking at these images, one immediately feels that one understands why listening to music, and especially making music, is so often termed "empowerment." Our head becomes a kind of power plant, every region is involved – with transfer effects not excluded. Judging by the images, music must open up completely different possibilities for the brain.

Two things, however, cannot be seen in those images: on the one hand, it is not visible what *type* of music the test subject has listened to. And, on the other hand, whether or not *any* music has been listened to at all. Perhaps there was dead silence. In that case, only the *thought* of music and the *anticipation* of music would have activated all those neurons. "If the notion was sufficiently vivid, we cannot distinguish by the image alone whether the brain was set in motion by an acoustic stimulus or just by the imagination," says Daniel.

Musical experiences that happen only in the mind are not all that uncommon. Who isn't familiar with the phenomenon of a tune that keeps catching up with you, drifting into your consciousness without having been invited to do so? Music can be imagined so forcefully that for a moment you don't quite know whether it is actually sounding from somewhere or whether it is taking place only inside your head. "Expectation and suggestion can greatly enhance musical imagery, even producing a quasi-perceptual experience," wrote the famous American neurologist Oliver

Sacks in his book *Musicophilia*. People's musical imagination is as diverse as the people themselves. We professional musicians make use of it all the time. When I read a score, I immediately "hear" the music; I *imagine* it. It has a sound, it has an auditory presence and it can move me even though it is only printed on paper. And when I am conducting, the music has taken hold of my brain long before the orchestra plays the very first note. How else could Beethoven have composed music in a state of complete deafness? The music wasn't played, he *imagined* it. His imagination must have been perfect, perhaps more perfect than the music played in real time, either then or now. For non-musicians, musical imagination might be more of a spontaneous experience, yet no less powerful for that.

Music is quite unique in this respect. Why? "I see my room, my furniture every day. But they do not re-present themselves as 'pictures in my mind,'" Sacks writes. "Nor do I hear imaginary dog barks or traffic noises in the background of my mind, or smell aromas of imaginary meals cooking, even though I am exposed to such perceptions every day." Nothing would even remotely correspond to the range of his musical imagery. "Perhaps it is not just the nervous system, but music itself that has something very peculiar about it – its beat, its melodic contours, so different from those of speech, and its peculiarly direct connection to the emotions." Apparently, music is so powerful that it can take over our imagination even without external acoustic stimuli. But I digress, so back to my initial question: Where does this power come from?

In the course of our conversation, Daniel becomes a little more specific. Biologically, the power of music is quite easy to explain. Music causes physical reactions in the brain and sets a whole cascade of chemical processes in motion. This has a positive effect on the well-being of most people. Music heightens oxytocin levels. Oxytocin is a hormone that increases our willingness to get involved with other people. It creates trust between people and is disseminated, for example, when singing together. Music also augments the production of the antibody immunoglobulin A, which is so important for our health. There are also studies that show that after only a few weeks of music therapy melatonin, adrenaline and noradrenaline levels increase. Melatonin regulates the sleep-wake rhythm and was proven to be effective in the treatment of certain forms of depression years ago. Noradrenaline and adrenaline put us in a state of heightened attention and excitement. They activate the reward centers in the brain. Listening to music and, of course, making music influence the serotonin level and thus the very neurotransmitter that is connected to the regulation of our mood.

"All these studies seem to confirm something the ancient shamans had long known: music – especially cheerful music – has a profound impact on our health," Daniel says. Music also significantly reduces the stress hormone cortisol – an experience that everyone knows when, after a hectic day, they put on music to relax in the evening. If different musical activities cause a change in the concentration of messenger substances in the brain, then the potency of sounds can hardly be doubted. "Music can move us to the heights or depths of emotion. It can persuade us to buy something, or remind us of our first date," writes Oliver Sacks. "It can lift us out of depression when nothing else can. It can get us dancing to its beat. But the power of music goes much, much further. Indeed, music occupies more areas of our brain than language does – humans are a musical species."

HAVE A GOOD CRY!

Many people love sad music, and I am one of them. Perhaps in my case, "sad" is the wrong word: melancholic, full of tristesse, plaintive, yearning – these terms would be more appropriate because after all these years it is impossible for me to associate music with one simple adjective. Anyway, music can move people to tears. I remember one night at the famous Tanglewood Music Festival in western Massachusetts. The Boston Symphony Orchestra played the last movement of Brahms' Symphony no. 1. The solo horn player made the long-drawn-out alphorn melody, in which we can so unmistakably detect nature itself, sound with such intensity that I was deeply affected.

Another time I listened to a recording of Bruckner's Eighth Symphony. I had recorded it with the Bavarian State Orchestra shortly before and was now checking the quality of our recording in a last run-through for the final version. My colleagues had played the opening of the slow movement very expressively. While I should have exercised the meticulousness of a bookkeeper to pick out every nuance that didn't correspond to my idea of the work, the music simply swept me away. I ended up with tears running down my face. Surely, in this case it was more about poignancy than mourning. But we all know from personal experience that music can actually make us sad, out of the blue. And that many people love precisely this kind of music.

That brings me to three questions. When does music sound sad? Why does it make us sad? And last but not least: Why do we want to listen to it, considering that melancholy and wistfulness are not exactly desirable mental states? After all, we prefer to be happy, animated and full of zest. The third question, therefore, contains a certain paradox, a phenomenon long known in science as the "paradox of tragedy": Why do human beings derive pleasure from unpleasant states of mind? It is remarkable that people – at least in Western culture – often experience the deepest, the most touching and also the most beautiful moments with sad music. Which, by the way, Aristotle already knew about. Catharsis – the soothing purification of the soul by ancient tragedy.

If you want to know about that, ask David Huron, a musicologist and cognitive scientist from Ohio, who has achieved world fame among psychologists and neuroscientists with his book *Sweet Anticipation*, and who has taught us so much about the phenomenon of expectation, which plays such an outstanding role in the power of music.

Sadness in music is a question of compositional technique. Sad music, says Huron, tends to be deeper, slower, calmer, darker in timbre and less agitated in its melodic line. The intervals between the tones are small and the melody does not consist of skips or big leaps. In that, the music keeps in line with the kind of language we all resort to when we have to break sad news. We tend to speak more quietly, more slowly and in a deeper voice. If composers want to express melancholy, they will instinctively switch to that mode. But can they also put *us* in that mood? This varies from person to person; we are either more or less receptive, depending on our natural disposition. But hardly anyone would doubt that music is capable of doing it.

Grief originates in the brain. The question of what exactly is happening there when sadness sets in, just by listening to a piece of music, is quite complicated – and has not yet been fully answered by the neurologists. How exactly visual or acoustic stimuli evoke emotions is still the subject of painstaking research. And the sensual pleasure of feeling sad is not to everyone's liking, either. Some experience it, and others don't. I vividly remember how in my early years the French mime artist Marcel Marceau, without uttering a single word, moved my friends and me to such an extent that our eyes welled up. We are still haunted by it, the more so because we actually *enjoyed* his undeniably tragic performance. And yet it was nothing more than a kind of silent movie.

David Huron offers three assumptions about this mechanism: Firstly, sad-sounding music may activate mirror neurons in the brain, which then trigger the corresponding feeling of empathy. Mirror neurons are nerve cells that exhibit the same patterns when observing an action as when the action is not merely observed but performed. The complex system of mirror neurons makes the ability to put oneself in the position of one's counterpart possible in the first place, thus inducing imitative resonance behavior. Music arouses corresponding feelings in people who are susceptible to it.

There are two further explanations of the fact that sad-sounding music can make you mournful. For one thing, there are acquired associations. Over the years we have learned that minor scales and chords sound sad. They are played slowly and solemnly at funerals or in gloomy movies. This experience is so deeply entrenched in us that we never really associate minor keys with great joy, but instead with melancholy, sadness or wistfulness. On the other hand, "sad" music induces musing or brooding, a kind of self-referential processing that clouds our mood. When test subjects were asked what was going through their minds when some "sad" music moved them to tears, the majority of them replied that it had evoked reflections on issues related to difficult life situations or, indeed, the very concept of mortality.

So music – if we are receptive to it – lets us experience sadness that is not caused by real events in our lives. At this point, it becomes abundantly clear that music creates a space for emotional experiences that are not directly connected to the reality of our existence. Apparently, we humans need that. But why do many people actually long for melancholy?

Here, too, David Huron has a theory to offer. Again, it is linked to our brain. When a person mourns – due to some event or other – the hormone prolactin is released in the brain. Psychologically speaking, this hormone counteracts emotional stress. According to the scientist, nature has installed a kind of emotional brake so that you don't let yourself become completely engulfed by grief. Music, on the other hand, can put people in a mood approaching sadness that causes the release of the very same messenger substances that normally result when "real" experiences aggrieve us. Here music works as the medium of a feigned state of mourning – of course only in those individuals who are receptive to it. The body reacts exactly as it has learned to do over millions of years of evolution: a messenger substance is released, a feeling of comfort arises. Normally, the person is facing an actual issue: the death of a loved one, the loss of a job. But in the case of music, nothing negative has happened at all – no drama whose effects would have had to be cushioned with the help of hormones. A pleasant feeling remains, and that's all. "Have a good cry!" says Huron on YouTube. "Nothing terrible happened. It's just music." A real experience, but without a real trigger!

"Music works like a drug," Daniel tells me in the course of our conversation. We humans, he continues, have discovered substances that cause chemical reactions in the brain and thus induce the release of messengers that put us in a different mode of sensation. Heroin, for instance, provides dopamine, that desired happiness or reward hormone that, usually after some success or accomplishment, ignites familiar positive feelings in us. Music, he says, acts like an opiate, deceiving the neuronal system to such an extent that it provides for the release of messenger substances that in turn influence our emotional state. That's where its power lies. David Huron recently wrote to me to say that the prolactin issue could not be clearly demonstrated in a study. Prolactin was found in the tears of the test subjects – but not in all cases. Nonetheless, it is easy to comprehend how music, which was created in the mind of a composer, has an impact on the mood of its recipient.

Worlds that are only created by music but which evoke real feelings and experiences in us account for some of the magic of music. "Music reveals to man an unknown realm, a world quite separate from the outer sensual world surrounding him, a world in which he leaves behind all precise feelings in order to embrace an inexpressible longing," E.T.A. Hoffmann wrote in his essay on "Beethoven's Instrumental Music," a slight variation on the previous quote. Sometimes you can literally yearn for melancholy. Music is a place of longing.

SWEET EXPECTATIONS

Music is a game with expectations, Daniel explains to me. And this is deeply rooted in our evolution. Anticipation or expectation is, in purely biological terms, a fundamental prerequisite for survival. Anticipation prepares us for the next event. Our ability to anticipate makes us fit for life in the first place. The brain controls that game almost perfectly; it is a kind of "anticipation machine" that continuously produces assumptions about the future, compares them with the event when it occurs and then makes new assumptions. Music has fixed structures we have internalized throughout our lives. "When we listen to music, the brain relates what we're hearing to everything we've ever heard," Daniel says. A strange phenomenon was shown in a series of experiments in which unknown melodies were played to test subjects and suddenly interrupted. Most people automatically continued to sing these melodies correctly. So, they were making adequate predictions, without which they wouldn't have been able to sing at all. "It has a lot to do with the structure of music," Daniel says. For centuries, our occidental music has been subject to strict rules and regulations, on the basis of which predictions about the further course of a piece of music are possible.

But not every prediction is correct. A composer may mislead us and break the rules in order to belie our expectations. That is the moment of surprise, which in itself creates emotion. It is part of the explanation of why we find music emotionally touching. In tonal music, the sequence is always the same: expectation, breach of rules, surprise, shock, shudder, finally a return to the rule and the redemptive effect: Ah! All of us are familiar with this. A composer repeats the same motif twice, then he changes it, leads us along a new path and again begins to play with our expectation of what might come next – for example, a resolving chord. In the end, our expectations are fulfilled after all – and it's back to the feeling of well-being.

"Musicians are magicians. They have control over us. Stage wizards have control over where you look; composers, over how you hear," says Daniel. And then he confesses something else he doesn't understand, namely, that a piece of music can surprise us even when we think we know it very well: "I am sure I have heard the end of Dvořák's Seventh Symphony more than a hundred times. And I still don't know exactly when the symphony ends. I am still being misled." At the very beginning of this book, I wrote that this is how I feel about Bach's piano music. My surprise is particularly great when I think I know the piece very well. Why?

"Since expectations can lead to different emotions, the manipulation of expectation provides one of the most potent resources available for playwrights, novelists, poets, film directors, choreographers, comedians, theatrical magicians, and others," writes David Huron in his book *Sweet Anticipation*. The matter is particularly difficult for composers, he argues, because music consists only of sounds. In return, I would say it is all the more effective for that. The hypothesis of the paramount importance of anticipation for physical survival, which I mentioned at the beginning, was formulated by Huron. Through music and its playing with expectations, the brain gets the opportunity to train the very skills that are indispensable for building and maintaining a society: tension and response, imagination and prognosis. This is the reason why Huron raises our ability to anticipate onto the level of the senses. Anticipation is our "sense of future." And that sense of future is trained by music. For me, this is a fascinating correlation, which contains much of what I myself experience every day. What happens on the biological or chemical level is a matter for the neuroscientists: hormones are released. If our anticipation proves to be correct, these hormones are different from those that are released when we are surprised, that is to say, when our assumptions are wrong.

HEARD A THOUSAND TIMES

Brain researchers and psychologists are not all that far apart; often their theories merge into one another. A musical experience can be regarded as a deeply psychological affair. And here, too, expectations play a special role. One could almost say that it is our expectations that give music incredible power over our intellect and our soul, that is, over the experiences we have gained and stored throughout the years. The sound waves produced by an orchestra become a melody only because our brain classifies those stimuli in the overall context of our life experiences. This context includes, as one of thousands of cognitive structures in the brain, our Western tonal system, as shaped by Bach's musical language. Then we feel comfortable. We expect certain chords to be resolved, we expect a piece of music to move toward closure, we expect the verse of a pop song to lead to a chorus. Without this wealth of cognitive background knowledge, musical experiences are hardly possible and one might perceive the music as mere noise or annoying clamor.

When Schoenberg composed his first works in free tonality, people were stunned. They deemed the tone sequences they heard unstructured; they had no experience whatsoever with this kind of music and were vexed by their own disorientation. Their brains couldn't process those acoustic stimuli because the necessary cognitive structures were missing. And even when Schoenberg used traditional forms, which were structurally, if not harmonically, derived from Brahms' aesthetics, his listeners in the concert hall flew into a fury. My relationship to this form of music is too organic for me to understand how difficult members of an audience might still find it. I have often heard this music and lost myself in its soundscapes. I have analyzed it, both in a historical context and in purely musical terms, and I conduct it frequently. My brain is programmed to have a variety of structures at its disposal with which to process my listening experience. This happens differently each time, which is why I never get bored with the music. Nevertheless, I feel empathy for the part of the audience that feels alienated.

A few years ago, I traveled with the Orchestre symphonique de Montréal to the Inuit in the Far North of Canada. It was the final leg of our first country-wide tour. It felt as if we were flying to the end of the world, to a wild landscape where nature is rough but pristine and unspoiled – a journey into the no-man's-land of the Canadian Arctic, where there are only a few isolated human settlements that seemed to have been scattered by a giant hand. This is where we took our music to. We performed in gyms, where the children crowded on the floor and pushed to the very edge of the provisional stage and marveled. Most of them had never heard classical music before and never seen instruments like ours, no more than we knew their sounds and tones.

The music of the Inuit is different from ours, considerably different. Throat singing is typical for them and very popular. It is more than just singing; it's almost a kind of party game. The singers rhythmically squeeze tones, noises and air out of their throats. They stand facing each other, staring at and singing to each other. They seem to be singing straight into their counterpart's mouth, so that the sound of one resonates in the head of the other. Even as a listener, you can observe it. But I wasn't able to recognize any melodic elements or lyrical moments in this kind of music, only an intensely rhythmic form of communication. Would this type of singing ever become music to me?

I still remember how, on an overland drive, our young chauffeur told me about his singing with almost touching enthusiasm. That, he said, was his hobby, a strenuous hobby. His face was radiant. Then he started humming and hissing at the wheel, wheezing out sounds. His counterpart, of course, was missing, but he didn't care about that. Maybe he was just imagining the other person. In between he laughed heartily. I listened to the song of that Inuit, a young fellow who enthusiastically squeezed all those sounds out of his throat, again and again in endless repetition. While I was listening, I was completely disoriented. Later I heard the same singing done on a different, professional level by two female singers. They performed together with our orchestra in *Take the Dog Sled*, a composition by the Canadian composer Alexina Louie, which I had commissioned and which incorporated Inuit music.

Only, in the course of time, when I got used to the sounds and heard how people imitated nature in their singing did those sounds become a song for me. I had found the Inuit music rather disconcerting until I began to learn more about this almost forgotten cultural asset and about the sounds' deep connection with nature, a way of singing in which people express their love for the land, the sea and the ice. Only then does one understand that their singing sounds like dogs chasing across the ice, folks running after them, breathing in the icy air, exhaling it again, the thin layer of snow crunching under their feet. And then one hears the screaming of the snow geese, the barking of the sled dogs. There is nature in the music – nature becomes music.

You first have to hear the silence in the Far North, which sets in when the wind has died down. The soundlessness of the snow, then the whoosh of the sea, the crackling of the ice. And somewhere, widely scattered, the sounds of people in their villages. When I learned all this on our trip to the Far North, I could make sense of the songs of the Inuit in a land we musicians from Montreal discovered like a foreign world, but which actually makes up a large part of Canada.

And so, in northern Quebec, at the age of almost sixty, I experienced once more what music actually is. Music, physically nothing more than an acoustic stimulus, whether a single chord, an arrangement of tones, an entire symphony or an Inuit song, basically originates in our own head and then spreads all the more powerfully within us. If one accepts this admittedly very reductionist view, it naturally implies quite a lot: I need to know something about music in order to fully enjoy its power. Or better still: the more I know about it, the more I immerse myself in its structure and its history or that of the composer, the greater and, above all, the deeper my musical experience will be. Not only do I need a certain basic understanding of the language of music, but perhaps I should also know something about the history of the period when, say, a symphony was written, or about the ideas that concerned the composer at the time. Depending on which aspect I am attending to, my perception of the piece of music will change yet again.

This is the secret of all great works. They offer an infinite number of possibilities of perception, transforming themselves again and again into a new experience, for the structure of classical music is so complex that I can discover something new each time I listen and thus penetrate deeper and deeper into the music and draw ever new inspiration from it. That's because of its indeterminate character. Music is not self-referential. For a start, it effectively means nothing. Or it means what our brain makes of it. If we know about Beethoven's initial admiration of Napoleon, and his subsequent disillusionment, we may hear those thoughts and feelings in his music. Perhaps we read a clever essay in the program before the concert begins. It will hardly leave our musical experience unaffected. Or we might just have studied the mysterious effect of the tritone and listened to that interval several times – and suddenly we recognize it in a symphony. And then we think about the reason why the composer employed it and what he might have wanted to express with it. Depending on what else we know about the composition, our way of listening will change.

Music may be about something, but its "content" varies, depending on the context. First of all, music is asemantic, not concrete; it is an abstract, nonrepresentational art. Thanks to this indeterminacy, great works become infinite, always raising new questions without ever providing a final answer. This is precisely where its power lies: in its manifold possibilities of effect that can set off a surge of emotions within us, put us into a state of heightened spirituality or help provide knowledge and insight. Music can change the brain, awaken memories or make them disappear; it plays with expectations and with our imagination. It nurtures our senses and our sensibilities, and it challenges us – comprehensively, with all our capacity for experience.

NOTHING COMES FOR FREE

If one is aware of these processes of cognitive perception, it also becomes clear just why classical music in all its complexity requires a little effort on the part of the recipient. It all starts with a moment of concentration. If I want to experience music, I first have to learn to listen carefully. This in itself is almost a provocation at a time when classical music often serves as piped background Muzak, or as an accompaniment for advertizing, such as Mozart's grandiose Piano Sonata no. 11 in A Major K. 331 (*Alla Turca*), used to promote a toilet flushing system.

Perhaps that is the reason why classical music can fascinate people more and more over the years, just as it has fascinated me from the beginning of my childhood: because of its complexity and depth, there is ever more to discover. A classical piece of music is multilayered. In its complexity it reflects life, which isn't a simple affair, either, and cannot be reduced to a few drumbeats and a catchy tune. To confront this complexity, you have to make an effort. You have to acquire some background information and ponder certain things. You also have to maintain a certain flexibility in dealing with what you have experienced. It makes a difference whether you listen to Vivaldi's universally known *Four Seasons*, or to the fourth movement of Beethoven's Ninth, where the intended message is supplied by Schiller's poem, or to a violin sonata by Witold Lutosławski, in which the movements do not bear titles that would let you know whether the music represents summer, winter or spring. Concentrated listening, the acquisition of knowledge and a good measure of flexibility in dealing with an aesthetic experience – it's quite a lot to ask.

But I do think that one should be permitted to expect a little effort from listeners, especially from young people. Classical music is no different from many other things in life where commitment, active participation and a certain amount of drive are required in order to achieve something. Does it always have to be plain sailing or passive entertainment, such as a trivial pop song with booming bass that sends the listeners into rhythmic ecstasy for a few days, but soon wears off and fades into obscurity? No, not everything is simple and easy, neither in life nor in art. A journey to the realm of classical music is not a jaunt to Cockaigne, the land of plenty, where milk and honey flow, and where sweet fruit hanging on the trees alongside rivers are ripe for the picking. It wouldn't at all correspond to human nature, which ultimately gets weary of effortless consumption, despite all those temptations. We are endowed at birth with a willingness to make an effort, just as we are endowed with laziness. We don't want to just lie on a triclinium, putting the sweetest grapes into our mouths; we also want to climb mountains, trudging around one bend after the other. Why?

We do it because even the effort gives us pleasure – and if not the effort, then the expectation of a wonderful vista, and a feeling of deep inner satisfaction after our work is done. That enjoyment is ensured by the release of some cerebral hormones. "It should be noted that pleasure does not trump all other values: the best music is not necessarily music that fills its listeners with pleasure. But without a significant dose of pleasure, no one would bother about music," writes Huron in his book. "Pleasure does not preclude effort. Minds need to reach, not simply grasp. Brains need to be challenged, not simply pampered." He is right. I'm not an ascetic. There may, indeed, there *must* be pleasure – not as simple self-gratification, but as a complex phenomenon. "If aesthetic philosophers are genuinely interested in understanding the phenomenon of beauty, they cannot achieve this goal without taking into account the operation of the human brain and its predilection for pleasure," Huron continues.

Whoever conceives the journey into the world of classical music to be a process of discovery and exploration, through which, layer by layer, he or she penetrates deeper into this universe, will experience many moments of pleasure in the process itself, whether these lie in the happy understanding of a structure, in the excited expectation of things to come, in our amazement at a witty twist in a melody or in our awareness that the music has just carried us to another place for a few minutes. Can you imagine how excited and happy I am when I suddenly recognize a new construction principle in a score I have known for a long time and my view is once again completely changed? I can promise you one thing: even if it doesn't always come easy, it is worth it. Whoever enters the world of classical music will never be disappointed.

That the beautiful things in life, the most formative experiences cannot always be gained without effort should also apply to young people. I learned this in my childhood when the pleasure of a musical experience lay first of all in finally being able to play a run fast enough and, above all, correctly – when I found that prowess it filled me with happiness. Until then, my mother had sometimes driven me uphill like a little donkey. In classical music, the mountain can be quite steep at times. But at the summit, a wonderful view opens up.

CLASSICAL MUSIC OR POP?

I have just made a rather provocative remark about pop music and termed it superficial, less profound and simplistic. At least it is less complex and therefore much more accessible to many people. Maybe the difference is like reading a cheap thriller much faster than Goethe's *Faust* or Dante's *Inferno*. But the gain in knowledge and the sense of satisfaction that comes from reading Goethe's *Faust*, once you take the trouble to tackle it, is many times greater than mere entertainment through a crime novel, even if its author is famous and the plot is immensely captivating. Admittedly, this comparison is rather foolish. Even I know that a good thriller can be high art. And the common classification of music as "light" or "serious," or as entertainment or art, is probably quite inappropriate. Not everything that is easily accessible is entertainment. And even the complexity of a piece of music as such is not a proper criterion for distinguishing "true" art from mere entertainment. Even Immanuel Kant, probably the most important philosopher of the Enlightenment, made an essential distinction between "pleasant art" and "beautiful art." Each of those has "for its immediate design the feeling of pleasure." But "pleasant arts are those that are directed merely to enjoyment" and "are only concerned with momentary entertainment, and not with any permanent material for reflection or subsequent discussion." The purpose of beautiful art is that pleasure accompanies the representations (of an object) not as "mere sensations" but as "modes of cognition."

Therefore, the subdivision of music already existed in the eighteenth century. Kant had linked it to purpose, not to any particular style of music, as is the case today. Just because I specialize in classical music I do not want to determine the quality of music of different genres, and certainly not decide what is a higher or lower form of art. Time will be the judge; time will prove the durability of a musical creation. Some of the sonatas from the hodge-podge of works even by renowned composers may be counted as entertainment rather than as serious music because they haven't stood the test of time. On the other hand, it can hardly be denied that John Lennon's not particularly complex song "Imagine" is a great testimony to his musical creativity and will endure – it is high art in the field of pop music, timeless not only in its musical form, but also in its political statement.

By profession I am a specialist for classical music and therefore by definition not a great fan of a genre that purports to highlight and combine the best of both serious and light music, the so-called "crossover." But perhaps even the term "crossover" is wrong. Maybe we should finally stop subdividing music into "challenging" and "light" music, but rather acknowledge the existence of different styles in all genres, and let time pass judgment. Great music is removed from time. It has something to tell us. And it's above any classification. It's just there.

What is interesting is that we like to ask of classical music whether it is still up to date. Who would come up with the idea of denying the importance and validity of texts by Aristotle or Saint Augustine, of plays by Gotthold Ephraim Lessing or of novels by Theodor Fontane simply because they are a few centuries or more than a thousand years old? When I ask Daniel if he could imagine that classical music might eventually disappear completely, he, the guitarist and rock musician, who can also play many classical compositions on the piano, looks at me aghast: "Never! It would be as if Shakespeare were to disappear at some point. Can you imagine that?"

A MATTER OF PERSPECTIVE

Music affects every person differently. Semantically, it is completely indeterminate and doesn't speak to us in concrete, but in abstract terms. It sets in motion a cognitive process, a reflectiveness triggered by emotion and ideas for our actions that might begin with a mere hunch. But it would be a mistake to expect a new impulse or a new idea, let alone a new social vision to arise directly from the experience of a symphony. It's not that simple. "Input" and "output" bear no proportion that could be formulated in terms of linear or similar functions that precisely calculate the yield of an investment to the last cent. There is no specific social return on the arts. Do I have to be able to predict how the policies of a head of government will change if they go to a classical concert every month for a year and preferably listen to the organizers' introduction beforehand?

"My favorite definition of music is that it causes you to look at the world differently than before," Daniel says. We've been sitting in his little office for two hours. His acoustic guitar is leaning against the wall next to his desk, always ready to demonstrate something. When you listen to a piece of music, Daniel says, you will perceive your environment in a different way – mostly inappreciably so. He is deeply convinced of this. Music leads to new connections in the brain. *How* the impact of music causes the brain to create those new connections is apparently still unclear. "This is the miracle that music works."

It is a miracle of considerable significance. The change of perspective, the possibility of seeing the world from a different angle, can be an opportunity to change relationships, to break with entrenched views and to solve questions in a completely new way. But how exactly does this change of perspective work? Why does music make us look at the world with different eyes?

"There are two states of the brain," Daniel says. He calls these the "task mode" and the "daydreaming mode." Our brain is in task mode whenever we attend to a task, be it learning a piece of music, preparing a meal according to a recipe or finding our way on a map. The "daydreaming mode" is the mental state of digression and contemplation that we are in when someone asks us, "What are you thinking of?" and we answer, "Oh, nothing" or "Don't know." "The daydreaming mode is relevant to our story here," Daniel says. Thoughts become free to create new connections, just as it happens in dreams when an armchair suddenly becomes the car in which one is driving across a sea. This happens only when the brain is free to make such connections. In that state, brain regions that are different from those necessary for concentrated work become active. Suddenly, a completely different neural network is in action. New thoughts or connections emerge that, speaking on the level of neuroscience, mean nothing other than that billions of neurons recombine via synapses. "If we want to solve a problem, it is often not possible with linear thinking only," says Daniel, "no matter whether we talk about aspects of climate change, of hunger in the world or of an imminent warlike conflict." Creative solutions are needed, not the straightforward thinking that determines our actions in task mode.

And what has music got to do with it? There is apparently a mechanism or "switch" in the brain that organizes the change from one state to the other. "In my laboratory at Stanford we have discovered where it is," Daniel says. It is located in the so-called insular cortex. Its mode of operation has not yet been investigated. What is certain, however, is that music acts upon this mechanism and is able to put people into a state of daydreaming that is different from their previous state of concentration. "A sunrise can do that, too," Daniel says. But in his opinion, music is rather unique. "It occupies us for a long time and in a way a painting or even a sunrise cannot." The pulse of the music synchronizes us. "We can't get away from it."

With music, the listener forgets time. Music is time-bound, yet the time we spend with it appears timeless – the "daydreaming mode" is a mental state beyond the physical dimension. You lose your sense of time and space, your sense of place, environment and surroundings. Sounds and melodies differ from paintings or a sunset in yet another respect. "With paintings, the feeling remains that they are somewhere out there, outside your body," says Daniel. But music penetrates us through our ears. We have it right in our heads. And when it has completely taken possession of us, when it has put us in a state outside of time and space, then the way is clear for new connections, for new thinking, for creativity. The brain researcher looks at me. He's laughing.

Our long conversation is over. Deeply satisfied, I leave Daniel's lab. Satisfied because I had the opportunity to look at music and think about it from a completely different perspective. Satisfied also because there is still no comprehensive answer to the crucial question: Why does music exercise that power over us? I have written down a few answers that seem fascinatingly plausible to me. There are countless other outstandingly clever and important explanations. The secret of the power of music, however, has not yet been unlocked. And if music is a synonym for life, nothing will change that. On the contrary, the more we strive to unveil the secret of music, the more complex it seems. A multilayered riddle. This is precisely where the elusive quality of music lies and, ultimately, its power.

BRUCKNER

Dissolution of Boundaries

Memories of my youth surface almost every time I think of Anton Bruckner. They take me back to Morro Bay, to a friend's house, to his family's living room with a grand piano that was always well tuned. It happened right there that Anton Bruckner's music broke into my life – I would almost say with its characteristic audacity: unexpected, powerful and at any rate unforgettable.

This sounds almost as emotive as Bruckner's music itself when conducted with too much vigor. But I'm not exaggerating. My discovery of Bruckner that afternoon was a formative event in my life. You would think that my friend David and I had put on a vinyl record of a Bruckner symphony, turned up the volume full blast, darkened the room, laid down on the floor with our eyes closed and let Bruckner's music unfold its effect on us. At the time, that was a popular pastime for my friends and me, which we pursued over and over again throughout our schooldays. But it wasn't like that. Things turned out a little differently.

David told me in the morning at school that he wanted to play something in the afternoon. He was a very good pianist even then. Today that's his profession. We were teenagers and occasionally played piano four hands together. In that respect, the invitation to his home wouldn't have surprised me if it hadn't been for his palpable impatience. Then I was really stunned by what he wanted to play.

When we arrived at his home, he showed me an edition of Bruckner's Seventh, Eighth and Ninth Symphonies, arranged for piano four hands. We started on the first page of the Seventh and played it with growing enthusiasm. Experienced pianists could cope with it quite well. Of course, we often struggled with it and had to start all over again. But we quickly got a good idea of the sound and pretty soon were utterly fascinated. David knew his way around music literature, including Bruckner's compositions. I, too, was familiar with Bruckner, at least with his choral works. Of course, we knew who Anton Bruckner was: an Austrian composer who had created virtually monumental music, which, however, was not recognized for a long time during his lifetime. Even in my own childhood and youth, his symphonic works were anything but usual items on concert programs. Nevertheless, this was different from anything I had heard and played before. There was probably nothing more absurd at the time than for two boys to play Bruckner on the piano four hands, especially in view of the ongoing youth revolt of the late sixties. But that's what we did do – play together once in a while.

I can't remember if my friend told me where he had got the sheet music. But in retrospect, it doesn't matter at all. What was important was that the music irritated us. We wondered, we marveled. It stirred us. Here was a composer who, unlike what we had learned from Professor Korisheli at school, did not engage in classical motivic development, but rather juxtaposed his musical ideas in blocks of themes. Even then, playing the piano, I noticed how difficult it was to connect those blocks. What did one idea have to do with the next? It seemed to me as if we were walking through a building completely foreign to us, looking around and becoming aware of how new spaces were constantly presenting themselves. We were about to discover something completely new, a music we didn't know and didn't really understand but that, we sensed, would have something to say to us.

I think everyone has such recollections of their youth – something full of surprise and wonder, something profound and of lifelong importance. It doesn't necessarily have to be music; for others it may have been the discovery of Hermann Hesse's novels, Friedrich Nietzsche's essays or Rainer Maria Rilke's poems. For me it was Bruckner. Such events form the substance of experiences that develop their full impact only over time because they do not fade but gain in significance with every year that passes, perhaps even triggering a lifetime passion.

Anton Bruckner's symphonic compositions have long remained a kind of musical mystery to me. Maybe they still are today, even though I have studied them as thoroughly as few other musical creations. What is their power? Why am I so moved by this music? Why is it that Bruckner's symphonies, of all things, can catapult me into a completely different world, a world of unbounded emotional and spiritual experiences? No predefined time, expanding space – that is Bruckner for me.

My discovery of Bruckner came at a time when general interest in his music, and especially in his great symphonies, seemed to be growing tentatively. In the sixties, renowned conductors began to perform and, above all, to record his works. First it was Eugen Jochum, who recorded all nine symphonies between 1958 and 1967. In 1926, at the age of just twenty-four, he had made his debut at the Munich Philharmonic with Bruckner's Seventh Symphony. Nearly four decades later, he was considered an almost incontestable interpreter of Bruckner. One of the first vinyl records I ever bought with my own pocket money was a Bruckner recording. It must have been one of Jochum's, probably the Seventh. Jochum was followed by many famous colleagues, two of whom were much discussed and praised for their Bruckner interpretations: Sergiu Celibidache and Günter Wand. Celibidache, who took over as conductor of the Munich Philharmonic in 1979, was particularly fascinating thanks to the breathtakingly slow tempi at which he performed Bruckner's symphonies.

My personal understanding of Bruckner has been shaped above all by Günter Wand, whose name is associated with that of the Austrian composer like no other. For many years, he used to study the score of a single symphony and its various editions before deciding in favor of one version and then performing it. He had so much to say about Bruckner. During our long friendship, I learned a lot from him, especially about Bruckner and what research into, knowledge of and faithfulness to a work actually mean.

Günter Wand was probably my last great teacher after Olivier Messiaen and Leonard Bernstein. Our relationship, which, after years of intense collaboration, developed into a close friendship, lasted until his death in 2002. When I met him, I was in my early forties. A few years earlier, I had taken over the direction of the Hallé Orchestra in Manchester, in addition to my engagement at the Opéra de Lyon. Wand was chief conductor of the NDR Symphony Orchestra (now the NDR Elbphilharmonie Orchestra) in Hamburg, which had engaged me as guest conductor for Mahler's fairy-tale cantata *Das klagende Lied* (*Song of Lamentation*). When the NDR musicians told me that Wand was to come to Hamburg and rehearse Bruckner's Ninth Symphony with them, I decided without hesitation to extend my stay by one day in order to attend the rehearsal. He hadn't invited me. I was bold enough to sneak into the concert hall and just sit quietly at the back.

This is quite uncommon among conductors. Conventions actually demand more respect, and you are at least expected to ask whether your presence is desirable. During a rehearsal break, one of the musicians came up to me and told me that the maestro wanted to talk to me. At first, I apologized nervously for my unsolicited presence. But even before I had finished speaking, Günter Wand dismissed my apology with a flick of his hand and welcomed me. It was, he admitted, the first time during his long years in Hamburg that another conductor was interested in his work with the orchestra. And soon we were – right on stage – in the middle of a discussion on Bruckner's Ninth Symphony and Mahler's fairy-tale cantata, which I had conducted.

After that first encounter, we met frequently. We talked about the orchestral works of Schubert and other composers, but mainly about Bruckner's symphonies no. 3 to 9. During our conversations, I absorbed his knowledge. Our examination of Bruckner's music soon led us to the very existential questions of life that touch not only on personal values and assessments, but also on faith. Of course, Günter Wand was an unchallengeable authority on Bruckner for me. Hardly anybody knew the work of the unconventional Austrian composer as well as he did. What he said was worth considering in every respect, even if we didn't always agree. Günter Wand often opted for later versions of the symphonies, which is to say, for Bruckner's revisions. In his opinion, they came closest to the ideals of the composer. But I began to become increasingly enthusiastic about the original versions ("Urfassungen"), which seemed to me much harsher, more vibrant, more radical and also more modern.

For Wand, Bruckner's symphonies were highly spiritual creations in which the composer dealt with the hereafter, couching his connection with God and the idea of an afterlife in sounds. Nature, too, is reflected in Bruckner's symphonies, but his views on nature are full of spirituality. Günter Wand once told me that he saw a kind of dichotomy in Bruckner's symphonies. The Fifth and the Ninth were very different from the Third, the Fourth, the Sixth, the Seventh and the Eighth. If one conceived the symphonies as dialogues with the beyond, then the direction of communication in the Fifth and the Ninth was from top to bottom, from heaven to earth. In all the other symphonies, however, that direction was reversed: people on earth sent their words up to heaven, hoping for an answer. I don't know if one can hear or feel such a thing. I don't even know if I can. In any case, Günter Wand gave me that interpretation as an incontrovertible fact to deal with.

Anton Bruckner appeared to the public as a rather contradictory person: a musical genius who, like almost no other, dared to take classical music to completely new dimensions. On the other hand, for decades there was the cliché that he was just a teacher's son from the countryside, servile, insecure and, at the same time, desperate for appreciation, a man whose groundbreaking musical legacy could not be reconciled with his personality. The weirdness attributed to him soon caused a large number of anecdotes to circulate. As a person he was taken even less seriously than as an artist. This discrepancy remained for many decades after his death in Vienna in 1896. Gustav Mahler's description of Bruckner being "a simpleton – half genius, half imbecile" was to influence public perception for years to come.

During much of his lifetime, Bruckner was largely unappreciated as a composer. As an organ virtuoso he was admired and acknowledged even beyond the German-speaking world, and as a professor for harmony, counterpoint and organ playing at the Vienna Conservatory, he was quite accepted. But as a composer he was controversial. The rejection of his music was the exact opposite of the recognition he longed for. His sometimes extremely submissive attitude toward political and artistic authorities could hardly be reconciled with his self-confidence and his ambitions as a symphonist. His breakthrough came only at the age of sixty, in 1884, with his Seventh Symphony. He had composed it between 1881 and 1883, the famous Adagio under the impression of the death of Richard Wagner, whom he deeply revered. Significantly, the world premiere took place in Leipzig and not in Vienna, where a merciless trio of critics under the leadership of the influential Austrian music aesthete Eduard Hanslick tried for years to discredit not only Bruckner's music but also the man personally.

A year later, the Seventh Symphony was enthusiastically received in Munich under the baton of Bruckner's friend and patron Hermann Levi. But the Vienna critics remained skeptical and deprecative. Hanslick, the leading critic at the time, described the successful Seventh as a "monstrous symphonic serpent." Even in this one, of all of Bruckner's symphonies, he missed "logical thinking, a refined sense of beauty and critical judgment," and declared it "a psychological mystery how this gentlest and most peaceable of men [...] in the very act of composing becomes an anarchist, who mercilessly sacrifices everything that we understand by logic and clarity of development, unity of form and tonality."

If I were to interpret that sentence today, I would think that the acerbic critic indeed characterized Bruckner splendidly, even if he didn't mean his comment in a positive way but had wanted to endow it with negative connotations. Driven by his inner need for expression, Bruckner simply had to ignore the common rules of composition because they had become too restrictive for his ideas of sound. Despite their enormous expertise, his critics, who were caught up in the spirit of the times, simply could not understand that this was precisely where the modernity of this artist lay. Perhaps it is the fate of all progressive artists that they have to pay a price for driving art toward the future too daringly.

Throughout his life as a composer, Bruckner actually paid a high price: that of loneliness. This does not so much concern the fact that he remained unmarried and largely on his own, but rather that he was completely misunderstood, and several of his important works were premiered only after his death – like the Fifth and Sixth Symphonies, whose performances he never witnessed. All his life, Bruckner had trouble finding a publisher who would take on his scores and pay him fees.

His symphonies were not only considered oversized due to their length, but they were also regarded as unplayable. The symphony as an art form seemed to have exhausted itself with Beethoven, who had perfected it with his œuvre. Could anything of symphonic significance come after Beethoven? If so, it could only be something utterly different. Beethoven was feted while he was alive; Bruckner was denied that treatment. One reason for this may be that Beethoven was already recognized as a composer of ideas during his lifetime, as someone who, in his works, addressed the seminal accomplishments of the Enlightenment and of liberalism, which revolutionized social conditions throughout Europe at the beginning of the nineteenth century. It is often forgotten that Beethoven composed his late chamber music works so differently, so innovatively that he was no longer understood by the majority of his audiences.

I often wonder how hard to bear it must be for an artist if there is not even the merest understanding of his works over decades.

Even Bruckner's friends had difficulty with his compositions and their exaggerated expressiveness. Hermann Levi's deeply shocked reaction when Bruckner, after three years of composing, sent him his Eighth Symphony, is almost legendary. Levi, whom Bruckner, in the first flush of excitement, had described as his "artistic father" after the successful Munich performance of the Seventh, didn't much care for the Eighth: "To put it briefly, I cannot find my way into the 8th Symphony and haven't got the courage to perform it," he wrote to Bruckner's student Joseph Schalk, who was charged with delivering the devastating news to the composer. Levi didn't want to pass judgment, but he was afraid of the orchestra's – and the audience's – resistance to the "impossible instrumentation." He was "particularly horrified at the great similarity to the 7th and at the stereotyped form," and recommended a thorough makeover.

Bruckner repeatedly revised his nine "valid" symphonies (he had disowned an early one in F Minor and another one in B Major, the so-called Symphony no. 0) – in some cases decades after they had been composed. This is why musicologists are confronted with the almost unsolvable task of pinning down Bruckner's artistic intentions, and conductors with the eternal question as to which version they should present to the listeners. For those revisions are not minor corrections of inherently consistent works, but rather drastic alterations with which he intended to adapt the all but archaic sound structures of the original versions to the spirit of the age. They were meant to sound smoother and to become more accessible. Again and again, his works met with incomprehension, not merely on the part of the critics, but also of friends and patrons. Not only did Bruckner always take malicious remarks to heart, but even more so sincerely meant advice. He then recomposed long passages or entire movements; he shortened and simplified.

I have studied and compared those versions countless times in detail, and I have often wondered whether Bruckner was even aware of the enormous innovative power of his original versions. Just as he had rigorously broken with traditional symphonic principles in his original versions, he rigorously set about revising them in order to withdraw what had been pioneering, to cut back their elemental quality, to endow them with greater compositional refinement – without respect for his earlier achievements and perhaps without recognizing the artistic aspirations permeating those first versions. Was he scared by his own modernity? There is no answer to this.

For me, the original versions of his symphonies are illuminating and fascinating. They are more modern, more visionary and more monumental than their reworkings, and they have much greater force. The power with which Bruckner's musical ideas were breaking new ground can be felt immediately. The original versions in particular prove how innovative and revolutionary Bruckner was in implementing his ideas, driving the harmonies forward and then destructing them. If I were to describe what his music does to me when it carries me away, it would be a change in my sense of time and space. Everything becomes grander and wider, time loses its absoluteness, space its limitation. For me, what manifests itself in Bruckner's music is the dissolution of our earthly dimensions. But how does Bruckner achieve this effect?

Not everything can be explained with his composition techniques, but some things can. I would therefore like to pick out a few points that can be identified without too much theoretical knowledge. Perhaps the next time you hear a Bruckner symphony, you will become aware of them.

Time is a dimension. With reference to time, Bruckner's symphonies, above all the Eighth, are oversized – according to the understanding of his era. Operas were known for their length, but a symphony that lasted eighty minutes had never been attempted before. That length, measured by our wristwatches, is unusual even today. Moreover, Bruckner's music is comparatively slow; it literally pushes the listener out of time – into extensive phrases, which usually run over sixteen bars. That, too, contradicted the composing and listening habits at the end of the nineteenth century. When a phrasing comes to an end, the listener has the feeling of having completed a journey. But before you become certain of it, Bruckner moves you into the next sound adventure.

All this leads to a gradual loss of any sense of time, something the composer may well have intended. Moreover, there is Bruckner's handling of his motivic and thematic material, which permeates the movement of a symphony in almost endless variations. Next time pay attention: the material undergoes an apparently never-ending process of development. Those variations take place only by degrees, like a very slow metamorphosis. Bruckner achieves this by making the repetitions of a motivic or thematic idea always sound similar, but nevertheless always providing new variations: sometimes he changes the key, thus giving the motif another tone color; sometimes he reverses or mirrors the theme; then again he varies the speed; another time, the context. The modification of the theme seems to happen in an almost associative manner, as though the composer were giving his thoughts free rein. The transformation happens almost imperceptibly. And it is only at the end of a movement that the listener realizes that he finds himself in a different world.

This handling of the material is completely new. If you engage with it and try not to listen for the beginning and end of a theme, then physical time loses its validity. If Bruckner had given his symphonies and their individual movements a customary, conventional symphonic structure, certain motifs would first be presented or introduced, then developed and varied and finally restated and brought to an end. But that's not what Bruckner does. That is why his music was disconcerting to the listeners of his time. They were missing structure. And perhaps his great critics didn't want to get lost in time at all ...

I want to give you another example of how Bruckner succeeds in changing our sense of time and thus abducting us from our everyday lives. He likes to use two and three notes per beat in turn: duplets and triplets. This way he creates an almost typical feature of his music, a simple "Bruckner rhythm" that pervades his entire œuvre. True, metric structures and all other rhythmic laws are precisely defined and strictly adhered to by Bruckner; nothing gets jumbled. But in the listener, the alternation between two and three notes per beat creates an unfamiliar sense of undulating movement. The listener begins to become oblivious to the measure line. He loses his sense of where the first beat is, or to put it another way: the downbeat loses its customary power. In music theory, the downbeat is the strong first beat of a bar, for instance in the ONE-two-three time signature of a waltz. The listener is used to those conventions.

But just imagine you didn't hear the ONE in a waltz anymore. If we can no longer hear the accentuation that we are so accustomed to, we get a feeling of being liberated, of floating in the music, of swimming in streaming water. Music becomes nature, be it the wind or autumn leaves whirling in the air, knowing no measure and no downbeat. If the listener no longer detects the classic division of time into individual bars, and stressed and unstressed beats, he is no longer aware of physical time and its menacing mechanics. Then the boundaries dissolve and the universe opens up.

The second dimension that Bruckner relieves us of with his music is space. The concept of "sound architecture" is frequently mentioned in connection with his symphonies. He designs edifices and chambers the way an architect does. His musical motifs appear abruptly – he constructs them in space. Bruckner often sets different groups of instruments, preferably the woodwinds, against each other to great effect, sometimes even setting a solo instrument against the whole orchestra. That contrast makes the sound space appear even larger. Then he stacks and piles up harmonies, story by story, to give the music its monumental character. He erects gigantic arches, which suddenly stand out when I analyze the score in detail. As a conductor, I have to make them audible to the listener. Bruckner works with repetitions, a technique that suggests a vacuum, i.e., space. He unexpectedly places new thematic material, sometimes only fragments of an idea, in a given musical context. Or he simply juxtaposes them to create a whole panorama. Buildings appear one after the other, or mountains, say, the Alps. One could think of a painting in which much seems accidental, but on closer inspection nothing is left to chance. Everything is connected.

Bruckner raises gigantic sound blocks, which lend his works their grandeur. As with the harmonies, the dynamics he employs contribute to highlighting the architecture of his works. Loud and quiet, sonic opulence up to a fortissimo, then again, almost abruptly, the lowest possible pianissimo, and finally dead silence during often-used general rests – all of this gives the architecture its contours. Sound spaces line up side by side, ever new spaces open up – sometimes in all their polarity, separated by a moment of absolute, tense silence. These contrasts constitute the perceived vastness of his music. Again and again, Bruckner uses a very simple, diatonic structure in which the subtle harmonies can almost inappreciably unfold their strength. A shadow falls upon the panorama, lends another color to it. Even before the listener becomes aware of this, the spell is broken and sunlight appears again.

In these composition techniques lies the sonority of Bruckner's symphonies, which, except for the Seventh, Eighth and Ninth with added "Wagner tubas," were written for romantic orchestras of a size for which Brahms and Schumann also composed. And yet the listener has the impression of having an almost oversized orchestra in front of him.

Bruckner's contemporaries were undoubtedly overchallenged by his compositional style. Gustav Mahler, while acknowledging Bruckner's greatness, described his unease as follows: "With Bruckner, certainly, you are carried away by the magnificence and wealth of his inventiveness, but at the same time you are repeatedly disturbed by its fragmentary character which breaks the spell." Others spoke of formlessness because Bruckner left the construction principles of "classicist" symphonies behind him. That is why it is so important for me to present Bruckner's works in a way that makes the construction principles of his symphonies become apparent. To do that, I have to recognize them first. As with all great composers, that process of cognition is a never-ending undertaking and a tribute to the infinite depth of their music. Every time I deal with Bruckner, I discover new elements of his "sound architecture," further connections and arches. It feels like visiting a famous building over and over again and penetrating deeper and deeper into the construction principles with each visit; first you see the arches, then you discover certain alignments and axes that are related to each other. This is part of the fascination of his works.

With the harmonic tensions he creates, the composer relieves his "sound edifices" of their gravity, which is what modern architects try to do when they give skyscrapers a twisted appearance or when they construct slanting façades that, against all physical laws, suggest a shift of the center of gravity. That way they come across as different and new. Bruckner pushes the boundaries of tonality and shakes the foundations of his "sound architecture" by removing the principal key so that the edifice seems to float. He often changes key, either by modulating from one key to another or by not committing himself to one key in the first place. He uses all twelve notes of the chromatic scale, and throws his listeners into abeyance because the tonal basis is missing.

This is of interest not only for experienced listeners, or for musicians who are particularly well versed in music theory and who recognize ambiguities when analyzing a score. It is something that can be experienced intuitively, because amateurs, too, can sense that the keynote is missing, which is to say, the start and end point to which the music normally heads. Bruckner was not afraid of dissonances. He draws them out and pushes them into space, as if he took it for granted that, long before Arnold Schoenberg, dissonance had already attained equal status to consonance and had emancipated itself from its subordinate existence as chords that must always be resolved.

Bruckner is famous for the *crescendos* and climaxes of his music. A symphony seems to begin out of nowhere, as if the music had always been present, if unnoticed. This gives it something absolute that is beyond the boundaries of time and space. But as soon as we do hear the music, it begins to develop, seemingly autonomously and independently of its composer. The music flows like a swollen, increasingly powerful river that slowly but irreversibly turns into a gigantic billowing wave, literally engulfing the mesmerized onlooker. Is this an expansion of the mind, the epiphany of a compositional genius whose works point beyond his person? Does the music defy the control of its creator?

I still don't know the answer. That's the mysterious thing about Bruckner's music, which occupies me whenever I include one of his symphonies in a concert program and bury myself in the score again. Sometimes, Bruckner was uneasy with himself. Frightened by his own audacity, he once asked a friend whether one was actually "allowed" to compose in such a way. Perhaps his receptivity to criticism is based on his discomfiture with the unruliness of his mind. So he willingly began to revise his symphonies to make them sound more "opportune." He tamed himself, he recanted. The recklessness with which Bruckner pushed his compositions to the limits of time and space had made them far too progressive; they were an imposition on the musical taste prevalent at the period and far ahead of their time.

For me, Bruckner's works present an expanding universe that continually nourishes an intimation of its infinite magnitude. This explains their power, that special quality that constitutes great works of art but which cannot be described with words, even when you have analyzed a piece of music in all details of its composition and grasped the musical idiom of the artist. There's something else, something grander. I don't know what it is. But Bruckner's music doesn't lose its hold on me any less than that of Johann Sebastian Bach.

The reason why it is so difficult for me to write about it in concrete terms is that I cannot explain it. Unaccountably, these two composers, each in his own way, have become an emotional constant in my life. The few thoughts I have written down here are completely insufficient to explain this fact. They are nothing more than a poor attempt to approach phenomena about which

I cannot speak objectively. In my enthusiasm for, and dedication to, Bruckner's music I would make the very worst Bruckner scholar. Perhaps you'd better forget what I have written about Bruckner. I'm thinking of his music. It is sounding in my head. And I'm speechless.

CHAPTER SIX

THE UNANSWERED QUESTION

"For once you have tasted flight you will walk the earth with
your eyes turned skywards, for there you have been and there you
will long to return."

Leonardo da Vinci (1452–1519)

There's not a day in my life when music doesn't matter. It's always
there. Either I rehearse, conduct, play the piano or study a score,
or I think about music – on my own or, preferably and much more
often, with others. Those conversations, especially with people
who haven't made music their profession, are not only stimulat-
ing for me, but extremely important. They are my connection to
the earth when I am once again losing myself completely in the
universe of music. Among the people I have spoken to are politicians, scientists, representatives of religions and other artists. In
our encounters I asked again and again about the significance of
classical music for their lives. How may music have influenced
their personal development? What role does it play in our society?
None of our conversations remained on a purely analytical level
for long. People's relationship with classical music, and their love
for it, is simply a deeply personal matter. I shall recount some of
those conversations here, at the end of this book.

HELMUT SCHMIDT: IN NO HUMOR FOR PESSIMISM

Helmut Schmidt's office at Germany's most important weekly *Die Zeit* was small, almost surprisingly so. Basically, I would have expected a much more spacious study for an elder statesman of such international renown, who from my American perspective was *the* political identification figure among Germans. But the former chancellor, co-editor of *Die Zeit*, to which on the occasion of his death in November 2015 the *New York Times* devoted several articles, did not *reside* and *hold court*. He worked like everyone else. That's what he was like – a real Hamburger, still very much down-to-earth, despite being held in such great admiration during the later years of his life. His Hanseatic understatement was typical of him.

It's been several years since I visited him at *Die Zeit* to talk to him about the importance of classical music, its connection to politics and the need for a permanent presence of the arts in a society that seems to be increasingly losing touch with them. Let it be said: talking to Helmut Schmidt about music was a great pleasure, enriching thanks not only to his deep love of classical music and his excellent musical education; it was also the sociopolitical context that he, as statesman and publicist, provided again and again – sometimes with a large pinch of the sardonic.

I remember him vividly: sitting behind his desk in a wheelchair, smoking. I take a seat opposite him. A question is burning my lips: Shouldn't politics be much more at the service of the arts, of music, so that classical music doesn't degenerate ever further into a mere pastime for the social elites? What answer could be more in the affirmative than that of great music lover Helmut Schmidt?

For a brief moment, a pause for effect, the former chancellor disappears behind a cloud of smoke. Then he opens the conversation in his own way: "Was it ever different?" he asks. "Literature and art have always been a matter for so-called elites. The need for art may also have existed among the common people. But most of the time, only a small part of society enjoyed access to music and theater. Today it's hardly any different from two hundred years ago or in antiquity. The need of ordinary people is for bread and water and a roof over their heads – elementary prerequisites for physical survival. That's much more important than satisfying a perhaps merely latent longing for music, painting or architecture."

Helmut Schmidt does not hide his skepticism toward social elites and their alleged love for the arts. "Allow me a cheeky remark, Mr Nagano. You also conduct operas. Some of these elites who consume opera are for the birds. They go to the opera because it's the proper thing to do and because their neighbors go to the opera. Bayreuth is a typical example of this. The opera audience in Bayreuth consists in part of people who earn many millions a year and who have no understanding whatsoever of the music. But once a year they make a pilgrimage to Bayreuth. A strange elite indeed. And I wouldn't even want to acknowledge them as an elite. In Bayreuth they perform Wagner. The old 'German Nationals' have always held on to Wagner. Wagner's libretti are very nationalistic, especially the *Ring*. The harshest critic of Richard Wagner's *Ring* was Friedrich Nietzsche. You must read *Nietzsche contra Wagner*," he recommends. "Nietzsche realized that there lies a national instinct behind it all."

"You don't like opera that much anyway. Why not?" I ask.

"I consider opera to be a misbegotten art form."

I look at him in astonishment. I know this isn't the first time he's said this. But it still amazes me to hear it so directly from his mouth. "Why?'

"Music as such is an international art, but opera needs language. Music exists as international art, as does painting, sculpture, architecture. All the other art forms, literature and drama, require language, and languages are national. That's why opera in particular is an imposition on the internationality of music. But I don't want to say only bad things about opera. It was a very important sociopolitical institution and probably still is today."

"Perhaps you could be described as an advocate of 'absolute music,' or at least as one of its great lovers," I say, "as someone who loves music for the sake of music, without lyrics, free of non-musical influences."

"Bach is my idol," he says straightforwardly.

"Mine, too," I agree.

"His music can move me to tears. However, I was never interested in the words Bach set to music. And I've always preferred concerts to opera."

"As a child, you received excellent training. You play the piano very well."

"That's right. But it wasn't just about playing the piano. When I was seventeen, I arranged many church hymns in four-part harmony."

I am amazed because I know what knowledge of music theory and what degree of compositional skills are needed for four-part harmony – and because it is a politician, of all people, who is telling me this. From a layman's point of view, this kind of arrangement requires a fairly comprehensive musical education. "How strongly has your musical education influenced you?"

"Unbelievably strongly, so much so that much else, and especially my general education, was totally neglected during my school days. It all started at the age of six or seven, and then, at the age of ten, even more so, phenomenally so. At school, I was brought up with music. Nowadays, I'm completely cut off from that world of music."

Again and again a deep wistfulness is discernible during our conversation whenever he mentions the loss of music, which his fading sense of hearing has been inflicting on him for years.

"When did you stop listening?'

"I haven't heard an orchestra or attended a concert for fifteen years. When I talk about music, it's only from memory." Schmidt pauses. "From the memory of an ancient man. Music reaches me merely as noise. I can't hear anything anymore, not even when I play the piano, which I still do two or three times a week. Today I can only *imagine* music. If you present me with a score, I can imagine what the music written there would sound like, but I will never again be able to hear it."

I can hardly put myself in his position, and can't imagine how quiet it would be if I myself couldn't listen to music anymore. "What does that mean to you?'

"I am a writer who can no longer enjoy music. Imagine that: I write one book after the other, without any music. That's terrible. Really terrible. It's a great loss to me. I used to find happiness mostly in music. Its loss is a great disaster. After all, I grew up with music. It was mostly for the sake of the music that my wife and I went to church at Christmas. I was friends with some famous conductors, Herbert von Karajan, Yehudi Menuhin, Sergiu Celibidache and Leonard Bernstein. I was once given a Walkman by Herbert von Karajan, which I often used when traveling. For me personally, music, whether sung or instrumental, was of incredible importance all my life – for as long as I could hear it."

I want to know where his fascination with conductors comes from. "Is it because conductors are leaders, just like politicians?"

"Conductors have always interested me greatly. And when I went to a concert, it usually was because of the conductor. I didn't necessarily have to hear a particular orchestra. Conductors are showmen who interpret music that is not their own. But the difference in showmanship between a man like Leonard Bernstein and Herbert von Karajan is enormous. One is feisty, excited, using grand gestures; the other, sparing and withdrawn. Both conduct Beethoven's Ninth, and it sounds completely different."

Schmidt lights another cigarette. I keep going: "With your passion for classical music, are you actually an exception among politicians?"

"I don't know. To what extent classical music had a similar meaning for Lyndon B. Johnson, I cannot tell you. I don't know whether what applied to me also applies to the mayor of Hamburg. It depends very much on the education of the individual, and what shaped him or her. In my progressive school, here in Hamburg, music and art were the most important things. Neither foreign languages nor the natural sciences played a particular role. That had a big impact on me. Until I was eighteen years old, my career goal was to combine my organizational talent with design in architecture and urban planning. But things turned out differently. I became a soldier. The Nazi era and the war made it all completely irrelevant. Any plans I had as a young man simply didn't matter."

"Would you say that classical music shapes the mind?"

Helmut Schmidt answers quickly. "Yes, that's true, without reservation."

"How often does a politician or a statesman attend a concert?"

"Rarely. All too rarely. I had very little opportunity to listen to music. A lot less than I would have wished for."

Does classical music transform politicians, make different, perhaps more prudent statesmen out of them? That's what I want to know from Helmut Schmidt. Or in other words: How does music mold one's personality?

"There are outstanding, first-class statesmen who have never needed a connection to music. So it depends on the person and on the coincidences of their life's journey, especially at the outset, during the first twenty years, or more precisely, in the second decade of their life, from eleven, twelve years of age to the twentieth year. This phase of life is crucial. When you grow up with music like I did, it shapes you. Then it will have meaning for your life. Maybe it becomes indispensable. But there is no general answer. There are politicians who don't need music at all. Instead, they need literature – say, Homer, Socrates, Plato, Aristotle, Sophocles, Anaximander and all the rest. I know only a few politicians among the outstanding figures who were really musically engaged. There are more musicians who are politically engaged, but even that is a rarity."

"Has classical music lost so much of its significance?"

"The difference between music and politics is very big. They are two fields that have very little to do with each other, actually barely touch each other."

And yet he points to a parallel that I had never thought of myself: "Musicians playing together all play a little 'uncleanly,' deliberately so, it's well-tempered or pragmatic tuning. It's only since Bach's *Well-Tempered Clavier* that they sound symphonious. Before that, a violinist playing an A sharp and a B flat played different tones. Since Bach, musicians have agreed to play in well-tempered tuning, and so the violinist plays both notes as the same tone."

Schmidt is referring to the well-tempered tuning that Bach perfected by deliberately tuning his keyboard instrument against the physically natural oscillations of pure intervals. "Unclean," in a physical sense, means impure, a compromise, if you like, but with the positive effect that all keys sound pleasant to the ear. From then on, interaction within an orchestra could function properly in every key.

"And what does that have to do with politics?" I ask.

"It's no different in politics. Everyone is playing a little dirty. The essential feature of democratic politics is compromise. Without the will to compromise, democracy is not possible. The typical politician, however, usually has less need for a classical concert. He prefers singing from the same hymn sheet. In unison, without compromise."

I ask Helmut Schmidt about the responsibility of politics for the arts: "Is there a political obligation on the state to promote the arts and, with them, classical music so that they survive?"

"My answer is a ringing yes. Absolutely. And there are enough politicians who understand that. By art I do not mean entertainment, i.e., music of inferior quality, which people are quite prepared to pay for. That kind of music finances itself. It has its own audience and doesn't depend on state support. It is part of the problem you raised. The public is literally flooded with light music. Serious music reaches fewer and fewer people. It is dependent on state aid. Whether this means that we really need that many opera houses is another question. Opera costs a lot of money. The Hamburg State Opera, for example, receives public subsidies to the tune of fifty million euros a year. However, the masses will never flock to a concert hall to listen to a symphony by Gustav Mahler, or to the opera for Verdi. You have to think about what you really want when you call for new opera houses. People who attend concerts or watch opera performances will always remain a minority. That doesn't mean that you as a musician have to give up Mahler's tradition. But you are cultivating the heritage of a cultural upper class and of some people who fund it – whether out of interest and passion or for reasons of prestige. You ought to be aware of this."

Should I, as an artist, be satisfied that we cater to upper class events? No. "Herr Schmidt, in the nineteenth century, opera was very popular and of such great social importance that it spread from the big centers of music to significantly smaller communities – in Italy, but also in Germany. Opera was a thing for many people, not just for an educated upper class."

"Mr Nagano, in the nineteenth century there were no records, no CDs, no Internet. People could only hear music in concerts halls and opera houses. That's why there was such a demand for opera. Operas were the only musical events apart from concert performances. We don't need additional opera houses. What we need are additional retirement homes! In Germany we already have nearly one and a half million elderly people with dementia who are in need of care. People used to die at the age of sixty. When Bismarck introduced a pension scheme in Germany, the retirement age was one's seventieth birthday. Most workers, however, never lived to see it. Today, workers on average live to be seventy-eight. We Europeans, however, refuse to recognize the economic problems that that entails. These problems have relatively little to do with music, and music has little influence on the solution of these problems." In our conversation so far Helmut Schmidt has mentioned only the classics of music literature, great composers and works that form part of the canon. "Do you also relate to new music?" I would like to know.

"Since the end of the nineteenth century people have experimented a lot in the field of serious music. But I was too old to develop a relationship with that kind of music – when I could still hear it. The music of Olivier Messiaen has reached me, of course,

Hans Werner Henze's operas less so, Stockhausen's compositions not at all. I don't know which of those will last. A lot will disappear. Only time will tell. Not everything, though. Certainly, even in the twenty-second century people will remember someone like Dante Alighieri, like Jean-Jacques Rousseau, Beethoven or Verdi. Music like the Chorus of the Hebrew Slaves in *Nabucco* will stay. Beethoven will stay. Bach will stay. Many others will vanish, regardless of their quality, just as Matthias Claudius' beautiful 'Abendlied' ('Der Mond ist aufgegangen') is almost forgotten."

"There's one question we haven't raised yet: What will be the future of classical music?"

"I'm not a prophet. Music has a chance. But to what extent that chance will be seized I can't tell you. Literature is more important an art than music. Its influence on man is far greater, and so is philosophy's."

As a musician, I can't and won't let that stand. "Are you really sure about that?" I ask guardedly.

"Yes. Very sure. Just think of Marx or Lenin and their enormous influence. Marx's *Capital* has indeed changed the world. It has survived for more than a century. The influence of music is much less pronounced. But the greatest influence is that of anodyne platitudes. Those one must endure with equanimity."

It's not an answer to my question. Once again I ask, "Herr Schmidt, classical music hardly plays a role in the lives of young people anymore. Is there a danger that this art will disappear completely?"

"I'm not so pessimistic," he answers thoughtfully. "There will still be young people involved in music."

Helmut Schmidt is no longer alive. He died on 10 November 2015 at the age of ninety-six. For his funeral he had selected music by Johann Sebastian Bach and Johann Pachelbel and Matthias Claudius' "Abendlied." I had the honor of conducting the Hamburg Philharmonic State Orchestra in the Church of St Michaelis. How many more heads of state will there be to whom classical music means so much?

WILLIAM FRIEDKIN: A TRIP WITH BEETHOVEN

What does a Hollywood director have to do with classical music? He uses it for soundtracks, like Stanley Kubrick in his movie *2001: A Space Odyssey*. That's what William Friedkin did, too. In *The Exorcist*, arguably his most famous movie, a good deal of classical music is used: Anton Webern, Hans Werner Henze, Krzysztof Penderecki and George Crumb. But William's love of classical music is by no means limited to this. Late in life, the filmmaker became an opera director.

I worked with him at the Bavarian State Opera. In 2006, he staged the erstwhile "scandalous opera" *Salome* by Richard Strauss and *Das Gehege* (*The Enclosure*) by Wolfgang Rihm. Right at the beginning of my engagement, I planned that evening as a kind of connection between tradition and renewal, past and avant-garde, and as an expression of the overall concept of my engagement in Munich, where avant-garde music has a long tradition. At the time, I had commissioned an opera composition from Wolfgang Rihm, which I wanted to place before *Salome*. It was meant to be an unusual evening: before the break, *Das Gehege*; after the break, *Salome* – directed by a Hollywood film director. I knew I needed William Friedkin, that maverick Oscar winner, who had already made history with his horror movie *The Exorcist* and his thriller *The French Connection* in the seventies. It wasn't his first opera engagement, by the way. In 1998, he had directed Alban Berg's *Wozzeck* in Florence, and later he made his debut at the Los Angeles Opera with Strauss' *Ariadne auf Naxos*, which I conducted. The initiative originated with Placido Domingo. After that, William staged *Aida* in Turin and *Samson and Delilah* in Israel.

William says two things about opera that express so much of what goes through my own head, as well: "Opera isn't life, it's greater than life." That might smack of pathos. After all, both of us are Americans. But William also says, "We directors have a mission to bring opera into the present." Opera is music theater: operas must be brought to life on stage. That is part of its fascination and its greatest chance nowadays. It is also the best way to demonstrate how contemporary the themes are that opera, and thus classical music, already dealt with centuries ago. I recently asked William about the importance of classical music in his life. It is a question we'd never talked about before, because I take music for granted.

"Classical music means a lot to me," he says, "an incredible lot. Kent, maybe you don't know this yet, but classical music has changed my life." He says it almost reproachfully, as if I should have known. After all, I have known him since my days at the Los Angeles Opera. At the time, he asked me if he could use my recording of Stravinsky's *Le Sacre du Printemps* with the London Philharmonic Orchestra for his erotic thriller *Jade*.

"My family hails from Ukraine. My parents left Kiev and came to New York. They didn't even speak the language. There was no music in my family. I grew up in an environment where the arts played no role at all. My parents fought for survival in a foreign world. They worked hard. There was no time for leisure, there were no hours when you could just sit at home in front of the radio and listen to music. We didn't go to concerts or to the opera. So my interest in music developed osmotically. I had to travel a long way to classical music. My encounter with it was pure coincidence. But before that coincidence could unfold its effect, I had to discover music in the first place."

William grew up in Chicago, where he fell for the blues. "Blues is the music of the South. Many African Americans came to Chicago by rail from the South. They boarded trains on the Illinois Central Railroad, which connected New Orleans with Chicago, and traveled north from Louisiana, Georgia, Alabama and Mississippi. Their music traveled with them. On the southern edge of Chicago they opened their clubs and played their music. I discovered these clubs at a young age. They really sucked me in. The premises were often no bigger than an ordinary room, but there were people there playing who would later become blues legends: Junior Wells, for example, or George 'Buddy' Guy."

Prior to his love of classical music, William was fascinated by blues and jazz: "Although I didn't understand the cultural roots of that music at all, I thought it was great. I got a job, and with the dollars I earned I bought myself tickets to the clubs. Blues and jazz was the music of Chicago, it was American music. In the famous nightclub The Blue Note I heard jazz clarinetist Artie Shaw, pianist Stan Kenton and the Duke Ellington Orchestra. It was a great time. One night I drove over to The Blue Note after some work on TV. It was the deepest winter. The streets were covered with snow. There was hardly anyone about. The only people I met that night at The Blue Note were the owner of the club, the manager and the bartender. Oscar Peterson was sitting at the piano, playing with his trio – three hours long just for the four of us. At the time I thought that his improvisations that night were the best I would ever hear in my life. So I went from blues to jazz."

Classical music was not far away for William. "I often listened to jazz on the radio, again and again in the car when I was on the road. There was a program dedicated primarily to classical jazz, playing the music of Louis Armstrong, but occasionally something new as well. I didn't like all of it. When I once again sat in the car driving home, that type of music was playing. Something must have made me change channels. I can still see my right hand suddenly moving toward the radio and turning the frequency adjustment knob. All at once, my car was filled with some extraordinary music, something I had never heard before. It was music for the brain, spiritual music. That's how I felt at the time. I was on an expressway and pulled over to listen to the music in peace. It had incredible depth – it was forceful, powerful, almost unsettling. When the last note had faded away, I heard the announcer's voice: it was *Le Sacre du Printemps* by Igor Stravinsky I had heard, conducted by Pierre Monteux, who had already conducted the premiere of this scandalous work in 1913."

In the fifties, William literally stumbled into the world of classical music. "The very next day I went to a record store and bought an LP. I desperately wanted to hear that music again. It was that moment in the car, actually an accident, that catapulted me into the world of classical music. That moment opened the door to an infinite number of other works that I listen to every day: Stravinsky, Bartók, Prokofiev, much later; first Beethoven, then Bach. Today, as we are sitting here, I am convinced that all the music that has ever inspired me is contained in, or at least suggested by, Mahler's Symphony no. 1. That's the work I listen to the most these days."

"But what is it that makes classical music so fascinating?" I ask.

"Great classical music in general is brilliantly conceived and carefully constructed, nothing is left to chance. Musical ideas are elaborated, the music is structured: notes, measures, rhythms, harmonies, movements, the sonata form. In addition, the composer always leads you to a musical climax. Those climaxes make up the basic principle of classical music. Great works take you on a journey, they transport you to another place, to a place of inspiration, memories, nostalgia and future visions. I have learned a lot from classical music that applies to film, as well: a movie has to follow similar structural patterns, you have to bring the audience to an emotional climax, as Beethoven does in his symphonies. With my discovery of classical music, I suddenly realized that the documentaries I made had no particular form. I had always followed my instincts in what I did. It was only when I encountered classical music and pondered why it so touched me that I realized that works of art require a particular structure. They don't start with the finale. You don't shoot your bolt right at the beginning. Beethoven's Fifth and Ninth Symphonies are journeys, genuine emotional 'trips.' Classical music introduces certain themes and then develops them. This makes for the voyage. I knew then that I would have to do the same thing in my movies from then on."

Traveling is a process of discovery that takes place in music as well as in a good movie. You can watch good movies over and over again and discover something new every time, William tells me, a detail that you hadn't noticed before, perhaps a connection, an allusion. "Every time I watch *Citizen Kane*, I notice something

I hadn't seen before," he says, "to this day, after all those decades."
Citizen Kane by Orson Welles, released in 1941, is considered a
milestone in the history of great cinema. "If these journeys do
exist, then the big question arises as to how we take the traveler to
the starting point of his journey. For me it was a coincidence, the
moment I turned the radio button in the wrong direction. Unlike
you, I didn't have any music education at school."

That's right. Professor Korisheli always brought me to that starting point. Regardless that today's technical possibilities make classical music available to everyone anytime, anywhere, it is by no
means certain that travelers will get to that starting point. Some
won't ever find it and cannot embark on their journey. They need
someone, a teacher, perhaps a friend, to guide them or to recom-
mend something to them. Today, the odds are long. William agrees.
But why are they long?

"Everywhere in the world culture is being pushed back," he
replies. "It's a kind of dumbing down. High culture no longer seems
to be vital, great works that were created in the past and have so
much depth hardly attract attention anymore – compositions,
paintings, literature. This phenomenon has become a problem for
classical music as well."

I ask him what exactly he means.

"When I teach at film schools, I quickly realize that the students
who are there to study cinematic history have never seen *Citizen
Kane*, for instance. They don't know who Orson Welles was. I
look at blank faces. However, they all know *Spiderman*. Like a
tsunami, movies of that genre have engulfed the entire history of
film and swept away everything else. But this is not only true for
film. Think of Rembrandt or Vermeer, their portraits and landscapes, those multilayered images of fascinating depth – what role
do they play today? Somewhere along the line came Andy Warhol,
then Jeff Koons with his blue balloons. What is this art compared
to Rembrandt and Vermeer? It's a joke that their works are sold
for twenty or thirty million dollars. You can think even further:
Who still reads Proust or Dickens today? No one. Everyone reads

novels by Jackie Collins, which sell millions. This is the problem of the arts today. Rembrandt and Vermeer are overlooked, as are Proust, Dickens, Shakespeare and Goethe, perhaps because access cannot be gained without making an effort. Music is made up of twelve tones. Today's composers of pop music have to use them, just like Beethoven had to use them. Twelve tones can become the Ninth Symphony or 'Kill the Bitch.' But the Ninth is simply overlooked in much of society. People listen to 'Kill the Bitch.'"

William is right. The point is not that great art, and thus classical music, is not available, or cannot be seen or listened to. It *is* available, more than ever. The new communication technologies are a great gift to the arts. But "can be seen or listened to" is not the same as "being seen or listened to." That is the real threat: bad luck for those who never come into contact with this music, those whom Fortuna doesn't smile upon, as she did upon William. They don't even know what they're missing. "Beethoven's symphonies are journeys," says William once more in conclusion, "the Fifth and the Ninth in particular. As long as music is played on earth, these symphonies will not perish. And everyone who has been on that journey will always want to return."

JULIE PAYETTE: GOOD MORNING, HOUSTON

Houston is located in Texas. Houston is home to the Lyndon B. Johnson Space Center, from which all manned space missions have been conducted for fifty years. There, in the Mission Control Center, flights to the International Space Station (ISS) are monitored. The name of the control center used for radio communication is "Houston." Julie Payette is well known in Houston. She is an electronics engineer and an astronaut. Raised in Montreal, she graduated in Wales and returned to Montreal to study. She has flown into space twice, in 1999 and 2009, to participate in the construction of the ISS, first on the space shuttle *Discovery*, the second time on the *Endeavour*. In Canada she is something of a national heroine, the best-known face of national space travel. For eight years, she headed the Canadian Astronaut Corps. She then lived and worked in Washington for a while. Between July 2013 and October 2016, she served as chief operating officer of the Montreal Science Centre. Today, she is Her Excellency the Right Honourable Julie Payette, the Governor General of Canada.

Julie Payette has received many awards. She holds the highest orders of the Province of Quebec and Canada. Personally, I have known her since 2013, when both of us were nominated "Great Montrealers" – she as an astronaut and scientist, I as chief conductor of the Orchestre symphonique de Montréal. However, more than that event unites us. We share a love of classical music, which for Julie, too, is much more than a hobby from her youth. "Classical music was and is an important part of my life," she tells me when I visit her at the Montreal Science Center. "The experiences we can have with classical music are very intense, and we never know what they might be good for." And then she tells me what she calls a "little anecdote," knowing full well that it is more than just an anecdote, but the beginning of an incredible experience: her journey into the universe.

"When I applied as an engineer to the Canadian Space Agency in the early nineties, there were 5,330 competitors for no more than four positions. An unbelievable dogfight ensued and a merciless sorting out over many application rounds. It's probably a lot harder than applying for an orchestral position as a musician. In the end, twenty applicants remained. We were all interviewed together, in a kind of panel interview," she recalls. When she was asked, "Miss Payette, what do you think makes you a team player?" she gave an answer for which she would have liked to bite her tongue afterwards, as she tells me. "I've sung in choirs all my life. I can hold a melody together with others, I can sing in harmony, at the same tempo. I've attended rehearsals for years. I've learned over time to respond to the most inconspicuous gestures of the conductor. What could make me more of a team player?" Julie Payette laughs as she tells me about it. It's not the first time she's told this story. "My goodness, what am I talking about? I thought then. I'm applying for a technical job in space and I'm talking about what it means to sing in a church choir." I wonder whether it might have been the deciding factor. "Maybe, but I don't really know."

Julie Payette learned to play the piano very early. Sometime in the seventies, someone recruited her for the church choir. Later, she sang in the Orchestre symphonique de Montréal Chorus, the Tafelmusik Baroque Orchestra and Chamber Choir in Toronto and, during her stay in Switzerland, the Piacere Vocale in Basel. Even as a child, she took the bus to choir rehearsals and mass on Sunday mornings. "And, of course, this is how I came in contact with the most wonderful music ever written: liturgical choral music." She would hardly claim to be particularly religious. Nevertheless, those moments of singing in churches are among the most intense experiences of her life. Suddenly, she lowers her voice, speaking very softly as if she were telling me a little secret: "What I didn't tell the Space Agency in that last round of applications was about those unique moments of utter bliss." She means the ecstatic moments into which music can propel you.

"Now and then one experiences this in science as well, moments of imminent discovery or insight. But they are very rare." In music it was different, she adds. "Most moments of pure, unadulterated bliss, of concord, which come to my mind, have to do with classical music." Once they sang an *a cappella* composition by Zoltán Kodály in the choir stalls of a cathedral. Half of the choir was seated on the left, the other half on the opposite side, on the right. The choir's vocal groups looked and sang at each other. "Suddenly, there was this perfect harmony," she recalls, "the tones seemed to dissolve, to lose their individual meaning. Our voices flowed into each other and combined to produce one great sound. I had never experienced anything like it before. It was as if we were all flying together toward another world." With classical music, she says, she also experienced moments of "total bliss," which arose solely by listening.

When Julie Payette talks about her two journeys into space, about her view of our blue planet in all its breathtaking beauty and vulnerability, one thinks that out there should, by default, be the sound of music. The view of the earth from a distance, where conditions are deeply hostile to man, underscores its uniqueness even more clearly. The atmosphere, without which human life would not be possible, surrounds the planet like a thin, sensitive membrane, a mantle of transparent silk, the outer edge of which can be seen from the windows of the space station as a bluish stripe. Julie Payette always pronounces the word "space" very softly. There are no sounds in space. There is nothing. Sound waves cannot be transported in a vacuum. There is complete silence, both felt and real. Julie lowers her voice yet again. "In the space station we always sleep at the same time. Every morning we are woken up by music played to us from the Control Center in Houston." Apparently, every astronaut may listen to his or her favorite music, which can then be heard throughout the station.

"One morning when I woke up I heard the first chords of what for me was the greatest soprano duet and men's chorus that had ever been composed: the 'De torrente' from George Frederick Handel's *Dixit Dominus*." *Dixit Dominus* is a setting of Psalm 110 that the young Handel composed in Italy at the age of only twenty-one. "De torrente in via bibet: propterea exaltabit caput" ("He shall drink of the brook in the way, therefore shall he lift up his head") begins with a soprano duet that was already etched in Julie's memory and will now probably be forever connected with that morning in space in 2009. "I had heard that piece a hundred times and sung it myself in the choir. That morning, the entire space station was suffused and pervaded by that music. First the chords in the strings, then the vocals. *My* music. Very quietly and very unexpectedly, it appeared to me in space, hundreds of kilometers above planet earth, in a state of weightlessness. And I knew that this soprano duet was not only heard by my colleagues in the space station, Japanese, Russians, Europeans, everyone who was assembled there; no, it was heard by many more people: the ground personnel in the control centers in Houston and Moscow, people who had done everything for us astronauts, who for years had researched, calculated, constructed and trained us. I knew that." Julie Payette surrendered to that moment, overwhelmed by the music and by her journey in orbit. "I still have a recording of that morning when, after a while, I answered the wakening call with a rather sleepy voice: 'Good morning, Houston.'" Then she looks at me with big eyes: "And now ask me again whether classical music is part of my life."

Julie Payette still remembers several other moments which she describes with the words "total bliss." Listening to her, I am thinking that the experience in space and a journey into the universe of music have a lot in common. "When you return to earth at 420 kilometers per hour in a space shuttle, it's a very special moment," she says. "Touchdown, the end of the STS-127 mission. That's when you realize that you've been able to participate in something much, much bigger than you are. And the borders have been pushed a little further. Overcoming borders is a deeply human need. The urge for the new is stronger than fear. Risks become secondary." I think about how often this need must have been constitutive for great music.

For the astronaut, music is much more than just a medium for creating feelings of happiness. Again and again she draws parallels between music and science. "Creativity is essential for the natural sciences," she says. For her, discoveries are based on the ability to think differently from the way everyone else does. Here it is important to leave the box of familiar thought patterns. "It's just like art. Research means finding new ways. You can't plan to explore something and assume to find this or that. When you do research, you don't know what you'll find. Anyone who doesn't have the courage to enter unknown territory will discover nothing – neither in art nor in science."

For Julie Payette these two domains are not separate: "They are not 'silos,'" she says, "both belong together. I would describe myself as a strong advocate of not separating art, science and technology."

This sounds just like Leonardo da Vinci, who was driven by unbelievable intellectual curiosity, coupled with a strong urge to express himself and to impart his knowledge to humanity.

The lead violinist in an orchestra must have tremendous discipline, and he or she needs sensitivity, creativity and, along with those, a basic knowledge of the rules and principles according to which music functions. "They must know and respect the code, otherwise they won't be able to make music with others." For a scientist or engineer, things are similar: they must have discipline and a knowledge of the code, of the language of mathematics or physics. "But a scientist must be creative in order to solve a problem. You have to be able to think outside the box, or just be brave and inquisitive enough to look in another direction, to ask questions, not to believe everything, to be open to new experiences with all your senses – just like in music."

DIRK NOWITZKI: BASKETBALL IS JAZZ

Every so often I have thought about the reason why Dirk Nowitzki has a grand piano in his living room. Of course, I had immediately spotted the instrument when it featured in *Nowitzki: The Perfect Shot*, a documentary film about the basketball superstar. It can be seen whenever Jessica Ollson talks about her husband. In the movie she takes a seat on the sofa, the black piano always at her back. The lid is propped open. I can't remember exactly where I saw that documentary – perhaps on one of my many long-distance flights, during which I often watch movies. But I knew instantly that I would one day broach the subject of the grand piano with Dirk Nowitzki. There was another, more far-reaching question behind it: namely, whether music had a deeper significance for sport than just helping a player to reach the required adrenaline level before a competition or to cope with defeat after a lost match. So I ask him straight out: "What significance does music have for sport?"

"Much greater significance than is commonly assumed," replies Dirk Nowitzki. "But I'm not speaking of classical music." Dirk used to listen to hip-hop and reggae, to Bob Marley, of course, to country music and Johnny Cash, and to classics like The Beatles and The Rolling Stones; certainly, in the early days, he listened less frequently to classical music. And he used to play an instrument himself. A competitive athlete must regard his own body as an instrument, he continues. Not only must he take care of it the way opera singers take care of their voice, but he must learn to *understand* his body in the first place. And he must develop an "I," a personality that can properly grow only if one listens to oneself. "Only when you know yourself from within do you know what strengths you will be able to display in a match." Music was a vehicle for finding out.

For us musicians this is almost self-evident. There is no other way. Music forces us to listen to ourselves, it throws us back onto ourselves. It seems logical to me that this also plays a role in sport, even though, in the case of sport, music is not the end but a means in the process of self-definition. I ask Dirk at what age he actually realized the significance of music.

"It has been my coach's concept that music is, almost perforce, part of the development of one's personality. And anyone who wants to achieve something in the game must develop a strong personality." Dirk is referring to his long-time coach Holger Geschwindner, whom he and everyone else usually calls "Hodge." Geschwindner is a former national basketball player who studied mathematics and physics alongside his sports career. He met Nowitzki when the latter was a sixteen-year-old player, and became his coach, mentor and friend, which he remains to this day. Nowitzki's rise to NBA superstar status is hardly imaginable without Hodge, even less so without Hodge's unconventional training methods. Geschwindner is a lover of classical music and jazz.

"Music always played a role in training. And he always explained to us players the reason why," says Dirk. Hodge took him to classical concerts and to opera performances, such as *The Marriage of Figaro* or *The Magic Flute*. Dirk Nowitzki even accompanied Geschwindner to Bayreuth's "Green Hill," where he had to "endure" Wagner's *Parsifal*. When he has a day off during the basketball season, he still occasionally attends a classical music concert. Of necessity, he always arrives a few minutes late and occupies a reserved box seat. There is no other way. If he were punctual and thus noticeable to everyone, the majority of the audience would probably not take their seats in time. He usually attends performances of the Dallas Symphony Orchestra, whose long-standing conductor Jaap van Zweden is a friend of his through his wife, Jessica.

Of course, I am interested to know what instrument he learned.

"At first the saxophone," says Dirk, "because it's such a great instrument." In 1998, when he turned his back on Germany, he even took it with him to Dallas. Later, when an opposing player accidentally knocked out one of his teeth, he switched to guitar and even percussion. The fact that he learned to play an instrument at all can also be traced back to his coach. "It wasn't until much later that I actually understood how many good reasons there are for an athlete to be involved with music beyond the usual fire-up songs," he admits. "When you are playing music, you have to listen to yourself. When it comes to joint music-making, you have to pay attention not only to yourself, but to others as well. You have to use your head and at the same time use your hands to operate the keys or strings." And: "You must literally *grasp* the instrument and understand it before you can play." During our conversation, the parallel with sport becomes clearer and clearer to me: understanding the game, taking advantage of the laws of nature, assessing the ball's trajectory, listening to oneself and to others. Besides, Dirk adds, making music shapes one's perception of previously unknown dimensions, not only those of space and time. His coach had taught him that as well. "Hodge is absolutely convinced of the validity of his ideas. The busters that train with him all have to learn an instrument, up to this day." His trainer would love nothing better than to make them play jazz or classical music. Dirk laughs.

I continue: "And what does basketball have to do with jazz?"

The answer to this question, too, seems intriguingly obvious. Jazz developed at a time when basketball was invented as a sport. Many decades later, there was a phase in basketball when priority was given to the players' athleticism. They were better trained and tactically more accomplished than ever before. But the ludic dimension of the game had been all but lost. "Overcoached and underplayed"; that was the saying among players at the time. Dirk says that so much more matters on the court than physical constitution, sporting talent or rehearsed tactical refinement. Creativity and ingenuity are of enormous importance, as is the ability to improvise and to dare sudden changes in rhythm. "Where better to learn that than in jazz?"

The connection with jazz goes back to the American basketball player Ernest Butler, who, as a member of the US Army, came to an American school in Giessen, Germany, in the early sixties. Together with Holger Geschwindner, he played for Giessen and after that for Bayern Munich. Later, he made a name for himself as a jazz saxophonist. His motto was "basketball is jazz," by which he meant the rhythm of movement when dribbling, passing or shooting at the basket. A scene from the documentary about Nowitzki springs to mind: Butler sits there with his saxophone, begins to play a little tune, places the instrument on his lap and imitates a basketball player's throwing motion. The game of basketball needs the playfulness of jazz, its unconventionality and exuberance, its abrupt changes of tempo, rhythm and direction, its zest.

"And something else," says Dirk. "Basketball is a sport in which your opponents on the court are constantly trying to prevent you from doing what you are intending to do. That's the basic pattern of the game." So, it's a question of surprising the opposing team, of devising new strategies, just like a jazz player devises new melodies, without falling afoul of the rules. Jazz, too, is based on rules of harmony and rhythm. "When you improvise in jazz, you apply the rules and methods that you have learned and create something new on that basis – be it at the saxophone or the piano. The same thing happens on the basketball court."

But music can do much more. "It trains the power of the imagination," says Dirk. "Which is absolutely essential for any sport." Something we musicians take for granted. Without some idea of how a note should sound, I couldn't sing it. Without my being able to inwardly hear a melody, I couldn't play it fluently and expressively on the piano, let alone conduct it. Anyone who makes music necessarily thinks several measures or – to stay with the analogy of sport – several steps ahead. We are conditioned to do so; we can't help it.

Not only in the big NBA arenas, but also in easily accessible inner-city basketball courts, players who, when receiving the ball, already have an idea of the story they are going to tell their opponent will play the better match. It is a kind of question and answer game just like in jazz, where the musicians relate to each other. For this, too, music is an excellent training field. "In sport, that ability makes all the difference."

I would like to know whether Dirk will take a few lessons at some point in order to be able to play the grand piano in his living room. Or his children? Certainly not, as long as he actively plays basketball, he replies. "And the children are a bit too small yet." But who knows what's to come?

The grand piano, by the way, has its own story. Back then, the Dallas Symphony Orchestra needed a new Steinway. Dirk heard about it. He thought of purchasing the orchestra's old grand piano at a donator's price. It didn't come to that. But his coach at the Dallas Mavericks, Rick Carlisle, who loves to sit down at the piano, remembered the keen interest his star had shown. In 2011, after the Dallas Mavericks won the NBA championship and Dirk Nowitzki received the Most Valuable Player Award, Carlisle presented him with a grand piano. "In a sense it's a Trojan horse," Dirk adds with a good portion of irony. He laughs again. "He probably gave it to me so that when he comes to visit he has a decent instrument to play."

YANN MARTEL: PERFECT SILENCE

The Canadian writer Yann Martel may not be familiar to everyone – the film *Life of Pi*, based on one of his novels, certainly is. *Life of Pi* was published in 2001 and was awarded the Man Booker Prize for Fiction in 2002. After its film adaptation by Taiwanese director Ang Lee, it sold millions of copies. Yann has written many other books. One in particular caused quite a stir in Canada a few years ago. It's called *What Is Steven Harper Reading?* For two years, Yann had sent a book to former Canadian prime minister Steven Harper every fortnight, explaining to him in a letter why he recommended that particular book. He never received a proper, let alone a personal, reply. Instead, it was always the same template letter posted by assistants of the admittedly busy prime minister, and betraying their (or his?) disinterest. Yann's letters to Steven Harper can be found in his book, which has become an impressive plea for the absolute necessity of reading, of literature and the other arts. Twice I asked Yann to write texts for my symphony orchestra in Montreal and printed them in our programs. Our connection is that of two artists who have two things in common: our concern for the continued existence of literature and music in the reality of people's lives, and our efforts to ensure that they are preserved.

"We wage the same battle," Yann once wrote to me in an email, "although your challenge is different from mine." It was not the case that people had stopped listening to music. "Your challenge is that they're only listening to one kind of music, the three-minute pre-fab American pop song. Death by Katy Perry, so to speak." But music was by and large still there. It was different with literature. "As a fiction writer, it's slightly more terrifying in that there is the specter of the person who reads nothing at all."

In a conversation, he blamed the threat to the arts chiefly on our economic way of looking at things, on the calculation of a return on investment. "I always think that you can't look at the arts from an economic perspective. That is a mistake. Of course, you can see how many people are working in the art industry, how much income is being generated there. But that's not the point. We humans do not create, or partake of, art for financial reasons. We create art for existential reasons. We write books, paint and compose music because art gives meaning to life," he said. "It's the same with religion. The comfort of God has nothing to do with financial comfort. People build temples, churches, mosques not because it pays off financially, but because they simply have to do it. The same is true of the arts."

Yann sees how problematic it is when politicians increasingly think in economic categories only. And he knows about the dangers if artists follow suit. Because they cannot offer a calculable return. That's why they will lose every battle in this field. They can quantify only what art costs, never what it achieves. "We artists should never emulate those standards," he says. "We must use a language that argues out of existential necessity." It makes no difference that people listen to anything from Benjamin Britten to Britney Spears. Those two artists served different markets. Both were valuable markets. "The problem with that money game is that serious art always loses out because it always costs more money than it generates. It doesn't yield the same financial return as a pop song. But what you get from it is worth it. It is the solace provided by wonderful music or a great book that makes life worth living. A life without art is an absolute inferno."

Yann Martel loves classical music. Not all music. But, he says, he doesn't like every book, either. Some music and some books don't appeal to him; they just bore him. "If we compare classical music with pop, the latter can be immensely appealing for a short while. Some pop songs are fantastic, but once you've heard them thirty times, you get tired of them. Classical music is different, much more complex. We can listen to Mozart and Vivaldi and Bach and Beethoven again and again, even though their music is hundreds of years old. There is something infinite in these works. This does not only concern the emotional aspect. There are so many different layers and a great depth." As a little boy, Yann listened to a lot of Vivaldi. He lost himself in those melodies, which the composer pushed forward in infinite variations and which seemed to always tell him something. "Vivaldi enabled me to dream, the music carried me away. I began to learn my own instrument so that I could play Vivaldi myself. While I was playing, I thought of stories. They just came to me through the music."

He doesn't know what the future holds. "We must get rid of this economic obsession – that it all comes down to money, that this is the only thing that counts. We have enough money! Instead, we ought to figure out how to put it to use, what to spend it on. If we invest in art, we will be richly rewarded. The solution to this whole problem is to get the young people excited about it."

The end of the email that I mentioned at the beginning is not quite as comforting as our conversations. He has a gloomy outlook on the future. "There is a complete absence of written words in their lives. Or there are only the words they text on their iPhones." This almost complete lack of written texts in the lives of young people is extremely threatening for literature. "There are more and more people who don't read anything. They get their narrative satisfaction from television." The new technologies drove back reading with a vengeance. Music, on the other hand, was quite well served by them, if only to a limited extent. "You rarely have that in the coming generation – a person who is averse to any kind of music, from pop to Beethoven, someone who prefers complete silence." During our conversation, he asks me, "Can you imagine living in absolute silence?'

Is music really better off than literature? I am mulling over this question, but I don't really know. Do we musicians have less reason to be pessimistic than writers like Yann Martel? "Well," he concludes his email, "there is always hope. Education is the key."

"For once you have tasted flight you will walk the earth with your eyes turned skywards, for there you have been and there you will long to return." Together with the crew of space shuttle *Discovery*, astronaut Julie Payette wrote that sentence by Leonardo da

Vinci in the logbook on board the iss shortly before her return flight to earth in 1999 because it probably best reflected her emotions. In this book, I have repeatedly described the world of classical music as an expanding universe whose infinity becomes all the clearer the deeper you delve into it. Anyone who has ever flown into this infinity and could guess the depth of classical music will long for that experience throughout their life. It will always draw them back into it.

BERNSTEIN AND IVES

Whither America?

Dustin Hoffman is a patriot. In that, the Hollywood star doesn't differ much from most other Americans I know. In our heart of hearts, we Americans are probably all patriots. This very special kind of patriotism is deeply American, a patriotism that comes from the soul, even if it is sometimes presented full of pathos. It is rooted in the very personal identification of each individual with a country whose social construction is barely three hundred years old and still in the making. Seldom do we realize that our history, which began with splendid ideas, is a history of strife, oppression and wars, of almost unbearable dissonances, of disappointments and hopes.

A touch of that patriotism, that mixture of pride and devotion, was felt when Hoffman set foot on the podium of The Broad Stage, the new theater in Santa Monica. That night in August 2008, he assumed the role of presenter. The newly opened Broad Stage, whose artistic advisory panel he chaired, was filled to the last seat. "America. That's our theme," he began, "a nation born out of discord, still happily thriving on discord." It was a memorable evening. Many prominent actors read the words of our country's Founding Fathers: George Washington, the founder of republicanism and democracy, Thomas Jefferson, author of the Declaration of Independence, and the radical democrat Thomas Paine, a fierce opponent of slavery.

The evening was conceived as a kind of return to what once made the United States so strong: the ideas of independence, freedom and inalienable human rights. The event was meant to be a direct response to the 2008 presidential election campaign, which had been marred by unprecedented ugliness and many untruths. The manipulative sophistication of the protagonists made it almost impossible to separate truth from lies. Looking back on the ideals of American history amidst the cacophony of the 2008 election campaign was to help people not to lose sight of more important things. We named our production *American Voices: Spirit of Revolution*. The music framing our play was that of Charles Ives (1874–1954). I had chosen some of his songs, the *Concord* Sonata, the composition *Three Places in New England* and the Fugue from his grand Fourth Symphony.

Charles Ives is perhaps the first composer in our short history to really succeed in writing *American* music. For me, he certainly is the most important one. "Charles Ives loved our American dissonance," Hoffman continued, "and put it to music. He once said he wanted to evoke those Town Hall meetings where they got up and said whatever they thought, regardless of the consequences." A question hovered over the proceedings, one that has outlasted the era of Obama and has arisen again even more starkly after Donald Trump's election victory. It agitates our whole country, it divides us, it incites people against each other. It is the unanswered question about which our American society is still at loggerheads: Whither America?

That evening was very important to me at the time. Barack Obama had a good chance of moving into the White House. For the first time, a black man was standing for election. Republicans and Democrats fought unscrupulously and had the effrontery to invoke the principles of our Constitution for each of their banal interests in order to make the electorate believe that their policies came closest to the American ideal. However, on the eve of the onset of the economic and social crisis, none of us realized that those were only the first cracks to appear in American society, cracks that in the future would run deeper and deeper through our country and lead to much dirtier and more violent political conflicts. None of us foresaw that just eight years later the highly controversial real estate and media entrepreneur Donald Trump would inherit Barack Obama's mantle and move into the White House. None of us imagined that two legislative periods later an era would begin in which untruths would no longer be propagated under the guise of respectable truths, but false assertions or "alternative facts" would be promulgated unashamedly and by the highest authority. Nor did we imagine that truths could be declared to be "fake news" with one stroke of the pen, or indeed with one tweet. If you are looking for answers to questions, you first have to deal with the truth and with facts. Rarely has it been more difficult for Americans to evaluate those.

I chose Ives because his music conveys American ideals, our values, our history, our tradition, our heterogeneous society, its sense of community, its unmistakable dissonances and, of course, our wonderful nature. In Ives' music, which in his lifetime found so few listeners, lies much of the United States, of sincere patriotism, of my homeland.

It was, in the main, Leonard Bernstein who rediscovered Ives for the Americans, for all of us – years after Ives' active time as a composer. Ives' works were largely unknown to the general public until his death. They were hardly ever performed. Leonard Bernstein once told me that he considered Ives to be the most important composer of serious music that our country had produced in its short history because "his music has all the freshness of a naïve American wandering in the grand palaces of Europe" and taking in the spirit of European music in order to transform it, in an almost alchemical fashion, into American music. Indeed, in Ives' music one can hear the United States – in all its diversity, yearning and dissension. That's why his music was so topical that night.

Bernstein loved the Second Symphony, which Ives composed at the age of twenty-seven. One could almost say that he discovered it, so that the world, especially the United States, could finally discover Ives. His music hadn't been played for almost fifty years. He himself had never heard his works in their orchestrated versions, because Americans had difficulties with their own art music. Longingly, they looked to Europe and didn't appreciate their own music for a long time. They didn't even take seriously their superstar Bernstein, who, as a composer, constantly wrote new music. The moment Bernstein rehearsed Ives' works with his orchestras and at long last performed them, he gifted Americans a music of their own, a music that couldn't have been more American.

The discovery of Ives began in 1951, three years before his death, when Bernstein catapulted the Second Symphony into public awareness. He performed it with the New York Philharmonic at Carnegie Hall and continued to include it in his concert programs. Decades later, at a concert at the Deutsches Museum in Munich with the Bavarian Radio Symphony Orchestra under his baton, he opened the program not by conducting but, rather unexpectedly, with a fifteen-minute introduction to Charles Ives, who had remained largely unknown to the German public until then. Ives, he said, was a child of nature, a country boy at heart, who in his Second Symphony successfully tried to write down the sound images of his world and to furnish them with quotations from works by great composers such as Brahms, Wagner, Bach, Bruckner, Dvořák and Beethoven. His music was original, eccentric, naïve and full of charm. Bernstein, then almost seventy years old, added with a raspy voice: "In fact there are those who think that Ives' Second is still the most beautiful symphony ever written by an American. Perhaps it is because it comes to us so full of his brave resolve to be American and to write American music in the face of an uninterested and uncaring world." Ives himself didn't want to attend its world premiere in New York. Perhaps he had lost the courage to listen to a work whose sounds he had only in his head. Three years later he passed away.

What exactly makes Ives' music so American? It is the folk songs and dances, the church hymns and gospels. You can hear the melodies and marches of the Salvation Army and songs like "Shall We

Gather at the River," "Columbia, the Gem of the Ocean," "Turkey in the Straw," "America the Beautiful" or "Old Black Joe." Humorous passages alternate with sad ones; profundity and banality, pomp and fragility are juxtaposed; there is unrestrained exaggeration, American pathos and the very subtlety with which Ives pares down the bombastically inflated passages of his works as soon as they threaten to slide into the trivial. This also is very American.

The composer Charles Ives is indeed a unique phenomenon in the world of music. He was a highly idiosyncratic person, driven by the urge to express himself in sounds, without having the need to earn money with it. Music already played an important role in his childhood in the countryside around Danbury, Connecticut. His father, himself a fairly unconventional musician, taught him. At the age of fourteen, Charles Ives was already so skilled at the organ that he was hired by the Second Congregational Church of his hometown. He later went to Yale to study but enrolled in the Faculty of Economics. Music was only a hobby, albeit at the highest level. For four years he attended music courses held by Horatio Parker, a composer trained in Europe, and studied harmony, counterpoint and composition.

Despite his fascination with music, he began work as an actuary in an insurance company at the age of twenty-four. In 1907, together with a colleague, he founded his own agency, which soon became very successful and later operated under the name of Ives & Myrick. As an entrepreneur, Ives attained considerable prosperity in the course of his life. Financially independent, he composed incessantly, at night and on weekends, for many years, to the point of physical exhaustion. As a boy, he was ashamed of his deep love of music, wondering whether it hadn't always been an effeminate art that not only he but many boys were ashamed of – an assessment that was unfounded, but which, probably due to the gender-specific education of the time, was deeply rooted in him and made him feel insecure.

That he should have committed himself professionally to the insurance business and not to music was due to the influence of his father. "Father felt that a man could keep his music-interest stronger, cleaner, bigger, and freer, if he didn't try to make a living out of it." Ives also found that the best way to compose was to never expect one's works to be performed in front of a large audience. Barely twenty years old, Ives lost his father and perhaps his only true friend – an experience he could not get over to his own dying day. All his works are dedicated to his father.

Can you really take a Sunday composer seriously? In the United States, no one did. It was a country where entrepreneurial spirit and entrepreneurial success was what counted, and in the end the money and the prosperity that a person gained. American composers and their activities scarcely played a role, especially not those of an alleged hobby or amateur composer. Ives' well-nigh revolutionary scores were hardly understood by the few people who concerned themselves with his music during his lifetime. They were often perceived to be a violation of the rules of composition as prescribed by the academy, or they were ridiculed because of their many writing errors.

Ives' successful existence as an insurance provider, his passion for music and his enormous productivity in both fields took their toll: he suffered two heart attacks. He no longer composed during the last twenty-seven years of his life. Soon, he also retired from his insurance business and left New York to return to his native Connecticut.

I often talked to Leonard Bernstein about Charles Ives. Through the conductor Seiji Ozawa, whose assistant I was at the time, I met Bernstein in the mid-eighties at the Tanglewood Music Festival. Again and again we met for analysis sessions during which we exchanged our ideas about various great works of the repertoire. And again and again our conversation revolved around the works of Charles Ives and the roots, sounds and peculiarities of original American music. When does music sound American? That question occupied Bernstein for a long time.

He, who was himself a composer, was looking for answers, for Bernstein, the son of Ukrainian Jews, was a patriot as well. In everything he did he was thoroughly American, as his sister Shirley wrote about him when he was still alive. He loved the United States and showed his love through his untiring commitment to American works. In his concerts he introduced many American composers. He adored George Gershwin and loved Aaron Copland. But Ives outranked them all. Bernstein gave his best explanation of what American music actually is, or better, what makes it sound American, to children. In one of his Young People's Concerts, he said: "One of the main personality traits that we have in our music is one of youth. It's young music; it's loud, strong, wildly optimistic. [...] Then there's another kind of American vitality, which is not so much of the city, but belongs more to the rugged West, full of pioneer energy. [...] Then there's a kind of loneliness in American music that's different from other kinds of loneliness. You find it in the way the notes are spaced out very far apart from one another, like the great wide open spaces that our big country is so full of." You can hear that in Charles Ives' music.

It could almost be described as historical irony that Bernstein should have made such an effort to win recognition for the unique quality of Ives' works, while he himself as a composer shared almost the same fate. Despite his popularity as a conductor and media star, the Americans struggled with him as a composer. True, he had a great success with *West Side Story*, premiered in 1957 and soon to become an American export hit. It was adapted for the cinema four years later and is still being staged again and again. But Bernstein didn't compose only that one musical. He wrote three symphonies; various other orchestral works; operas such as *Trouble in Tahiti*, *Candide* and *A Quiet Place*; and four other musicals, film scores and chamber music.

Many of his works had hardly a chance during his lifetime, something Bernstein knew and regretted. For over a hundred years, the majority of Americans seemed to be wary of American composers and their avant-garde works, as if they didn't dare to offer some opposition to Europe with its dazzling composers, its long music history and its great interpreters – to offer something that wasn't rousing jazz or moving gospel songs and therefore genuine American music creations, but something within the genre of classical music.

A look at the history of American art music makes this wariness understandable. We Americans didn't have much time to develop serious American music. As a nation, we are not even three hundred years old. The beginning of our history was burdened with existential challenges. Moreover, our roots are polyglot because our ancestors hailed from all over the world. They first settled on the East Coast and then moved further and further West. Around the turn of the century, when Debussy, Schoenberg and Stravinsky were inventing completely new music based on the harmonic foundations of classical music in Europe, Americans also began to compose, among them such renowned artists as Walter Piston, Virgil Thomson, Roger Sessions and Aaron Copland. They had all been to Europe, had studied harmony, counterpoint and composition and created works that – frankly – didn't sound American at all. They were beautiful but they were all borrowed from the European tradition and not really American.

Gershwin and Copland used jazz, but so did Ravel and Stravinsky. The use of genuine American material alone does not make music American. American compositions seemed to be a specific genre of European music. The European style of music still appeared to have a lock on the Americans. Thirty years later, with the wave of emigration before the Second World War, European music came to the United States in the persons of Schoenberg, Stravinsky, Hindemith, Bartók and Milhaud, who settled, composed and taught in the United States. The American music world remained firmly in European hands. And the search of American composers for the ingredients of their very own American classical music was far from over.

There was only one composer who remained untouched by all of that because of his chosen life plan: Charles Ives. The eccentric from New England had little to do with the European circus around classical music. He didn't care about the rules of tonal music, about form and sound, counterpoint and the conventional sequence of harmonies. He had, in fact, learned the rules of the art from Horatio Parker at Yale, but only – as Bernstein once said – to break them. Ives' memoir bears witness to that: he despised Parker's obsession with rules and declared him to be the gravedigger of the genre. Under the tyranny of the rules of classical compositions, music would soon become an impossibility. "I am fully convinced [that], if music be not allowed to grow, if it's denied the privilege of evolution that all other arts and life have, if [in the] natural processes of ear and mind it is not allowed [to] grow bigger by finding possibilities that nature has for music, more and wider scales, new combinations of tone, new keys and more keys and beats, and phrases together, if it just sticks (as it does today) to one key, one single and easy rhythm, and the rules made to boss them – then music, before many years, cannot be composed – everything will be used up – endless repetitions of static melodies, harmonies, resolutions, and metres – and music as a creative art will die."

Ives wanted freedom – with youthful enthusiasm. He was looking for new possibilities based on the model of nature, he wanted to create more comprehensive scales, new tone combinations, new keys and an overlapping of different keys, time signatures and phrase lengths. Even in a free United States such a bold ambition had no chance: "In the music courses at Yale (four years with Parker) in connection with regular college courses, things or ideas of this nature [...] were not so much suppressed as ignored. Parker, at the beginning of Freshman year, asked me not to bring any more things like these into the classroom." In the music courses at Yale, Ives' revolutionary ideas were simply hushed up. His father had been more generous: "Father used to say, 'If you know how to write a fugue the right way *well*, then I'm willing to have you try the wrong way – *well*. But you've got to know [what you're doing] and why you're doing it.'" Ives heeded that advice. He would not let himself be restrained.

Ives didn't look to Europe. He didn't even notice the dramatic developments in Vienna at the beginning of the twentieth century:

the division of the world of music into champions of atonality and defenders of traditional harmony. He heard nothing of the sneering, almost hateful bickering about the future of classical music that took place in the European music metropolises of Vienna, Paris or Prague. Even before Schoenberg wrote his famous Second String Quartet, with which he finally went beyond the boundaries of Bach's cosmos, Ives experimented with polytony and atonality, with quarter tones and with polyphonic and polyrhythmic structures. He wrote serial music, used collage techniques, composed works with different layers, which were completely independent of each other, and tried out different sources of sound in space. With an almost carefree attitude, Ives took the lead of the avantgarde – unintentionally and unambitiously. But in his lifetime, hardly anyone noticed it. In Vienna, fierce arguments were continuing, while on the other side of the Atlantic something completely new emerged.

Ives was self-contained. In his music he wrote down what he saw: the small towns and communities of New England, the gathering of people in wooden churches and town halls, at parades, in football stadiums. He described nature, the sweep of the country, the patriotism of the Yankees. Ives' music had developed its own musical aesthetic. For decades, he was completely alone with it. Ninety percent of his orchestral music had not yet come to the attention of any conductor, as he wrote in later years. To his knowledge, in a period of thirty years only four conductors knew any of his scores. One of them, by the way, was Gustav Mahler, who had Ives' Third Symphony, completed six years earlier, sent to him in 1910. How different would Ives' life have been if Mahler had performed his Third Symphony? But Mahler died a short time later. It wasn't to be.

Leonard Bernstein dealt in detail not only with Ives' Second Symphony, but also with a short, breathtakingly modern orchestral work by his fellow countryman: *The Unanswered Question*. Ives had added the subtitle "A Cosmic Landscape." This short chamber music work is more pioneering, perhaps even more profound than all the new developments that Europe had to offer at the time, a daring composition by a thirty-four-year-old, written during the crisis of tonality that was shaking the foundations of aesthetics in Europe in 1908.

Even the orchestration of that miniature defies all conventions. A string quartet, a solo trumpet and four flutes, placed far apart in physical space. Never before had there been anything like it. The musical structure, too, offered something completely new: like a collage, trumpet, strings and flutes act rhythmically and harmonically almost independently of each other. Extensive consonant string chords form the tonal basis on which the trumpet repeatedly pushes a question into space, an atonal motif, oblique, unmelodic, unrelenting. The flutes respond six times – each response more dissonant, impatient and desperate. The seventh time, the question remains unanswered. According to Ives, the trumpet's enigmatic phrase poses the "perennial question of existence," to which humans find no definitive answer.

Bernstein, however, understood Ives' *Unanswered Question* – how could it be otherwise? – to be not of a transcendental but of a deeply musical nature. He named a world-famous cycle of lectures, broadcast on television and later published in book form, after Ives' work. His own unanswered question was the question of in which direction music would drift in the twentieth century. Whither music? Could the dilemma of the new century, the antagonism between tonality on the one hand, atonality and ambiguity on the other, be solved? If one understands Ives' unanswered question the way Bernstein did, then that unique composer addressed the question earlier than all of his European counterparts, who were to become much more famous. The question kept Bernstein busy all his life: the eternal rivalry between dissonance and traditional melodiousness, harmony and free tonality, that manifests itself, and is resolved, in Ives' works. The same confrontation takes place in Bernstein's own compositions, in which he portrays the struggle between both schools of thought. Bernstein was firmly convinced that the origin of all music was tonal because it corresponded to human nature, and that tonality would remain the natural basis of all composition, the grounding of all musical development. Every craze, exaggeration and intellectual gimmick would always have to return to it if music were not to lose its right to exist.

And Bernstein believed that new music would have to be eclectic, i.e., combining different styles and schools – always on the basis of the natural overtone series, which was an unchanging acoustic reality valid for the entire cosmos. He composed that way himself. His music included classical harmonies, jazz and blues, the unmistakable sound of Broadway, Latin American rhythms and Schoenberg's twelve-tone music. Basically, Bernstein has been proven right.

Ives' work *The Unanswered Question* allows for many interpretations. Personally, I can't help applying his unanswered question to today's United States. Whither America? In the years of my collaboration with Bernstein, that question would certainly not have occurred to me.

I learned a lot from Bernstein. I remember one of our first encounters that went quite unexpectedly. Bernstein broke off our conversation about Tchaikovsky's Fifth Symphony to spend the rest of the afternoon with me at the Guggenheim Museum. Had I been too ill-prepared for him? Was I an inadequate interlocutor? I don't know. On that day, at any rate, we no longer talked about music but about expressionist painting. It was only much later that I understood Bernstein's holistic approach to art. Art included language and poetry, painting and, of course, music. And to understand these arts, a sharp intellect was as important to him as the passionate mysticism he found in Ives' works.

During the last days of his life, I visited Bernstein once more. I called him and received an appointment. I really wanted to see him – perhaps driven by a hunch that there wouldn't be that many opportunities anymore. He was already quite ill, and his lungs were affected. Many expected his imminent demise. I went to his house in Tanglewood. He knew that life was coming to an end. I suddenly knew it, too. As always, he was smoking. In one hand, the right hand, he held his cigarette; in the other, the oxygen mask, which was supposed to help him through phases of respiratory distress. We talked about personal matters and about music, this time about the music he himself had composed. That had very rarely been the case. In most of our encounters we had discussed issues concerning the repertoire he was engaged with.

"Kent," he said pensively, "there is some strong music in *A Quiet Place*." He said it with deep conviction, but also with a touch of disillusionment. He was of the opinion that some of his late works in particular were good music. As a composer, however, he had to witness how controversial he was and how, right up to the end, many of his works convinced neither the critics nor the public. The world premiere of his opera *A Quiet Place* in 1983 was the best example. The *New York Times* wrote: "To call the result a pretentious failure is putting it kindly." The paper recommended an extensive revision of the material. Later, the opera was performed in Vienna, where I had accompanied him a few years earlier. Here, too, he met with only moderate success. "There is some strong music in *A Quiet Place*," he repeated almost casually. It was one of the last sentences that he left me with and would later motivate me to look for that strong music.

Bernstein would regret it if his musical ideas were lost. His words never released their hold on me. We had all turned this brilliant, generous person, with his outstanding talent and charisma, into a celebrated pop star, who, so to speak, had to constantly stand on his head in order to entertain everyone. However, many critics – and, perhaps, colleagues as well – still don't believe his compositions to be profound. I couldn't get his sentence out of my head for years. For a long time, I wasn't sure of Bernstein's importance as a composer. Time has not yet given its verdict. Would more of his works than just *West Side Story* make it into the canon of important compositions that are accepted worldwide? I wanted to free his opera *A Quiet Place* of all the pomp and circumstance in order to uncover its musical foundations. Layer by layer, I wanted to remove every-thing that disguised the true substance of his music, due to an all too opulent orchestration. I had in mind a chamber music ver-sion that would show what this work really entails: American sounds, unique music, all breathtakingly well composed. As I later learned from members of his circle, Bernstein himself had already thought about that.

Some time ago, I rehearsed this new version of *A Quiet Place* with Ensemble Modern. The result amazed us all. Bernstein was not only the composer of *West Side Story*. He was not only one of the greatest teachers of classical music, perhaps its most gifted protagonist, a titan on stage, whether he taught, learned, played or conducted. He was a unique composer who eclectically mixed everything American music has to offer, true to his own prognosis. Bernstein's music is American – if very different from Ives', more urbane and confrontational. He was right: his compositions con-tain strong music, even those that failed so badly at their world premieres that they threatened to fall into oblivion.

Ives and Bernstein are two composers who represent the United States like no other. Ives' music is my home. Its suggestive power takes me back to my country, to its value system and its great sense of independence, and to the close cohesion of our commu-nities as I remember it from my childhood. In Bernstein's music I hear the great cities, the multitude of social conflicts in our immi-grant society and, repeatedly, the topic of human alienation. Both composers were – each in his own way – patriots, inspired by the ideas of brotherhood, communal spirit and peace; they conjure up that ancient and yet so fleeting sense of community for which we Americans are still fighing today. Ives and Bernstein did so with their music.

In a profoundly American context, those two composers belong together. We know Ives' music thanks to Bernstein's inexhaust-ible energy in helping that composer to posthumously achieve the reputation he was entitled to during his lifetime. And we have to set out to discover more of Bernstein's music, so that it won't be lost at some point, and so that something of this universal artist survives other than *West Side Story* and the increasingly diffuse memories of how striking he was as a human being and as a mediator of music. As a media star, Bernstein will vanish over the years. However, the themes he dealt with in his works are still topical today. The way he addressed them may have been too provocative and too exposing for a puritan, often bigoted American public. I think that the time is ripe for Bernstein's works, especially today, in this deeply fractured and divided country. We have only just begun their rediscovery. Not only Donald Trump's United States will need Bernstein's music.

The United States has not overcome its identity crisis. What would Ives and Bernstein say to that? At best, our sense of community and cohesion is undergoing a profound change; at worst, it is in tatters. And the American dream – the idea that everyone can make it to the top in this young, once so free country – has long since faded. Many are beginning to question that dream. The United States is currently showing its ugly face, one that could already be glimpsed a decade ago in the 2008 election campaign. Intolerance and deep resentment characterize today's political altercations. You would think that society had ossified. In large sections of our society, curiosity and gumption seem to have disappeared. The long-awaited awakening from paralysis after 9/11 has not yet taken place. Whither America? For me, *that* is the unanswered question that we Americans are faced with today.

I, too, am an American – with heart and soul, hopelessly so. And I don't know the answer to that question. That night on Broad Stage, we should perhaps have played Ives' *Unanswered Question*, which emphasizes less the United States' spirit, its diversity and also its dissonances, but rather confronts listeners with that unanswered question. At the time, however, it wasn't yet possible to foresee the deep rifts running through our society. "And even with revolutionary thinkers [...], the Declaration of Independence, the Constitution, and the Bill of Rights, the nation still faced an uncertain future," Dustin Hoffman reminded the audience of American history toward the end of the performance. No one could have guessed that ten years later our society would not be in better shape, but in a much more worrying state of disorientation.

At the end of Ives' *Unanswered Question*, only the string players can be heard, who, with their consonant chords, had provided the bedrock of the work for the entire six minutes of its duration. Unperturbed, they were playing a G major triad. The basis of the composition is tonal. The dissonant quarreling of the woodwind quartet has ceased. The solo trumpet has blown its question into space for the seventh and last time. Whither America? There is no answer. The piece ends quietly, tonally, harmoniously. In the affirmative, as Bernstein said at the end of his famous lecture cycle. Hope dies last.

ACKNOWLEDGMENTS

I would like to thank all those who have greatly influenced the development of my creative voice over so many years and who have contributed to the outcome of this book:

Professor Dr Dieter Rexroth, a brilliant musician, musicologist, dramaturge, advisor and social scientist who has never tired of supporting creative colleagues with his comprehensive knowledge and whose influence and guidance has been essential.

Master designer and visual artist Peter Schmidt for his continuous provocation, aesthetic inspiration and friendship.

Gabriele Schiller, with whom I have been collaborating creatively and conceptually for over twenty years to help fulfill the ambassadorial role of an artist.

Madeleine Careau, CEO of the Orchestre symphonique de Montréal, and Jean-Pierre Brossmann, former director of the Théâtre du Châtelet, and their rare ability to see the future before it arrives and who have unconditionally supported a complex artistic vision through tirelessly helping to implement my ideas, some of which I have described in this book.

David Sela, a community leader, avid supporter of the arts and indefatigable advocate of classical music whose generosity made this English publication possible.

Professor Dr William Kinderman, influential musicologist, pedagog and concert soloist who consistently brings deep and fresh insights to music.

Professor Dr Edward Houghton, music historian, conductor and leading specialist in medieval and renaissance music whose pioneering, creative research has helped provide a foundation for understanding the European music tradition and its development during and since the Enlightenment, and whose encouragement led me beyond composition toward performance.

My career began more than forty years ago in the United States – at the beginning there were great teachers who deeply influenced my understanding of music and gave me the substance that generates the curiosity and discipline necessary for the lifelong search for profundity that lies beyond the obvious, and the status quo.

Some are mentioned in this book. I would also especially like to thank the celebrated piano professor Goodwin Sammel and of course my beloved mother, Ruth Nagano, both of whom opened the world through their piano instruction and without whom I would never have discovered the world of imagination, expression and universality that lies within the world of sound, color and light.

Above all, my heartfelt thanks to my wife, Mari Kodama, without whom my cultural identity and artistic voice neither would nor could have gone beyond normal limits, and without whom I would not have had the courage to write this book.

Finally, my daughter, Karin, who is a source of never-ending joy, truth and life, and who constantly challenges us toward actuality with today as tomorrow – all of which are essential qualities of life.

LITERATURE

Adorno, Theodor W. *Introduction to the Sociology of Music.*
Translated from the German by E.B. Ashton. New York, NY:
Seabury Press, 1976.
– "Scientific Experiences of a European Scholar in America." In *Critical
Models: Interventions and Catchwords.* Translated by Henry W.
Pickford. Introduction by Lydia Goehr. New York, NY: Columbia
University Press, 2005, pp. 215–42.
Bauer-Lechner, Natalie. *Recollections of Gustav Mahler.* Translated by
Dika Newlin. Edited and annotated by Peter Franklin. London:
Faber and Faber, 2013.
Bernstein, Leonard. *Young People's Concert: "A Tribute to Teachers."*
The Bernstein Experience on Classical.org (8 May 2018).
Cott, Jonathan. "Leonard Bernstein." In *Back to a Shadow in the
Night: Music Writings and Interviews 1968–2001,* 187–217.
Milwaukee, WI: Hal Leonard, 2002.
Floros, Constantin. *Anton Bruckner: The Man and the Work.*
Translated by Ernest Bernhardt-Kabisch. Oxford: Peter Lang, 2011,
2015.
Forbes, Elliot, ed. *Thayer's Life of Beethoven.* Princeton, NJ: Princeton
University Press, 1964.
Frisch, Walter, ed. *Schoenberg and His World.* Princeton, NJ: Princeton
University Press, 1999.

Frye, Northrop. *The Educated Imagination*. Bloomington, IN: Indiana University Press, 1964.

Göllerich, August. *Anton Bruckner: Ein Lebens- und Schaffensbild*. Nach dessen Tod ergänzt und herausgegeben von Max Auer, vol. 4, part 2. Regensburg: Bosse, 1974. English translation of the Levi quote by Hans-Christian Oeser.

Gradenwitz, Peter. *Leonard Bernstein: The Infinite Variety of a Musician*. With personal contributions by Leonard Bernstein [et al.]. New York, NY: Wolff, 1987.

Hanslick, Eduard. "Bruckners III." In *Die Moderne Oper*, vol. 6: *Aus dem Tagebuch eines Musikers: Neue Kritiken und Schilderungen*. Berlin: Allgemeiner Verein für Deutsche Litteratur, 1892. English translation of the Hanslick quote by Hans-Christian Oeser.

Hessel, Stéphane. *Time for Outrage!* Translated by Damion Searls, with Alba Arrikha. Foreword by Charles Glass. London: Quartet Books, 2011.

Hill, Peter, and Simeone, Nigel. *Messiaen*. New Haven, CT: Yale University Press, 2005.

Hoffmann, E.T.A. "Beethoven's Instrumental Music." In *Musical Writings: Kreisleriana, The Poet and the Composer, Music Criticism*, 96–102. Edited, annotated, and introduced by David Charlton. Translated by Martyn Clarke. Cambridge: Cambridge University Press, 1989.

– "Review of Beethoven's Fifth Symphony." In *Musical Writings: Kreisleriana, The Poet and the Composer, Music Criticism*, 234–52.

Hugo, Victor. *William Shakespeare*. Translated by A. Baillot. With illustrations. Boston, MA: Estes and Lauriat Publishers, 1864.

Huron, David. *Sweet Anticipation: Music and the Psychology of Expectation*. Cambridge, MA: MIT Press, 2006.

Ives, Charles E. *Memos*. Edited by John Kirkpatrick. New York, NY: Norton, 1972.

Kant's Critique of Judgement. Translated with introduction and notes by J.H. Bernard. Second edition, revised. London: Macmillan and Co., 1914.

Keats, John. "Ode on a Grecian Urn." In *The Complete Poems*, 344–5. Edited by John Barnard. London: Penguin, 1988, 2006.

Korisheli, Wachtang Botso. *Memories of a Teaching Life in Music: The Autobiography of Wachtang Botso Korisheli*. Morro Bay, CA: Wachtang Botso Korisheli, 2010.

Krautscheid-Albiez, Christiane. "Richard Strauss 'Ein Heldenleblen'": Dichtung und Wahrheit. In *Programmheft der Berliner Philharmoniker*, 11 April 1999. English translation of the Strauss quote referred to in this program note by Hans-Christian Oeser.

Leonard Bernstein's Young People's Concerts. Drawings by Isadore Seltzer. New York, NY: Simon and Schuster, 1970. Edited by Jack Gottlieb. Newly revised and expanded edition. New York, NY: Doubleday, 1992.

Levitin, Daniel J. *The World in Six Songs: How the Musical Brain Created Human Nature*. New York, NY: Dutton, 2008.

– *This Is Your Brain on Music: The Science of a Human Obsession*. New York. NY: Dutton, 2006.

Loewe, Andreas. *"Musica est optimum": Martin Luther's Theory of Music*, academia.edu (The Melbourne College of Divinity).

Luther, Martin. *The Familiar Discourses of Dr. Martin Luther*. Translated by Captain Henry Bell. A new edition, revised by Joseph Kerby, etc. Lewes: John Baxter, 1818.

Martel, Yann. *What Is Stephen Harper Reading?: Yann Martel's Recommended Reading for a Prime Minister and Book Lovers of All Stripes*. Toronto: Vintage Canada, 2009.

Masur, Kurt. "Ich bin vorsichtig mit den Plänen." In *Focus Online*, 11 September 2013. English translation of the Masur quote by Hans-Christian Oeser.

Messiaen, Olivier. *Music and Color: Conversations with Claude Samuel*. Translated by E. Thomas Glasow. Portland, OR: Amadeus Press, 1994.

Plato. *Republic*. Translated by John Llewelyn Davies and David James Vaughan. With an introduction by Stephen Watt. Ware, Hertfordshire: Wordsworth Editions, 1997.

Rexroth, Dieter. *Beethoven: Leben, Werke, Dokumente*. Mainz: Schott, 1988.

Rousseau, Jean-Jacques. "Essay on the Origin of Languages in Which Something Is Said about Melody and Musical Imitation." In *The Discourses and Other Early Political Writings*, 247–99. Edited and translated by Victor Gourevitch. Cambridge: Cambridge University Press, 1997, 2003.

Sacks, Oliver. *Musicophilia: Tales of Music and the Brain*. New York, NY: Alfred A. Knopf, 2007.

Schiller, Friedrich. *On the Aesthetic Education of Man*. Translated with an introduction by Reginald Snell. Mineola, NY: Dover Publications, 2004.

Schoenberg, Arnold. "To the National Institute of Arts and Letters, 22 May 1947." In *Letters*, 245–6. Selected and edited by Erwin Stein. Translated from the original German by Eithne Wilkins and Ernst Kaiser. Berkeley, CA: University of California Press, 1964.

– *Style and Idea: Selected Writings of Arnold Schoenberg*. 60th Anniversary Edition. Edited by Leonard Stein. Translated by Leo Black. With a new foreword by Joseph Auner. Berkeley, CA: University of California Press, 1984.

Schweitzer, Albert. *J.S. Bach*. Preface by C.M. Widor. Translated by Ernest Newman. London: A. & C. Black, 1923.

Vargas Llosa, Mario. *Notes on the Death of Culture: Essays on Spectacle and Society*. Translated by John King. New York, NY: Farrar, Stauss and Giroux, 2015.

Webern, Anton. "Schönbergs Musik." In *Arnold Schönberg*, 22–48. Mit Beiträgen von Alban Berg [et al.]. Munich: R. Piper, 1912. English version at https://schoenberg.at/index.php/en/anton-webern-schoenbergs-musik-2.

Williamson, John, ed. *The Cambridge Companion to Bruckner*. Cambridge: Cambridge University Press, 2004.